WOMEN WORK & WORSHIP
in The United Church of Canada

Shirley Davy, Project Coordinator

PERMISSIONS

Quotation from *The Church in the Canadian Era,* by permission of the author, John Webster Grant.

Quotation from *In Times Like These,* by permission of The University of Toronto Press.

Photo of Nancy Rowell Jackman, by permission of The Globe and Mail, Toronto.

Music *Minuet* and *Meditation,* by permission of the composer, Gwendolyn Richardson.

"Women and Power in The United Church of Canada", by permission of the author, Shelagh Parsons.

"Christian Feminism in the United Church: Resources in Culture and Tradition", by permission of the author, Randi Warne.

"Liberating Christianity", by permission of the author, Margie Whynot.

"Side Road on the Journey to Autonomy: the Diaconate Prior to Church Union", by permission of the author, Diane Haglund.

"Pouring the Tea and Hiding the Wine Bottle: Reflections on the Role of the Minister's Mate", by permission of the author, Andrea Shaver.

"The Influence of Ruth Tillman on Women in Ministry", by permission of the author, Marion Pardy.

Editor: Nancy Hardy
Cover Design: Heather Dau

The publication of *Women Work & Worship* has been made possible by the Jackman Foundation.

THE DIVISION OF

MISSION IN CANADA

CONTENTS

PREFACE

Sin, Sex, and Money could have been the title of this book. Why? Our sin, in the church's eyes, seems to be our sex—female, and our value—money!

When I went to theological college in the sixties, church history included a lot of things, but not how we women have ministered throughout the history of the church.

Ruth Tillman's memorial service that chilly November, 1978 evening at Metropolitan United Church in Toronto gave us a sense of deep loss, not only of Ruth, but of a segment of United Church history. Some of us had gone to the United Church Training School, and some to Covenant College, as it was renamed. We were conscious of our own tradition as deaconesses, but felt that the rest of the church was not. Ruth was dead and her life and work commemorated in that one service. How would the next generation of diaconal ministers know about her leadership in the church? How would they know about that particular time to which she belonged?

We gathered in the narthex to talk about how the life and work of people like Ruth could be recorded for our sisters and brothers, and I decided to do something about it. This book, for me, is a tribute to Ruth Tillman who gave me a chance to write an article for CGIT and thereby recruited me to church work as a profession. It is also a tribute to all those women who have gone before us, and to those who are to come, who need to know who we are, who our foremothers were, and who our granddaughters and grandnieces will be.

Nancy Rowell Jackman

INTRODUCTION

Two years ago, when I first became involved in "The United Church Women's Project" (we hadn't found our name at that point), we were thinking about producing a history. Not long into our conversations, however, we (the United Church committee appointed to oversee the project) realized that none of us felt quite comfortable with a "story" that would be library-researched. Besides, there was no place to research women's work and worship: the whole area had been ignored by both religious and feminist scholars. After a good deal of reflection about how we might get at women's work and worship, we decided that I would spend the first of the two years encouraging women of the United Church to gather their own materials locally, and to send me what they found out about themselves, and their heritage. This part of the project involved travelling, meetings, telephone calls, letters. Then, responses started coming in! In fact, Women, Work and Worship (WWW) assisted several local projects through a Local Research Funding Program; we were determined that already stretched resources should not be stretched further for the sake of the project.

The next six months of the project were spent reading materials—and every word of everything that reached the office by the end of February, 1983, was read. With all the concerns, joys, fears and hopes of the contributors combining like a stew in my head and heart, a final view of what was required in the book started to emerge.

First, there needed to be an overview of the materials sent in and other research resources that was tied together by some analytical perspective. Since I am trained in the social sciences, I have used that approach. And since I am also a specialist in religion, I have tried to ground that perspective in my understanding of Christianity. Someone else might have gone about this process differently.

The first section of the book presents such an overview. These four chapters are offered not as the last word on women in our church, but as the beginning of a conversation among us. I do not ask you to agree with what you read, only to "hear" it. This may be a starting point for a creative dialogue that can help us all grow toward the potential given to us by our Creator.

There also needed to be a place to share some of the stories and reflections. Sections 2 and 3 have been written by you and your sisters in the United Church. Each item was selected for what it can tell us about ourselves and about our church.

Since we hoped to stimulate research within the academic community and in our own church, we offered six research grants for papers related to the project. These are included as Section 4.

There are many areas that have not been considered in this book, particularly the women of the United Church in French Canada and in Native Ministries. If this project stimulates further research in those important fields, then it will have succeeded on those grounds alone.

Throughout the two years of the Women, Work and Worship project, this question has arisen over and over again. Why is it about women? What about the men of the church? There are two answers. First, although the book focuses on *women's* work and worship, it *is* also about churchmen and about the church in general. In fact, since the United Church has been dominated by men (in terms of determining policy and administration) since its inception, men form the context within which the story of the women must be told. Second, the "history" of our church has been developed almost entirely from a male perspective. Even women who do not consider themselves feminists would recognize that *their* experience of church is quite different than that described by Canada's church historians. Most historians have considered the church primarily as a legally constituted institution and discuss individual people only to the extent that they have effected some change in the status of that institution. Since women have, in the past, had little say in the administration of the church at any level, they are, not surprisingly, absent from the scholarly accounts. An account of church life from the perspective of its women (who constitute the *majority* of members and adherents) is essential to any balanced view of what our church is.

In closing, I would like to acknowledge the help and support of the members of the Ministry with Adults Working Unit, of Ruth Evans, who kept us on course, and to the members of the WWW committee: Margaret Torrance, Janet Silman, and Nancy Jackman. And a special thank-you, too, to my sisters at Women's Inter-Church Council of Canada, with whom I "lived" for the length of the project. I will miss them all as I begin a new adventure in the fall.

Shirley Davy

The joy of women sharing,

  the delight within their souls

Will release the soaring eagle in us all.

*(Nancy Telfer)**

*Nancy Telfer is a composer and member of The United Church of Canada. The above lines are from her hymn "The Spirit is Among Us" which is part of a larger work, *The Journey,* commissioned by Women's Inter-Church Council of Canada for its 1982 national gathering, "The Female Connection". (Copies of both the hymn and the choral work are available from the publisher, Gordon V. Thompson Limited, 29 Birch Avenue, Toronto, Ontario M4V 1E2.)

Section 1

Our Story:
Christian Liberation

SECTION 1: OUR STORY: CHRISTIAN LIBERATION

Chapter 1: WOMEN TOGETHER: THE CALL TO COLLECTIVE ACTION

Why Women's Organizations Were Formed

The Call to the "Christ-work"
The Call to Social Action
The Desire for Education
The Need for Community
The Need to Support the Church

Why Women's Organizations Thrived

Fellowship
Political Bonding

What a Churchwoman's Organization Offered Its Members

Joy-Giving Self-Concept
Joy-Giving Group Expression of Emotion
Joy-Giving Location in Space
Joy-Giving Attitude Towards the Past
Joy-Giving Work
Joy-Giving Focus for One's Life

Conclusion

Chapter 2: FAITH AND FINANCES

In the Congregation and Community

The Financial Ability of Women's Groups
The "Value" of Women's Groups
Something Out of Nothing
Who Spends the Money?

In the National Church

More Than Meets the Eye
Money, Power, and Partnership

Chapter 3: SOCIAL CHANGE REFLECTED IN WOMEN'S WORK AND WORSHIP

Church Union: Building and Breaking

Chapter 1 WOMEN TOGETHER:
THE CALL
TO COLLECTIVE ACTION

*One day we just decided to get
organized as a Woman's Association of the
United Church, with an elected slate of
officers. I believe we did it that same sunny
afternoon, without even consulting the
minister and without being or having a
congregation. Just because we wanted to
belong. I didn't know any better. As we
walked out the gate, somebody behind me
said, "We have a WA, now we'll get a
church!" We broke a rule. Our faces may
have been red, but a minister and a church
building did come.*[1]

The women of Sault Ste Marie may not have "known
any better," but they were continuing work that
had been part of The United Church of Canada for
many years. Long before the first churchwoman's association came into
being, women were contributing to church life in a variety of ways. As
Christian mothers they were instructors in the faith, and as Christian
neighbours they were, at best, living examples of Christ-like caring.
Individual acts and influence tended to be invisible, however, and the
women did not expect either reward or recognition. Even today women
in the church make their contributions in much the same way that they
might have before there were organizations in which to participate. Since
that is so, we must somehow account for the appearance of women's
groups. Why were they formed? Why did they thrive? What did they offer
their members above and beyond the personal satisfaction?

Excellent books have been written about the two national organizations that amalgamated to form the United Church Women in 1962. *Wide
Windows* by Jean Gordon Forbes traces the development of The Woman's Missionary Society from its Methodist and Presbyterian roots to
1951; and Ethel M. Bird presents a similar historical overview of The
Woman's Association in *And Their Work Continueth*...Both accounts
focus on the formal organizations and the work accomplished by their
emissaries. They tell little about the thousands of churchwomen in con-

5

gregations across Canada who were the sole support of the grander mission. By contrast, this chapter will attempt to convey some of the flavour, the vision and the energy of women's organizations at the congregational level.

WHY WOMEN'S ORGANIZATIONS WERE FORMED

The Call to the "Christ-work"

> ...to relieve the wants, assuage the griefs and mitigate the suffering of many of the wretched and destitute of our fellow creatures.[2]

It is difficult from the perspective of the 1980s to imagine a society without social welfare programs. Unemployment insurance, hospital and medical insurance, mother's allowance, sick leave and old age pensions help ease the pain of economic crises. But before the existence of such programs, women, and primarily churchwomen, responded to the human suffering around them, performing the "Christ-work" of the church: feeding the hungry, healing the sick, comforting the bereaved and teaching the disadvantaged.

The Halifax Wesleyan Female Benevolent Society (whose purpose is given above) was organized in 1816 to cope with a severe depression that hit Halifax after the Napoleonic and American wars. Society members distributed clothing they had made themselves, blankets, and food parcels to households in which breadwinners were either unemployed or absent. They also sought donations in money or products from local businesses. In the first year of its existence, the Society had collected over one thousand dollars and relieved nearly three hundred distress cases. Within two years of its formation, the Society's charity was extended to thousands—Methodist and non-Methodist alike.

Churchwomen not only served their own communities in times of local need, but also assisted their sisters and brothers in other parts of the country. Maritime women recall packing barrels of clothing and salt cod for the prairie provinces which were doubly devastated by depression and drought in the thirties. The enormous task of prairie relief resulted from the concern of one United Church woman, Annie Entiknap, who was President of Assiniboia Presbyterial of the Woman's Missionary Society.

> It was a time of real struggle and hardship for the people of southern Saskatchewan. Annie's visits to the WMS groups brought sympathy and encouragement. She listened to their sad stories, and her concern for people led her to contact Dr. Dorey, Home Missions Secretary for Saskatchewan, to try to get some help for these people.

6

> The result was astounding. Dr. Dorey, through church
> contacts in the East, was able to achieve a generous
> response of food and clothing. The result was that Annie
> was in the used-clothes business. Bales of good used
> clothing came and were distributed from Annie's front
> porch. People came from miles around to get help, and
> none were refused. The hospital in Kincaid was supplied
> with layettes from the bales and could not have continued
> without this help. Annie became known as "The Missionary
> Lady". It was a huge tusk for a small woman.[3]

In many areas of Canada, people would not have survived the Great
Depression, dignity intact, without the efforts of organized churchwomen. Soup-lines were organized (usually an ecumenical effort), and
blankets, clothing, and fuel were provided to those unable to attain such
necessities for themselves.

> ...by 1930 the Great Depression was affecting the lives
> of everyone, particularly many families in our downtown
> district. In retrospect, one realizes how well the church
> responded to the people's needs... We visited families
> where the breadwinner was unemployed, carrying food and
> showing our concern. A clothing centre for the needy was
> established, and a Mother's club, so they could share and
> enjoy a social time while volunteers cared for their infants
> and young children. Christmas baskets were packed and a
> gift and toy centre was available. The Senior Citizens' Club
> was formed, meeting one afternoon a week for games, sing
> song, worship and tea. A few of the younger members of
> the WA organized a summer nursery school to keep small
> children off the streets. It was so successful we decided to
> keep it going all year, and invited the help of non-
> Metropolitan friends to finance it.[4]

Other churchwomen taught their poorer sisters how to sew and then
provided them with patterns and fabric so they could clothe themselves
and their families and, perhaps, earn some money to better their lives.

Two world wars saw women organize to "support the war effort"—a
phrase and a stance that might tug at the consciences of peace advocates
today. Bandages were made by every woman's group, it seems, for
distribution by the Red Cross. Soldiers overseas were remembered on
birthdays and holidays with "parcels from home" which contained
homemade preserves, baked goods, hand-knitted socks and caps. Soldiers in Canada were taken in and entertained by hospitable families
when they were in port cities or training camps far from their own homes.
The end of war meant making quilts and packing bales of clothing for
shipment to war victims abroad. Churchwomen cheered the return of
their local "boys" with supper celebrations and, after World War Two

especially, set up groups to befriend the war-brides who accompanied so many young soldiers home.

Churchwomen responded to local disasters with generosity and imagination. The First-St. Andrew's (London) anniversary book tells of flood relief organized by women.

> When the disastrous flood of the 1930s swept over the London West breakwater, seventy homeless people lived in our Sunday School hall for a month. The women were kept busy running a dining-room, a nursery in the parlour, and making over clothing for the guests on sewing machines in the Board Room.[5]

Mount Paul's (Kamloops, British Columbia) anniversary book gives a similar account of work done by its women:

> During the 1948 flood, the ladies fed many flood victims and workers and even housed one family in the church basement. [6]

Every community has its own story of hurricane, tornado, fire, flood, explosion or some other catastrophic event. What is common to these stories is the immediate response of churchwomen, many of whom were affected as much as their neighbours, to the suffering of those around them. Whether gathering furnishings for a burnt-out family, hauling sandbags to keep ahead of rising water levels, or supplying meals and dry clothing to men involved in emergency relief work, the greater part of women's gift to others was the caring, the spiritual aspect of the practical task.

The needs of individuals were not neglected. An amusing trip through the Minutes of the Birtle (Manitoba) Union Ladies Aid (1917-1923) keeps us in touch with a mysterious Mrs. Conway and her successor.

> 1921   For some unrecorded reason the Aid gave $2.00 per month to a Mrs. Conway, and supervised the spending of this.
>
> 1922   In March 1922, the ladies were concerned about getting Mrs. Conway ready, mended, sewn for the Old Folks Home. They bought materials and got her ready.
>
> The ladies received some dishes from Mrs. Conway (whom they had assisted) and the proceeds of $16.00 from the sale of her stove and bed.
>
> In December, the ladies were going to each send Mrs. Conway a gift. She was not forgotten. Also, they were still sending her $2.00 a month. (This is in the days before Old Age Security.)

1923   *In November 1923, the ladies were again planning to
        send Mrs. Conway parcels for Christmas—she was
        not forgotten.*

1924   *The ladies often sent items to Mrs. Conway; for
        Christmas 1924 they bought flannelette and made
        two nightdresses.*

1925   *Now the ladies take on a new case—Mrs. Talbot—
        $2.00 a month to be used to purchase goods when
        needed. Later they just gave her the money.*[7]

One wonders just how many Mrs. Conway's and Mrs. Talbot's were being assisted by churchwomen across the country before a universal old age pension was introduced.

That some groups formed because of a call to Christ-work is evident in their statements of purpose: "to serve God and fellowman"; "to visit the sick and needy"; "to help lighten one another's burdens by kindly deeds"; "to help in the everyday life of the women." And that the church saw the Christ-work as the province of its women is evident in a statement from Prince Edward Island: "One of the big social events of 1902 was the Methodist Ladies Aid Strawberry Festival that raised $102.00 for the *women's work.*"[8] (italics added)

The Call to Social Action

> *...women tend to be very modest about their
> contributions to the church.*[9]

The influence of churchwomen on both church and society has seldom been acknowledged, even in accounts of their own organizations. There is a growing body of evidence, for example, that women provided much of the impetus for the Social Gospel Movement early in this century, a movement which saw social activism as a necessary expression of faith. The commitment to shaping God's kingdom on earth obligated each Christian to recognize and denounce injustice wherever it was found and to eradicate its cause where possible.

One of the earliest attempts of organized churchwomen to effect social change in Canada was made by the Women's Christian Temperance Union, an ecumenical organization whose aim was to lessen (not to ban as is commonly believed) the sale of intoxicating liquors and to prohibit their manufacture. (That the WCTU has become trivial and ridiculous in the popular imagination is some indication of how our society regards women. Temperance work was also being done by men's groups, none of which have become the butt of beer-bashing jokes; in fact, Jesse Ketchum donated the land for the building of Temperance Hall on Temperance Street in Toronto.)

The increasing consumption of liquor was seen, by Methodists especially, as a threat to the stability of Canadian society in the last quarter of the nineteenth century. It incapacitated some men to the extent that they were unable to work, or consumed their earnings when they were able. The wives and children of these men were left destitute and wholly dependent upon the charity of others for their survival. It was a situation with which churchwomen, already engaged in charitable work, would be all too familiar. The extent of the problem can be seen in statistics quoted in 1895 by the president of a local WMS (Methodist) in Prince Edward Island.

> Canada spent 80 million dollars annually for liquor, an average of $16 per capita, while against that Canada gives only half a million dollars for missions, which amounts to ten cents per head.[10]

Although some WCTU tactics, such as having Sunday School children sign pledges that they would never consume alcohol (one wonders how many of those pledges have been kept),[11] may be questionable by today's standards, it was that organization which led the battle for voting rights for women and which was the first advocate of equal pay for equal work. Their argument, couched in the philosophy of maternal feminism,[12] was that women must have the opportunity to influence public policy if the whole spectrum of human understanding was to be incorporated into public affairs. Women, because of their predisposition for nurturing, would improve society through a more humanistic approach to government and legislation. It was that same argument that eventually led to the election of Nellie McClung to the Parliament of Canada, and to the "Persons Case" in 1929 in which women were declared to be "persons" under Canadian law.

John Webster Grant conveys the scope of the Temperance Movement in his church history, *The Church in the Canadian Era.*

> Although prohibitionists made much of the harm done by liquor, it would be a mistake to regard the movement as essentially negative. Its advocates had in mind not the eradication of a single evil but the formation of a new type of man and thereby the creation of a new type of society. A sober Canada would be an approach to Methodist perfection, an updated version of the Scottish covenanted nation. Prohibition could be regarded either as the keystone of a broad program of reform or as a reform sufficient in itself to usher in utopia.[13]

The twists and turns of local temperance activity since church union are brought to life in an account received from the Watrous UCW in Saskatchewan. Here we see that the social concern remains even if the offending substance has changed over the years.

10

Temperance work is ongoing and supported over the
years by the various women's groups. It began June, 1924,
when they endorsed the Temperance Resolution passed by
Saskatchewan Provincial Convention, that urged them to
pray, work, and vote for prohibition. Speakers were
brought in for the WMS and Sunday School...Beginning in
1932 and continuing until the late 1940s an Annual June
Temperance Meeting was held. During regular WMS
meetings the Temperance secretary provided informative
articles, telling facts such as one glass of milk contains more
nourishment than 13 glasses of beer.

1935   *The WMS and WA protested the sale of beer in*
         packages and the extended parlour hours.

1942   *Saskatoon Presbyterial forwarded a resolution to be*
         sent to provincial and federal governments urging
         refusal of sugar for the making of beer and other
         alcoholic beverages. (Sugar was rationed during
         the war.)

1944   *The University of Saskatchewan requested money in*
         order to train teachers for temperance work.

1970   *UCW catered to Alcoholics Anonymous banquets.*

1976   *They protested the increased liquor outlets in*
         Saskatchewan.

1982-83 *The UCW supports the local ministerial association*
         in sponsoring a Drug Awareness Program.[14]

World peace was another issue around which churchwomen organized. Although they had prayed together within their own congregations
in 1895 (Anglican women had named St. Andrew's Day as a Day of
Intercession for Missions), the first ecumenical prayer meeting of regional
scope occurred in 1920 when women conducted services throughout
Ontario to affirm and participate in what the organizers had named
"Women's Interdenominational Day of Prayer for Missions." This enormous organizational task had been initiated in 1918 by a Presbyterian
woman, Bessie McMurchy, who had enlisted the aid of the Women's
Missionary Boards of the Anglican, Baptist, Congregational, Methodist
and Presbyterian Churches.

It is no accident that this process of calling women to collective prayer
coincided with the end of World War One. Although not explicitly a
pacifist movement like some other women's organizations of its day
(Voices of Women, for instance), the intent to influence public policy was
evident at the outset in McMurchy's hope of "promoting the spread of
Christ's kingdom by United Prayer, United Action, and a stronger voice
in national questions."[15] By 1921 the women's service was being held
throughout Canada, and in 1922 Canadian women joined hands with
their American sisters, and the "Women's World Day of Prayer" (now
called "World Day of Prayer") became a truly international event.

Women were also making statements about peace within the confines of their own congregations. Birtle Union Ladies Aid[16] held a "Peace Day" on November 11, 1920, in their local community hall. Churchwomen in Watrous (Saskatchewan) report that their group circulated a peace petition in 1931[17] and, two years earlier, the women of Marshall United Church (Saskatchewan) had sent a resolution protesting cadet training to their local newspaper.[18] Women in Prince Edward Island took time from their Depression relief work in 1931 (they were packing boxes for Western Canada) to circulate a Disarmament Declaration within their community.[19]

Until recently, the world has paid scant attention to women's organizations, church or secular, which advocate peace through disarmament. But it is a tribute to those pioneers—who understood that a balanced and sane public policy depends upon the equal participation of women and men in the making of that policy—that so many denominations have taken up the cause of peace today. It is easy to forget that The United Church of Canada was less than kind to the pacifists among its ranks, whether lay or clergy, when Canada became involved in World War Two.

In some parts of the country today there is an urgency to the discussion of war and peace. Uranium is mined in Saskatchewan, and the "yellow cake" (the raw earth from which the uranium is extracted) travels by truck close to many residential communities. It is not easy for Saskatchewan to struggle with the realities of uranium mining. On the one hand, the mines provide employment for husbands and sons; on the other hand no one knows for certain how the work affects the health of uranium miners. The levels of radiation exposure are generally set by governments which are aware of the economic and political benefits that result from the mining of uranium.

Alberta and Ontario churchwomen have different reasons for their immediate concern about peace. Canada has agreed to let the United States test its cruise missile in Alberta. Quite apart from the danger they may pose in themselves, the tests violate the consciences of all Canadians who do not wish to be a party, however far removed, to massive nuclear destruction. Ontario churchwomen face a similar issue of conscience in regard to Litton Industries, the manufacturer of the delivery system for the cruise missile. Whether in Saskatchewan, Alberta or Ontario, these groups must deal with the somewhat demonic argument that Canada and Canadians are not producing nuclear weapons. Churches and churchwomen's groups across the country are courageously acknowledging that our responsibility is no less because we are merely accessories to the nuclear industry. In the event that nuclear weapons *are* used, the parts of the process will be judged as guilty as the whole.

The concern of United Church women about the nuclear issue (energy as well as weaponry) was evident in the United Church sponsorship to Canada in 1981 of two women from Japan and Papua New

Guinea. Through local UCW organizations, hundreds of women in the western provinces heard Aiko Carter speak about the continuing effects of bomb shock on Japan years after the nuclear devastation at Nagasaki and Hiroshima. They also heard Lina Volkus tell about Pacific islanders evacuated from a nuclear testing zone in the 1950s, who were allowed to return to their island in the 1970s. Twenty years after the testing, many of those who elected to return experienced radiation poisoning and found that crops did not grow as they should because the soil was still contaminated. Both women called for an end to the uranium industry in Saskatchewan and urged women to become active in their opposition to governments which affirm the principle of nuclear testing *anywhere* in the world.

Churchwomen have responded to social issues whenever they have understood that to do nothing would be unChristian. Often they have been the first to reach such an understanding and lead the rest of the church into battle. The call to social action is still heard and heeded by many women of the United Church even though the opposition to "intemperance, cigarettes and profanity"[20] has been transformed into opposition to more contemporary evils such as sexism in advertising and outright pornography

The Desire for Education

> ...the women knew more than the men about missions.[21]

For the greater part of the nineteenth century, a Canadian woman had no access to formal higher education beyond the "ornamental" training that prepared her for "any woman's best and highest sphere ...aiding some good, honest, faithful man in discharging the duties of life."[22] Mount Allison (Sackville, New Brunswick) was the first Canadian institution to admit women to degree programs, and it was that university which awarded the first Bachelor of Science and English Literature degree (Grace Annie Lockhart, 1875), and the first Bachelor of Arts degree (Harriet Starr Stewart, 1882) to women. Although the voice advocating women's equal access to academic education was growing stronger towards the end of the century, it was, as is frequently the case, economics rather than any principles of fairness that accomplished that goal.

> It is likely that the decision to admit women was hastened by the financial crisis that arose at Mount Allison in early 1872, with the cutting off of the provincial subsidy from New Brunswick in the wake of the 1871 Common Schools Act.[23]

In a society which discouraged women from pursuing serious study,

13

an interest in mission fields provided an excellent (if unconscious) compromise that women with enquiring and competent minds could make with prevailing values and expectations. Women gathered together to learn not only about their missionaries, but also about the countries, the cultures and the politics within which their missionaries lived and worked.

Antigonish (Nova Scotia) women had been interested in missions since 1846 when one of their sisters, Charlotte MacDonald Geddie had sailed with her husband to the New Hebrides. So when the minister called the ladies together in 1878 and proposed the formation of an auxiliary to the Halifax Woman's Foreign Missionary Society (formed 1876), "his request was received unanimously."[24]

The women of South Gloucester (Ontario) report that a Woman's Foreign Missionary Society (Presbyterian) was established there in 1902 and that the members studied books on mission fields. A young girls' group, "The Pearl Seekers" was initiated by that society the same year "with the object of interesting children in the work of foreign missions and educating them in the grace of giving."[25]

Mission study included practically everything. In Comox (British Columbia), women prepared and read papers on leprosy, the work of medical missions in India, the new China, native peoples, welcoming strangers into the church, "map talk" (overseas missions), war and "women who weep" (the last topic probably had to do with World War One since the date of its presentation was 1915).[26] Clearly, these women were as interested in the sociology and psychology of their times as in the geography and history of their missions. And it seems they did not hesitate to explore their own relationship, as women, to the broader issues.

At the instigation of Thora Mills, some women of St. Andrew's United Church (Toronto) formed two book clubs in 1941 that took seriously women's need for intellectual stimulation and creative expression. The clubs were unconventional for their time in two respects: they did not confine their interest to religious or church issues, and they were deliberately free, at least at their beginning, of the traditional "women's work" ethos. The following accounts paint a picture of churchwomen as complete human beings—heads as well as hearts, thinkers as well as doers.

Westminster-Central United Church Book Club[27]

....Some of the younger women became identified with the Book Club because of its nature, freedom from bazaars and ticket-selling.

A prize was offered for the best short story written by a member and at a special meeting the winning essay was read aloud. This opportunity, cultural and educational, was enjoyed for several years. For at least three members it provided the start for writing professionally.

Subsequently the members decided to do some social work to help underprivileged families. Packing hampers at Christmas was the first undertaking. Other help was provided, including a holiday at a summer camp, for such families.

An annual Book Club Party was held when special speakers, authors, and travellers gave illustrated talks. The chief money-raising event was a home-baking and sewing table at the annual bazaar. Recently the Book Club has sponsored an evening of songs from well-known musical comedies. The Book Club has also arranged joint meetings with other congregational groups and continues in its twenty-ninth year.

(The above account was written in 1969. The Westminster-Central United Church Book Club continues in 1983 as the St. Andrew's United Church Book Club.)

The Mary Firth Book Club

Meetings were held in the homes of members every second week. Here there grew a warm and personal interest in each other's work, family, pleasures and problems. Many lasting friendships developed. This close-knit feeling was responsible for an average attendance of twenty-two in a membership averaging twenty-five to thirty.

Meetings were opened with a chosen devotional, followed by business and a book review, social evening or special event. The wide variety of subjects of the book reviews should be noted. There were newly published novels, comedies, plays (these were acted), modern poetry, instructional books and escape books. In addition, guest speakers told of their own special knowledge or work, or showed entertaining moving pictures.

The social events were many. Advantage was taken of all the parties the calendar dates offer—Valentine, St. Patrick's, Hallowe'en, culminating in the Christmas special as guests of Mrs. H. Bacon. Other events were visits to cooking schools, the Crippled Civilians' Workshop, television tapings, and to The Globe and Mail and the Bell Telephone Company.

Last, but not least, were the group's efforts to give help where and when it was needed. During World War Two it undertook the task of befriending a young English soildier. He enjoyed the attention so much that he dismayed the group by suggesting he come over after the war! Also, the group undertook to send layettes to English Lucy of London, who needed them with astonishing regularity! At home, help was given many times when no welfare assistance was to be had. An Indian school in Manitoba, the Retarded Children's Association, and other worthy organizations were aided with gifts of money. Each

Christmas, gift cheques were sent to three missionaries in Africa—Miss Amy Schauffler and Dr. and Mrs. W. Strangeway...

(The Mary Firth Book Club, named after a deaconess at St. Andrew's, disbanded as its membership of young mothers found themselves at new life stages.)

United Church women's understanding of their own mission and ministry has broadened over the years. Study topics today include human rights issues such as Latin American politics, sexism, racism, and discrimination against the disabled; and other issues of social conscience such as consumerism, poverty, and violence. One of the major concerns is the environment, especially pollution and contamination, and our relationship to it. The old interest in missions has been translated into "outreach" at the local level, and into the study of ecumenical policy and activity overseas at the international level, by virtue of United Church work with overseas partners and participation in the World Council of Churches.

That "education is the child of religion"[28] has certainly been true for women in Canada. Until the twentieth century the church was the only acceptable context within which most women could stretch their intellects. In that sense the church has provided, and continues to provide, a framework within which women can liberate themselves. Bible study remains the bread and butter of churchwomen's study groups, of course, and women are beginning to find their own truths revealed in scripture, and to trust their own interpretations.

The Need for Community

...both congregations used the facilities together and attended services together. I came to Hines Creek (Alberta) in 1944 and did not know until the 1950s who were United Church members and who were Anglicans.[29]

Churchwomen's organizations have traditionally provided a medium through which women could keep in touch with each other and thereby keep *all* family members in touch with local activities. This function, generally misunderstood and devalued in our society, was absolutely essential to both the formation and continuing existence of community. So-called "gossip" kept women abreast of marriage possibilities for daughters and sons, impending births, and the general physical, emotional and even financial states of almost everyone. In this way they could respond to birth, marriage, sickness, poverty and death.

Being part of a community of women was obviously important to Rainy Creek (Alberta) settlers who would walk six miles or ride fourteen miles on horseback to their Ladies Aid meetings in 1906.[30] It was important too, to women of East Sault Ste. Marie (Ontario) who distinguished themselves in the United Church by forming their own Woman's Association *before* their congregation came into being.

> *One day we just decided to get organized as a Women's Association of the United Church, with an elected slate of officers. I believe we did it that same sunny afternoon, without even consulting the minister and without being or having a congregation. Just because we wanted to belong. I didn't know any better. As we walked out the gate somebody behind me said, "We have a WA, now we'll get a church!" We broke a rule. Our faces may have been red, but a minister and a church building did come.*[31]

Judging from one report, however, there were limits to how far some women would go to attend their meetings.

> *One enterprising young farmer decided to kill two birds with one stone. Seeing he had to take his wife to the Ladies Aid meeting in Duff (Saskatchewan), he would take a load of pigs to the stockyard at the same time. After finally getting his pigs loaded in the front of the sleigh box and his wife settled in the back, they took off for Duff, only to get half way there and upset the lot—pigs, wife and all—out into the snow. Well, his wife, being somewhat ruffled both in attire and temper by that time, insisted on returning home. Now it is no mean feat to reload pigs out of a snowbank, but after much undignified squealing and scuffling, back they went to the farm. The wife never did get to her meeting and the Ladies in Duff wondered at her absence, but knowing the person involved, I doubt whether they were ever duly informed.*[32]

Churchwomen initiated, organized, cooked and served community suppers all across Canada. These would often be the social high point of the year, attracting families—even those who were non-churched, or churched within other denominations—from miles around. Such occasions provided young people with an opportunity to look over local marriage prospects, men with the opportunity to talk shop, and newcomers with the opportunity to get to know their neighbours and become known themselves. This was particularly important in farming communities where families lived some distance from each other. A New Brunswick women writes about the 10-cent teas at her local church.

> *Perhaps the greatest lasting value was the social atmosphere they generated. Held in the different homes of the community, a Saturday evening 10-cent tea was a chance for everyone to get together for an evening of music, games and good fun. We were supposedly in the midst of a*

17

*depression but nowhere was there gloom and doom in
those gatherings. Such gatherings were one of the factors
which made a close community from a scattered
countryside.* [33]

Women are the nervous system of the church; through them all the
messages of human pain and joy circulate. And until the establishment of
social service agencies, women's organizations were the nervous system
of their communities. To some extent they still are. Meals-on-Wheels,
blood-donor clinics, hospital auxiliaries, transition houses, distress centres, local charitable organizations—all provide contexts within which
churchwomen continue to affirm and enhance their social environment.

The Need to Support the Church

*...in our particular situation, if there were no women
there would be no church.* [34]

No cause was as successful in organizing churchwomen as the need
for money—to build or furnish a church or manse, to pay off existing
mortgages, to expand or renovate, to roof, heat, paint, and to install
modern kitchen facilities that would enable them to raise more funds
more efficiently. Even groups that formed primarily for other purposes
generally found themselves contributing to the financial operation of the
physical church. The reasons for this will be considered in the next
chapter.

WHY WOMEN'S ORGANIZATIONS THRIVED

Fellowship

*...there were many lonely housebound women. I
remember one who told us how much the fellowship meant
to her—to have tea out of somebody else's cup.* [35]

Whatever their *stated* purposes for organizing, women hungered for
the companionship of their sisters. "Fellowship" and "friendship" are the
words which appear most frequently in the Women, Work and Worship
reports—not as *causes* of the organizations, but as heartfelt after-
thoughts. The bonds women formed with each other eased the difficult
tasks, it seems, and lent dignity to the most menial jobs women did in the
church. And it was "fellowship" that helped women survive in an institution which deemed them unfit for positions within its courts. A woman
from Steep Rock Community Church (Manitoba) speaks for hundreds of
churchwomen when she writes:

If we sat at the front or at the back is not important.
Being there, supporting each other is what has made us
strong and successful.[36]

The view that churchwomen can be "strong and successful" *apart*
from the wider church without being "strong and successful" *within* it will
be discussed in a later chapter. Disenfranchised people everywhere *are*
strengthened by community, and community often becomes the most
valuable and valued aspect of its members' existence. Today feminists
speak of support groups, and workers of solidarity: both are "fellowship"
in a secular sense. In significant ways, women's sense of their own special
fellowship within the church emulates the earliest Christian experience of
community.

Some groups have been straightforward about the importance of
companionship. Maple Hill Ladies Aid (Ontario), for example, stated
boldly at the outset that its purpose was "to provide a monthly outing and
to raise money for the church"[37] Young mother's groups continue to
form so that women may support each other in the onerous task of
parenting. "Fun, fellowship and music" was the goal of "The Joymakers",
a Hamilton ensemble of guitars and banjos formed in 1975,[38] as it was for
the ukulele band formed in Moncton in 1949.[39] Even women who were
not church members participated in churchwomen's groups; doctrine
was apprently secondary to friendship.

> ...women's groups were organized where every woman
> in the community was welcomed, for fellowship was so
> necessary in those early days when distances were travelled
> by foot, or by horses or dog-sleigh over bad roads, often
> through extreme cold and snow.[40]

As one begins to appreciate the importance of "community" to
churchwomen, one also begins to understand why quilting was a favourite endeavour. Sitting around a frame in this collective creating was both
productive and therapeutic. The quilt was merely the occasion and the
excuse for the larger work being done—telling stories, sharing problems,
discovering themselves by discovering each other—doing what women
have done together for ages.

Women are social creatures, and the church has provided a medium
through which sisterhood could be affirmed. It was the "fellowship"
women found there that caused them to continue in church groups.
When they found it elsewhere, churchwomen's groups began to decline.

Political Bonding

> ...women had received the right to vote in national
> elections and to sit in the Parliament of Canada before the
> women of St. Paul's (Prescott, Ontario) were admitted as
> members of Session.[41]

Most churchwomen do not give much thought to their political status within the church. Yet the organizing and naming of any special interest group is essentially a political act. The women of the Halifax Wesleyan Female Benevolent Society could have come together informally to perform their charitable work. Money could have been raised, missions studied, manses painted, and suppers cooked without benefit of statements of purpose, constitutions and slates of elected officers. The need to organize formally and to identify their organizations as a continuing presence within the congregations, demonstrated women's sense of alienation from churches which did not accept them as fully participating members.

It is difficult from our perspective to imagine churchwomen's groups as radical or subversive. In the nineteenth century, however, they were met with suspicion and were carefully watched over by clergy or laymen. In her account of early Presbyterian groups in the the United States, Elizabeth Verdesi writes about women's meetings held in 1811.

> *One minister, after opening their meeting with prayer (since women were not permitted to pray in public at this time), was invited by the ladies to leave. He declined, explaining, "No one knew what they would pray for if left alone."*[42]

This situation in Canada was not much different. Dr. Christine MacInnes points to the novelty of Halifax women even thinking they might organize a society of their own:

> *A very daring idea for women of that day! That they might draw up rules and even have a name?*[43]

Even when ministers were sympathetic to the idea of women's organizations, other members of the congregation didn't hesitate to oppose them.

> *It was June 3, 1897 when Rev. Dr. Hincks and Rev. George McCullough gathered seven women of the congregation to organize a Woman's Missionary Society in the Victoria Square (Ontario) Methodist Church. Women's organizations were frowned upon and so a cloud of criticism and stiff opposition came from the men of the church...*[44]

Another account tells of a heated debate that went on in the newspaper of a small Ontario town after a "Mother's Meeting" had been organized in 1900 to do WCTU work.

> *This drew a rousing letter from a man in the Methodist*

> *congregation who denounced that idea of married women meeting in any organized manner and neglecting their children. The following week an angry mother wrote a scathing letter of reply in the newspaper. She lashed out with "I think it's high time for fathers to turn a new leaf and stay at home one evening in the week and give the mothers a chance." She then attacked the Methodist with this comment. "I am sorry this Methodist cannot find some better employment than trying to put out a flickering flame that a few praying women are trying to fan. Our meeting will be open to all, but there will be no tea drinking. We thank "Pro Bona Publica" for his suggestions, and will make him welcome to some of our gatherings."[45]*

By signing his letter "For the good of the people", the Methodist gentleman provided a clue to the nature of the objections to women's groups. "People", in his patriarchal thinking, meant "*male* society". Obviously the Mother's Meeting" was committed to what *they* understood to be the "good of the people" in a more inclusive sense.

Women in most congregations worked under the direction of clergy or church officers. A Ladies Aid formed in 1929 stated in its constitution that it would

> *...with the consent and approval of the minister, session and officers of the Church, try with God's help to do our bit towards building up the work in our midst.[46]*

One wonders what might have happened if God had called these women to a task that the minister, session and officers of the church did not approve. It is this very issue—the direct access of each individual to God—which prompted the Reformation. The women of church, it seems, were the only Protestants still in need of intercession.

There were some cases when women had to seek permission from their Board before they could clean the church. Others had "to receive the permission of the session" to hold a bridal shower for the minister's daughter in the church.[47] In another area, women frequently found themselves locked out of their church on their meeting days, and met in the church shed.[48] All of these situations suggest that women had no real "ownership"—spiritual or material—of their churches. Here, as in the broader society, they were regarded as non-primary human beings who, in the proper ordering of things, should commit themselves to the comfort, the support and the continuance of those humans who *were* considered primary.

To the degree that women's groups could achieve their goals without disrupting or threatening the existing power relationships between men and women, they were generally supported by the church as a whole:

> *...the men of the church were only too ready to accept*
> *contributions of money and prayer from women, but could*
> *not abide their speaking in public.[49]*

It was only when they began to have a sense of their own calling and mission and developed autonomous enterprises that the church became uneasy about its women's groups.[50]

While many churchwomen have remained unaware of the political implications of their organizations, some others have been quite deliberate about their strategies to overcome gender-discrimination. The current issue of inclusive language, for example, is one with which Methodist women in Saskatchewan would have been familiar in 1906.

> *At the Methodist General Conference of 1894, the*
> *Presidents of Ladies Aids were admitted to Quarterly*
> *Boards, and in 1906 a motion was introduced to change the*
> *term layman to lay member, which would automatically*
> *admit women to church courts. (It was defeated, but only*
> *by 42 votes.)[51]*

Perhaps those brave pioneers felt the same way their sister from British Columbia does today when she writes, "enough is enough!"[52]

Formal organizations strengthened the political status of women in the church both collectively and individually. The first women to sit on boards or sessions were usually there as representatives of their group. Many congregations did not admit women to their policy-making bodies until representation of the United Church Women became mandatory in 1962. Now increasing numbers of women are serving on their own merit, not as representatives but as partners with men in the community of the church. Even so, although women constitute the majority of its membership, the United Church continues to be dominated by men.

WHAT A CHURCHWOMAN'S ORGANIZATION OFFERED ITS MEMBERS

> *Ministry is the process of equipping one another, not to*
> *run away, or to hide from life—but to survive and to*
> *overcome, joyously and generously.[53]*

Sociologist, Orrin E. Klapp, has suggested that there are six conditions essential to human happiness.[54] These can be examined in relation to churchwomen and in doing so, we may see more clearly the hidden benefits individual women derive from their organizations.

Joy-Giving Self-Concept

Western culture has not been kind to woman. Philosophers and scientists have told her she is defective, and religious leaders have defined her as lesser than man in the divine order. The creation story which presents women and men as equals (Genesis 1: 27), neglected by Paul and by most scholars since Paul, has almost passed out of the Christian story. Instead, we continue to teach our children the *other* creation (Genesis 2: 22) which suggests that woman is derivative of man, a non-primary human. Patriarchal scholarship ignores those passages of scripture which would undermine its political "rightness". And since patriarchy depends upon the premise that women are inferior, any passage suggesting otherwise would be ignored, refuted or twisted to conform to the prevailing mode of thought.

The problem this poses for women is that they have been conditioned by patriarchal values. They come to believe in the inferiority of women and, therefore, of themselves. This is hardly conducive to a "joy-giving self-concept."

In the late 1960s, some sociologists in New York City wanted to test the theory that everyone in a society is socialized to the values of the dominant power group. To do so they assembled pictures of children, arranging them by skin colour from the blackest to the most fair. Then black school children were asked separately to select the child from the pictures that they would prefer as a best friend. They chose the blond. The difference between what these children valued in people and what they saw every time they looked in a mirror would have a profound effect on the directions their lives would take. The "black is beautiful" movement was a systematic attempt to neutralize this phenomenon.

By coming together formally, churchwomen could develop a sense of their importance as a group; this in turn contributed to the individual's sense of her own value. In their work together women experienced each other as competent and intelligent human beings and that produced in each a new confidence in her own capabilities. Even while excluded from the mainstream of the church, women could, in their own circles, meet as whole thinking and caring people.

Joy-Giving Group Expression of Emotion

Experience has taught me that churchwomen like to sing and dance. As I travelled around the country with the Women, Work and Worship project, the hymn most sung in our meetings was, in fact, "Lord of the Dance". Therefore when several women in different parts of Canada told me that their ministers "did not allow" this beautiful hymn to be sung at Sunday service, I suspected that here was an important separation between women's "God-wardness"[55] and conventional patriarchal worship. Whether in singing together, dancing together or celebrating communion together, the spirit is evoked, for women, through the sharing, the blending, the touching, the speaking and the hearing. It seems that

23

God is experienced in relation and is in no sense an abstraction.

A shared ministry also brings out a sense of spiritual sisterhood, and this seems to have been as true of the early organizations as it is today. From participation in a group, churchwomen have learned that there is a female experience of God. Their Creator is more readily found in the circle than in rows, and the fact that women frequently called their groups "circles" suggests that at some level they understood women's worship to be qualitatively different from worship as it was practised in their churches. This understanding could only enhance the "joy-giving expression of emotion" that occurred in their shared worship.

Joy-Giving Location in Space

George Carlin, a comedian, performs a routine in which he talks about the importance of having "a place to put your stuff". Although laughable, the importance of his observations cannot be denied.

Before they had organized, women in our churches had no place to put their talents, their skills or their vision. Permitted only passive access to the sanctuary and excluded entirely from the Board rooms, women assumed control of church parlours and kitchens. Here, at least, they could carve out a "space" for themselves. Many women, to this day, feel more comfortable using the "back doors" of their churches which are somehow theirs in ways that sanctuary doors are not. Perhaps the back doors lead more directly to those women's "joy-giving location in space".

Joy-Giving Attitude Towards the Past

The church as a whole has not given its women much in the way of a past. Even scripture is directed towards men, a fact which becomes apparent in a reading of the Ten Commandments. Churchwomen's organizations gave women an opportunity to discover their ancestors in the faith. Studies could focus on women of the Bible, for example, or on Jesus' interaction with women. This "reclaiming of heroes" has helped women to feel less alienated from their faith in some ways, and has also helped them to understand that their lesser status was certainly not Christian in the sense that it had any basis in Christ's teachings. How liberating a discovery that has been!

Women's groups, especially the missionary societies, gave women a chance to see competent women in action throughout the world. Their sense of history and of woman's place in history must have been greatly expanded by mission study. Some must have wondered why their sisters who were medical doctors could practise overseas but not at home, or why Chinese mothers felt obliged to cripple their daughters with foot bindings. All that was learned about other times and places would teach them something about themselves as women. In spite of the indifference of the wider church to women's story, women could, in their own groups, pursue a "joy-giving attitude towards the past".

24

Joy-Giving Work

Doing meaningful work is, perhaps, the greatest single source of personal satisfaction. Churchwomen's groups allowed individuals to extend the range of their concerns and activity beyond immediate family and friends into the wider community. Whether organizing a soup-line, packing bales for a distressed part of the country, or participating in a peace march, churchwomen are doing either what they have *chosen* to do, or what they have felt *called* to. Even the more mundane tasks such as peeling potatoes or washing up are "joy-giving work" because of the environment of fellowship in which they occur.

In terms of good works we have already seen that churchwomen have every reason to feel good about themselves. Disadvantaged by gender in the world of paid employment, a source of personal satisfaction to many men, churchwomen made their mark as volunteer workers and helped to humanize Canada in the process.

Joy-Giving Focus for One's Life

The sense that one is about God's work, helping to bring about God's kingdom, lends an ecstatic energy to the task at hand. The notion of "calling", however, has a special significance to those who are disenfranchised, because it assigns absolute authority to God. It provides a moral justification for defying convention, tradition and legislation, all of which are (in a literal sense) man-made. This "joy-giving focus", in both its spiritual and political senses, enhances all the other conditions for happiness and supplies the bond that unites the women of the church. As churchwomen's groups become secularized and lose touch with this focus, the ecstatic aspect decreases, and so does the commitment of individuals to the group.

Conclusion

This chapter is perhaps best concluded with the final paragraphs written for "The Story of Women's Groups in Brooklyn Sunday School—Harcourt Memorial United Church: 1887-1982." The author, in considering the twenty years since the formation of United Church Women, provides a summation that captures the essence of this chapter.

> Over the past twenty years, the Purpose of the UCW has remained the same—only the methods have been changed. Although some areas of the world are still in need, we no longer send bales of clothing. Instead, we send seeds and agricultural experts so that the people learn to help themselves.
>
> Our studies now focus on acid rain, nuclear disarmament, and world peace—and Faith/Justice, our

current study. Financial contributions have been made when and where a need is seen, in church and community.

Most of what the women do cannot be measured in financial terms. There are the multitude of little things done day by day, consistently, quietly and unobtrusively, ministering to each other, in the same spirit of love and concern that has been evident in the organization from the beginning.

Most importantly, the Vision which began the UCW in 1962 has remained. "With enlarged vision and deepened consecration, teach us to meet each new challenge with a fresh way of thought and action. In all things keep us close to thyself so that thy life may make our organization a living thing growing in spirit and activity". (From the UCW Inaugural Service, January, 1962.)[56]

Chapter 2 FAITH AND FINANCES

I t was not originally intended that an entire chapter would be devoted to churchwomen and finances. However, so much of the material sent in to the Women, Work and Worship project focussed on money—how we raise it, how we spend it, who controls it—that it seemed an area which cried out for further exploration. In thinking and reading about the subject, I began to realize that this preoccupation with cold cash reflected some profound truths about women's role in the church. The following sections consider women's "faith and finances" at the congregational and national levels. Any insights they contain have been distilled from the hundreds of submissions from across Canada.

IN THE CONGREGATION AND COMMUNITY

The Financial Ability of Women's Groups

The ways devised by churchwomen to raise money demonstrate entrepreneurial skills that boggle the mind. Quilting, bazaars, rummage sales, book sales, bake sales, plant sales, auctions, economy stories, catering, church and community suppers—the list of fund-raising activities goes on and on. In spite of all evidence to the contrary, however, churchwomen do not see themselves as engaged in business, nor does the local church, in most cases, recognize or credit those skills of administration and organization that are necessary to fund-raising.

A woman from Saskatchewan wrote about four catering groups that supported her church.[1] When I met her at a conference and commented on the talents of those business women, she laughed and replied, "I'll have to tell them that; they've never thought of themselves in those terms." The social myth is that competence in the arena of public enterprise is not a feminine quality. That churchwomen *have* managed to make such financial contributions to both the local and national church *without dispelling the myth* indicates how deeply lodged it is in society. In at least one case, the responsibility for the church rested almost entirely with the women in its congregation.

27

> *For the latter fifteen years our church was so lacking in men that had it not been for the women of the church we would have had to close as in both work and attendance the women were the only ones to assist, and the finances too depend upon them.* [2]

Some fund-raising activities demonstrated a unique blend of imagination, initiative, and faith. One in particular involves the "Hotplate Cookbook" compiled by women of Vancouver Presbyterial. This contained nutritious and easily prepared recipes for people with limited cooking facilities—mostly the elderly and the poor. The group borrowed $1,200.00, printed 3,000 books and sold them in lots of 10 for $5.00 to those who could distribute them to the needy. When all of those were sold, the women applied for a grant to New Horizons, an organization which assisted senior citizens. After a Board of Directors (with ten members over sixty-five years of age) had been established, the churchwomen received a grant of $4,875.00 and ordered 3,000 more copies. These were soon sold, but the story doesn't end there.

> *At this time we were being urged by the Public Health Nurses, who were distributing the books to their patients, to take a long look at our recipes and try to find some with more nutrition. We had decided to revise our book, each of the board members looking for recipes that contained more nutrition and bringing a recipe made up to a luncheon so we could try them out and decide which ones to use...The revision was made and a decision to order 11,000 more copies, which put us in the bracket of being a bestseller.*
> *...In the spring of 1977 it was decided to phase out the project. We were almost out of books again and had made money in spite of intending not to, and we felt that we had completed the project.* [3]

Another group added a little spice to its plant sale by calling it a "Slip and Bloomer Tea". Apparently they had a record crowd! [4]

Many churchwomen's groups began as "Parsonage Aid Societies". Their work did not end with the provision of funds to support their minister's residence, it seems.

> *The care of the manse was left to the Ladies Aid and feelings often ran high when it was time to do painting and paper-hanging as some of the members had very definite ideas on what they considered "good taste". Before a new minister and his wife and family arrived the manse was given a thorough cleaning by the group. One of our ministers brought his new bride to Stockton (Manitoba) and never before did the manse get such a cleaning. Would you believe that two of the women returned to the manse after*

*the others had gone home and tied a cow bell under the coil
springs of the bed?*[5]

The care and upkeep of churches fell to the women's groups. In fact,
the first act for one Ladies Aid, after it had been duly constituted, was to
decide to buy a dust-mop for the janitor, and to outline the janitor's
duties.[6] For most, however, paid caretaking staff was a luxury and the
actual dusting, polishing, scrubbing and waxing was the women's work.
As if that were not hardship enough, at least one group had to ask the
board for permission to clean the church.[7] Women also sawed wood,[8]
varnished floors, laid carpet, painted,[9] shingled roofs (by tying themselves to the chimney),[10] and even made trousers for the preacher.[11]

The remarkable thing about women's support for the church, particularly in the area of finances, is that they started with few resources and
practically no access to money of their own. The funds were produced
through wit, imagination, initiative, organization, and those skills they
had acquired in other facets of their lives. To start with so little and
accomplish so much is one of the unsung tales of our time.

The "Value" of Women's Groups

> *Through the years more and more has had to be done
> to cover the expenses of running a large church besides the
> offering which is given Sunday by Sunday. Many
> organizations have faithfully undertaken this task but the
> women have always done a superb job, raising money
> through quilting, bazaars, garden parties, church socials,
> teas, catering and suppers.*[12]

When the Woman's Foreign Missionary Society (Western Division)
was formed by Presbyterians in 1876, several ministers expressed a fear
that their church finances would suffer as a result.[13] That simply did not
happen. Canadian women, like their American sisters, developed a pattern of "double-giving". The fear expressed by the clergy, however,
suggests a more deeply rooted anxiety that lay organizations engaged in
God's work are somehow in competition with the church. Such an
assumption was particularly hard on churchwomen who had no access to
policy-making positions in the church at any level, and could *only* heed
their call to mission work through their own societies.

Any misgivings churchmen may have had about churchwomen's
groups faded before the obvious benefits. Women demonstrated a
remarkable ability to raise money without disrupting their other church-
related tasks, and were undoubtedly encouraged in this enterprise. Here,
finally, was a contribution they could make without rocking the boat.
Money and all that it accomplished was tangible evidence that women
had an active and meaningful presence in the churches. Important as a
source of self-esteem and also as a source of positive recognition from the

wider church, money seemed to become the focus (and the justification) for women's groups. This was especially so for groups such as Ladies Aids and Woman's Associations which worked on behalf of their local churches.

It wasn't long before the wider church *expected* its women's groups to make money. As a result, the groups *constituted* for other reasons, such as study or consciousness-raising, were frequently made to feel guilty (by the congregations and by other woman's organizations) for their "selfish" pursuits. Many such groups eventually bowed to the pressure to raise funds even though doing so destroyed any possibility of continuing their fellowship of reflection and contemplation.

The money contributed by women's groups to their congregations is generally thought of as "secondary" income. There is ample evidence, however, to show that several of our churches were built, and are sustained, by women. A group in British Columbia reports that their church has been financially dependent on the UCW for the last fifteen years.[14] Another in Manitoba took a $10,000.00 loan during the Depression and made payments of $750.00 per year in order to pay off the large debt on a new church building.[15] Churchwomen across Canada write that the funds they've raised have been *essential* to congregational life: paying the minister's salary; building, buying, renovating, furnishing and insuring church and manse; purchasing pews, hymn books, Sunday School materials; paying off debts; and paying for emergency repairs made necessary by such natural calamities as fire, flood, hail, and wind.

A report from Caledonia, Ontario, tells of a group's decision to disband itself some years ago: "It didn't take long for the minister of the church to re-organize the Ladies Aid!"[16] Obviously its contributions to the church had not gone unnoticed. Another report from Campbell River, British Columbia, demonstrates that churches depended upon funds raised by the women. Old Minute books contained the following entries:

> *$50.00 short on minister's salary. Contact WA for help.*
>
> *Oil bill owing. Contact afternoon WA group.*
>
> *Mortgage payment overdue. Use stained-glass window fund.*

The study-oriented WMS groups, because they were part of a structure that was financially and administratively independent of the church, did not have to justify their fellowship through endless fund-raising activities. They *did* raise money, but it was for projects chosen by themselves, or by their parent organization. In these groups money was only the means to further the mission work; in the church-related groups such as Ladies Aids and Woman's Associations, money became an end in itself. In most cases it was simply handed over to the managers of the church, and did not represent any special ministry for the women who had raised it.

One last point must be made about women's financial contributions to the congregation. There is a tendency to equate women's givings with the givings of their organizations. If the UCW contributes $5000.00 to the church budget, we tend to think that $5,000.00 is the amount women have given. However, women form sixty to seventy percent of the membership of the United Church and, as members, they also contribute their Sunday offerings. And half of family givings (from families in which the woman is financially dependent upon her husband) must be credited to women in any modern understanding of family finances. Therefore *the amount of money given by women to their congregations is actually far greater than the amount given by their organizations.* Far from being "secondary" or auxiliary givers, it is not unreasonable to speculate that women are the *major* source of funds in our churches.

Something Out of Nothing

Young Susan came home from Sunday School with a mite box. "Why do you call it a mite box, Mother?" "Because," chirped in her brother, "You might put something into it and you might not!"

Considering that until recently few women had access to money of their own, the amount they have been able to contribute to their churches is astounding. For most churchwomen it has not been a matter of transferring money earned elsewhere to church coffers, but of turning imagination, wit, talent, and the raw materials of the household into hard cash. Domestic skills—cooking, sewing, knitting—have become the primary source of their income; millions of dollars have been raised with church suppers, quilts and bazaars. Some enterprising groups have moved their activities into the public marketplace, serving meals at local exhibitions or fairs, or operating secondhand stores on a full-time basis.

The ability of women to raise money without an initial capital outlay is evident in the variety of schemes they developed. "Slave markets" were held in which the skills of group members were auctioned to the highest bidder.[19] Several groups had periodic penny-per-inch waistline measurements taken of its members, or issued sunshine bags into which members put a penny on nice days. A "travelling apron" went from person to person and each woman sewed a coin into it.[20] The Sunday egg project of churchwomen in Manitoba built a basement for their church; the money was raised through the sale of eggs collected by members on Sundays.[21] Other Manitoba women staged a play and charged admission in order to pay for a piano for the newly opened public school.[22] Talent money was also a favourite way of raising funds. In one group, a woman produced an acre of wheat with her dollar, and two others bought an ice-cream freezer and sold ice cream. When all the receipts were in at the end of the year, the group had realized $385.00—a respectable sum for 1906; enough, in fact, to purchase two lots for a church building.[23]

Several churchwomen's groups have raised money by catering. In some cases, three or four catering groups have been formed within one congregation. Saskatchewan women bleached sugar-bags and transformed them into pillow cases, tablecloths, tea towels, dresser scarves and aprons by adding some "fancy work". These were sold at "very reasonable prices".[24] Perhaps the most unusual fund-raising was done by a group in Mansonville, Quebec—they bought a cow and then hired it out to members by the year. These same women were encouraged to pay their dues in yarn, knitting or weaving; any wool received was woven into flannel.[25] Another prize for entrepreneurial know-how would have to go to women in White Rock, British Columbia. This group rented a television set and charged admission to people who wished to watch the coronation of Queen Elizabeth.[26] At least one group raised money by not spending it; they took over the caretaking chores of their church to save up for a new furnace.[27]

Individual churchwomen have also made an impact on the finances of their churches. Christina Kerr, a widow since World War One, challenged her congregation to a building program in the early fifties by starting a building fund with a $10.00 pension increase she had received. She continued to put the extra $10.00 into the fund every month, and eventually the new church was built.[28] The first amount of money offered towards the construction cost of the new J. Wesley Smith Memorial Church in Halifax was a contribution of $2.00 by a woman who was earning twenty-five cents a day washing clothes.[29] Mrs. James Dawson of Crapaud, Prince Edward Island saved all the money she made from crotcheting lace for pillow cases until she had enough money to purchase chimes for the church steeple in 1951.[30] In 1982, two women, Mrs. Coltart and Mrs. Jarvis, donated seventy-five quilts to help their Portage la Prairie (Manitoba) UCW meet its 1983 budget.[31]

The size of a churchwomen's group does not seem to affect either its enthusiasm or its ability to make money. Eileen McLeod of Herschel, Saskatchewan, speaks for many United Church Women when she writes that the lack of a large membership "never seems to keep the group from tackling any project."[32] Perhaps there is a good lesson in faith here.

There is also a lesson to be learned from the means by which women raise money. After reading about the hundreds of ways devised to collect pennies, nickels and dimes, a member of the Women, Work and Worship Advisory Committee wondered aloud why women didn't just pay $2.00, $5.00 or $10.00 in dues at the beginning of each budget year. The answer is that most women did not have direct access to money. Had there been substantial fees payable all at once, many women would have been unable to participate in the group. The strategy of collecting little bits of money through the year, whether in sunshine bags, mite boxes, travelling aprons, birthday boxes, waistline measures, or miles of pennies, allowed the poorest women to contribute as much as the wealthiest. It was a way by which women could protect each other's dignity and discourage social class hierarchies in their own groups, even if such hierarchies were part of the dynamic of the wider congregation.

This same principle is the basis of The Fellowship of the Least Coin, an international fellowship begun in 1956 by an Asian woman, Shanti Solomon, to help Christian women in every nation to "become aware of their relationships with the rest of the world-wide family."[33] The participants set aside the "least coin" in their currency (a penny in Canada) each month and this is contributed annually to a common fund which is used for ministries all over the world. These pennies, and their international equivalents, grew into a quarter million dollars in 1982. The important aspect of this fellowship is that the poorest women from the most desolate circumstances were able to participate as fully as their affluent sisters around the world.

The penny collections, whatever form they took, and the fund-raising projects in which all group members participated equally, reflected a concern with human dignity and an understanding of stewardship that transcends church finances...

Who Spends the Money?

...the men, as officers (elders, stewards), must still think
they run the church and support it financially.

In many congregations the money earned by women's groups is still handed over to the church managers. This was almost always the case in the past. The Victoria Square (Ontario) United Church History, for example, states that the proceeds from the annual fowl supper "are always turned over to the Church Treasurer by the UCW, a gallant band of hard-working women who do much towards the upkeep of the church and manse."[35] Another group reported that when the church treasury was short of cash, "our treasurer was instructed to pay what was required."[36] The disposition of their money in this way would not be a problem if women were represented, equally with men or proportionately, on their boards. This was seldom the case, however, so the money earned by the women was spent on whatever the governing men of the church thought important. The frustration this caused is evident in several reports. Some groups, denied any official control over their money, devised informal strategies of control of both their finances and their fund-raising activities.

In some cases women took on specific expenses as their special responsibility. It does not take a great deal of imagination to understand why so many women's groups assumed the caretaking costs. The Birtle Union Ladies Aid, after protesting about uncut grass and badly needed church repairs for a year, finally took matters into their own hands and hired a grass-cutter and repair man themselves.[37] In 1941, there was some discussion about whether women's organizations would be a necessary part of a church newly formed through the union of two congregations. The general conclusion of the congregation was that "their financial assistance would be very much appreciated." In spite of that appreciation the Minutes of 1944 indicate that the women "interviewed and bothered the men until they got the church cleaned and provided someone to assist with the weekly cleaning." In 1982 these women were still "bothering" the Board about a caretaker![38]

Some groups were quite adamant about what they would and would not do for the church. Minutes of a women's meeting in Kamloops, British Columbia, tell a terse but interesting tale.

> *September 1925: Special Meeting*
> *The Management Committee asked to meet a committee of*
> *the Ladies regarding a Congregational Social. After some*
> *discussion, however, it was moved by Mrs. Colley,*
> *seconded by Mrs. Lee, that the men be asked to take the*
> *Social in hand in view of the fact that the energy of the*
> *Ladies was being taken up at this time with preparation for*
> *the bazaar.*[39]

Not all "Ladies" felt so comfortable about telling their managers to "do it themselves", however.

Another strategy of control was to establish a fund. When their church board asked to borrow $150.00 in 1923, the women of Birtle (the same ones who hired the grass-cutter) "voted by secret ballot, and overwhelmingly said 'no'! They were saving for a manse!"[40] A report on the Duff (Saskatchewan) Ladies Aid tells us the story behind a motion passed in 1927 to donate $100.00 to a church building fund.

> *Apparently the Ladies heard in a roundabout way that*
> *the men were about to approach them once more for help*
> *with the minister's salary and so they called an earlier*
> *meeting than usual to discuss the matter. They decided that*
> *perhaps the men might dig a little deeper if they started a*
> *building fund for their new church, and the women would*
> *not be at their beck and call every time the need arose.*
> *They did build up a fund of $600.00 which went towards the*
> *construction of the church basement in the Fall of 1929.*

Several women's groups have tried to dispense with their fund-raising, only to discover how essential such activity is in church life. A UCW group in Waterloo (Ontario) passed a motion in 1971 *not* to do any more catering. However,

> *Eight months later...our missionary treasurer reported*
> *our M & S fund was short $80.00, so we catered for the*

34

> *Inter-Varsity Christian Fellowship banquet and made*
> *$117.00 profit—$100.00 of which went to the M & S Fund.*
> *We have been catering ever since.*[42]

Another group in Manitoba voted in 1966 to eliminate all outside catering. By 1972 church expenses had become very heavy and "the old motion re catering was rescinded."[43]

Women in Prince Edward Island were obviously aware of the pressures on their groups to raise money; they deliberately planned their kitchen "on the basis that the UCW would *not* pay for the new church from the kitchen." Apparently the pressures did not go away, however, for these same women were to wish on several occassions "for a few extra stove burners and an extra oven or three."[44]

The lessons to be drawn from the Women, Work and Worship materials about churchwomen's faith and finances are inescapable. In any accurate reflection of their contributions (both within and outside their organizations), women are primary sources of church income, and not secondary givers as is commonly believed. This perceived "auxiliary" status has prevented women from asserting their share of rightful authority in regard to church funds, and has supported the notion that women are supporters, helpers, assisters of those *men* who do the *real* work of the church.

The money-earning capacity of women led to the acceptance of their organizations by the wider church, the same ability that is most valued today. This is evident in the opposition met by women who have attempted to form study groups free of fund-raising activity, and also in the difficulty churchwomen experience when they try to curtail some of their money-oriented projects.

Although women have been a major source of funds, they have had little say in the disposition of those funds. If women *did* have equal representation with men in the policy-making bodies of their congregations, strategies for maintaining some informal control over their money would be unnecessary; the ministry as perceived by the church would then reflect the ministry as perceived by the women of the church. Without such representation, however, churchwomen and their groups are alienated from their congregations and the institution of the church remains something "other" and apart from them.

IN THE NATIONAL CHURCH

> *In 1980 the M & S Fund raised a total of $20,526,113 of*
> *which a little over $2 million came from United Church*
> *Women groups. Most of the money comes from the M & S*
> *side of duplex envelopes used in most churches.*[45]

As in the congregations, women's financial contribution to the national church budget tends to be minimized. Their givings are far more than the givings credited to the UCW organization, for most women including those who do not consider themselves UCW, give through regular Sunday offerings. Since women comprise from sixty to seventy percent of the total United Church membership, it would be on the conservative side to estimate that money contributed by the UCW and single women, plus women's share of family givings, adds up to at least *half* of the total budget of the Mission and Service Fund from which the church is administered. Even if we take *only* the UCW contribution to the M & S Fund into account, we find that women give roughly one-tenth of the whole budget, and one-third of the budget for the Division of Mission in Canada. It is this Division from which the UCW receives its staff support and educational materials.

In spite of the magnitude of the UCW's financial contribution, the national church does not seem to accord the organization an appropriate degree of recognition in terms of staffing or programming. A recent statement from the Secretary of the Division of Mission in Canada, for example, refers to the UCW and "men's networks" as though the two groups shared the same status.[46] They don't. The "men's networks" consist of United Church Men, an organization that is practically extinct except for Hamilton and Maritime Conferences, and AOTS ("As one that serves") Men's Clubs, an organization that is independent of the United Church structure, with its own constitution and in control of its own finances. In 1980, AOTS reported 100 clubs across Canada, with approximately 3,000 members. By contrast, the UCW membership in 1980 was 139,603.[47] There is no doubt that the men's groups are important to the people they serve. However, in terms of size of membership and financial contribution, their importance to the national church cannot be equated with that of the UCW. If they *are* valued equally, it can only be because men are generally accorded higher status in the church than women.

Money, Power and Partnership

> ...*co-optation effects a change in the organization, and this results in a dilemma; how to provide sufficient participation in the organization to satisfy the co-opted elements without losing control.*[48]

Several reasons have been given for the amalgamation of the two women's groups into United Church Women. The Dominion Woman's Association and Woman's Missionary Society both had national study programs and already shared an educational ethos. In many congregations, women had already unified the work of the two organizations. Although the WA had a larger membership, the WMS had a stronger national organization and it was thought that the combination would draw on the strengths of each to unify all the women of the church. The process, it was thought, would also unify women and men of the congregations across the country, as women began to play a more active part in the "total mission of the church."

At the national level it seemed expedient to amalgamate overseas mission work so that the United Church was not perceived as a divided house by those being served abroad. Unquestionably, the administration of one mission board would be more efficient than the administration of two. There was some intention too, that a Board of Women, equal in status to the Board of Men, would assist the integration of women in the offices of the national church. After much negotiation the WA and WMS combined to form the UCW in 1962.

That same year saw another amalgamation. A new Board of World Mission and a new Board of Home Missions (later to become Division of World Outreach and Division of Mission in Canada respectively) was set up, incorporating work formerly done under the direction of the WMS. At the time of this amalgamation, the WMS was responsible for half the overseas mission work being done by the United Church, and for one-third of the home missions work.

The 1963 Reference Edition of *The Observer* shows the transfer from WMS to the General Funds of the United Church at $1,680,802.00. A slightly different (and more complete) picture of the finances can be seen in the following.

> *In 1961, members provided 92.96% of WMS income; total receipts for the General Fund were $1,607,539.51; allocations to Conference Branches, $1,500,000. At the end of this year with the transfer of the WMS Retirement Fund to the church went $3,252,000 as a paid-up fund to provide for active and retired missionaries' pensions. The traditional "money in hand before spending"* policy made it possible for the WMS to turn over to the Church Treasury $1,850,000 for the Stabilization Fund.*[49]
>
> (Author's note)* Unlike the United Church, the WMS established its budget on the receipts of the preceding year. That is, money spent in 1962 would have been taken in, in 1961.

The formation of the UCW involved years of study and negotiation on the part of the executive of the women's groups and the commissions and committees established by General Council. The intentions of all involved seemed to have been motivated by a sincere desire for greater unity among churchwomen and among women and men, and for a more efficient realization of God's will as expressed through The United Church of Canada's work in the world. In spite of that, and without questioning the motives of the individual players, there is a nagging familiarity to the process that brought the strong and powerful Woman's Missionary Society (the Woman's Association had nothing to lose by amalgamation) under the control of the United Church. The same process, called "co-optation" by Verdesi in relation to the American Presbyterian Church, seems to be a predictable pattern. It is interesting to note that the United Church AOTS Men's Clubs, which also share a mission with the church, have retained their autonomy and remain in a relationship with the church (after attempting other forms of relating) that is similar to that of the WMS before the amalgamation. One wonders if they too might have been "co-opted" had they achieved the membership and financial status of the women's organizations. In 1982 the men's group (AOTS and UCM) did not produce any revenue for the national church, and received $8,500.00 in support from the Ministry With Adults Working Unit. By contrast, UCW received $22,100.00 in support and contributed three and a half million dollars to the M & S Fund. (This amount does not include money generated through the sale of supplies such as membership pins, certificates, cards, envelopes or study resources.) United Church Women must judge for themselves whether they have been provided "sufficient participation in the organization" to justify their lack of political and financial autonomy within the institution of the church.

Chapter 3   SOCIAL CHANGE
REFLECTED IN WOMEN'S
WORK AND WORSHIP

The United Church of Canada, as a participant in society, is both a reflection and shaper of the Canadian consciousness. An ongoing dialogue between "the world" and the church constantly modifies each to affect public opinion, public policy, and church doctrine.

In some cases secular movements have led our church into social issues by challenging the institution on its own ground of faith and justice. Of all the denominations, the United Church has been in a unique position to respond. Because of the nature of church union, it is an institution *committed to the church that could be,* rather than to the church that has been. The twentieth century has seen some major changes in Canadian life and through the interplay of church and society these changes have affected women's work and worship.

CHURCH UNION: BUILDING AND BREAKING

>...the history of the Christian tradition is filled with the stories of people who have had to make hard political choices because of their faith.[1]

It is easy to forget that when we speak of Church *Union,* we are speaking from the perspective of The United Church of Canada. For many Canadians the event was a rupture—not only in their churches, but in families and communities as well. Little has been written about women's part in this process. Of the 342 signers of the Document of Church Union, only four were women.[2] Unofficially, however, all the women of the uniting churches would have been very much affected by the local lobbying on both sides of the issue.

The first proposal for church union in Canada came from the Anglicans in 1889. It was actually part of a world-wide movement to breach some of the divisions between Protestant denominations. Early talks with Methodists and Presbyterians faltered on Anglican insistence on an episcopal structure—a hierarchical and centralized form of church government under the direction of a Primate. Since there seemed to be little chance of surmounting the structural problems involved in union with the Anglicans, the non-episcopal churches participating in the discussion began to think in terms of union among themselves. In 1902, Presbyterians proposed union with the Methodist Church. Congregationalists soon became involved in the process, and all three denominations set up union committees and established a joint committee to iron out the details of their unification.

Church historian, John Webster Grant, names three reasons for the interest in union: a new understanding of theology and biblical criticism had blurred traditional denominational lines; a "bad conscience" about Protestant sectarianism had been awakened by theological movements of the late nineteenth century; and there was a growing sense that competition among Protestant denominations was counter-productive to the mission of the church[3]. Perhaps it was this latter sense of mission, linked as it was with "Canadianism", that eventually resulted in successful union in this country while union talks failed elsewhere. The Joint Committee had prepared the Basis of Union by 1908, and in 1925 The United Church of Canada became a reality.

Around the turn of the twentieth century, women had little authority in their churches or in society. They were second-class citizens—legally and politically—in both. Higher education was becoming more accessible but only up to a point. A woman who received a medical degree in Canada in 1900, for example, had to go to the United States to complete her internship, since no Canadian hospital would accept women doctors.[4] Some older members of the congregation in Prince Edward Island recall when women of the church,

> ...did not teach Sunday School, sing in the choir, assist with midweek catechism classes, or testify and pray aloud during a church service or prayer meeting. Although these women were devout Christians and were concerned about the spiritual welfare of their children and other people, they held no office in the church, did not serve on any committee or attend any meeting in connection with church business.[5]

When women did work in their churches, particularly with the Presbyterian tradition, they were generally under the supervision of men. Female Sunday School teachers, for example, worked with male superintendents. In a taped interview, the late Beatrice Wilson tells about ministers or elders handling the devotional at women's meetings because of the strong feeling about "what a woman was fitted to do." There was some fear, apparently, that left on their own women might even try to lead in prayer![6] The subordinate status of one congregation's women is amply demonstrated in the following account from Bay of Quinte Conference:

> *In 1894 an organ was purchased for $80.00, the money
> raised by serving a Harvest Dinner...The trustees and
> stewards arranged for the dinner and the ladies were to do
> the cooking and the proper arrangement of the tables.*[7]

The irony about women's position in their churches was that their own independent organizations were thriving. All three of the uniting denominations had established missionary societies in the nineteenth century, and all but the Congregationalists were supporting women in both foreign and home missions. (The Canada Congregational Woman's Board of Mission supported overseas missions only; the home mission work was administered and funded through a general church board.) By the turn of the century all of these societies were well established testimonies to the ability of those same women who were "unfitted" for office within their churches. In addition, by 1900, ecumenical women's groups, especially the Woman's Christian Temperance Union which had been founded in Canada in 1874, were becoming a political presence throughout Canada. (The World Convention of the WCTU was held at Allen Gardens, Toronto, in 1897.[8])

Women involved in any of these organizations were growing into a new sense of their own competence and, simultaneously, beginning to understand the impact of acting together. In short, during this period many women were becoming "politicized". Elizabeth Ross, President of the Methodist Woman's Missionary Society for twenty-three years, wrote in her Introduction to *The Story of the years 1881-1906* of

> *...a revelation of the new life, the expanding vision that
> came to Christian womanhood during the latter decades of
> the nineteenth century. The women of Christendom have
> come into great possessions. Their ideals have changed;
> individual responsibility for the betterment of the world,
> both at home and abroad, has been borne in upon them,
> and the growing power of being able to bring things to pass,
> of planning and of being responsible for the carrying of such
> plans to successful completion, has given to them an added
> dignity, a new courage, a more intelligent devotion and a
> deeper spiritual life.*[9]

One missionary (male) was so impressed with the work of the women in his mission field that he told an audience: "If one or the other must leave, I would say, 'come my brethren, let us go home and leave the work to the women'."[10]

The early years of the twentieth century saw Canada prosper and expand. Immigration rose from 17,000 in 1896 to 200,000 in 1906[11] and began to include eastern Europeans. Most settled in the prairie provinces to establish farms, but many found their way to cities which were also beginning to attract rural youth to jobs in industry. The Protestant denominations, founded largely on rural values, were forced to devise ways of dealing both with the urban influx and the isolated constituents in the West. The Catholic Church, with its tenuous balance of French and Irish leadership, now found people among its membership who spoke neither French nor English, and who had their own distinctive notions about the substance and ritual of worship.

Churchwomen were not passive onlookers in this expansion through immigration. Rural settlements required farm workers, and the affluent city households required servants. To fill this need, the YMCA, National Council of Women, IODE, and some of the church-connected women's groups actively recruited immigrant women for domestic labour. In fact the Protestant Directorate of Female Immigration reported in 1915 that 129,000 domestic servants had entered Canada in the decade 1904-1914.[12] Most of these were British.

The practical work involved in recruitment occupied many churchwomen. Indeed the process was inspired with both religious and patriotic fervour. Prospective servants were encouraged to think of themselves as participants in a grand scheme, and tempted by talk of all the land-owning bachelors in Canada. The recruiters, on the other hand, held the somewhat self-serving belief that these women recruited from among the poor and widowed in a depressed Britain, were being saved from a life of degradation. They were assisted in this view by The British Women's Emigration Association, a group of upper-class English women who understood very well that British society was being threatened by "overpopulation, high unemployment rates and severe poverty," and that a mass relocation of women to Canada could only help Britain's economic problems. The members of this agency stressed the selflessness of their mission as they,

> ...snatched up people who otherwise would sink, that they saved them from crime and penitentiaries, and gave them health and hope...that this work of emigration was a very noble work in its relation between themselves and their fellowmen, between themselves and their Father who was in heaven...that it was the purest philanthropy because it was so absolutely unselfish...that there was a higher ground, that it was a religious work.[13]

In addition to recruiting, churchwomen operated hostels, organized job registries and provided travel aid. This latter service was offered to all immigrants by churchwomen across Canada as a way of making new church contacts. Clinics and missions, staffed largely by female volunteers, were established in the major cities where unskilled immigrants tended to congregate. In rural areas, hospitals and schools were founded and maintained with the financial assistance of the woman's missionary societies. The determination of the Protestant churches to "Canadianize" the immigrants reflects an imperialism that was like the overseas missionary societies' commitment to "converting the heathen". They were quick to learn that immigrant communities were less than responsive to church assistance if the price were loss of religious or cultural independence.

Adaptation to new rural and urban problems enhanced the Social Gospel movement in Canada, which was committed to setting up on earth,

> ...the kingdom of God as a social organization based on the Golden Rule of Christ.[14]

Along with this movement was a growing sense among many women of the church, particularly Methodists, that women had a special role to play in social reform because they were, after all, "mothers of the race." Temperance activity and prohibition had already brought churchwomen into the arena of public politics, but now a few began to fight for the vote so that women could direct determination over the policy-makers, if not over the policies for which they stood. (See Warne's consideration of "maternal feminism" in Chapter Nine.)

On the whole, the problems associated with mass immigration and the general fervour for the social mission of the church brought about more cooperation among the churches committed to union. Churches worked together, sharing resources, issuing joint statements on social policy and establishing, in 1912, a program of interdenominational theological teaching for Anglicans, Presbyterians, Methodists and Congregationalists. Many churches in the west had amalgamated locally when the Basis of Union was formulated in 1908. Eventually these would form a General Council of Local Union Churches and, as such, enter into The United Church of Canada. Cooperation, consensus, and local unions seemed to assure the easy formation of the new denomination. However, World War One and a bitter controversy within the Presbyterian Church were gathering clouds on the horizon.

Canada entered into World War One with the blessing of its churches. In fact some denominations (especially Methodist) used their pulpits to recruit young men, going so far in some cases as to say that any young man who could go to war and didn't was "neither a Christian nor a patriot."[15] The war involved churchwomen in a new kind of work— knitting socks, scarves and hats for soldiers, sending bales of clothing to distressed areas where the war was being fought, providing day-care for women entering the work force, and comforting each other in their private fears and tragedies. They also continued the fight for prohibition until Canada became totally dry in 1919.

The end of the war and the return of the men from overseas had another kind of sobering effect on Canadian society. The increasingly sophisticated technologies developed in the nineteenth century had been viewed as gifts which would help usher in the new fair and just society.

The war, however, had taught that technology could also be a powerful destroyer. The notion that machines enslave humans rather than liberate them was to remain a feature of the western world's literature and film for decades to come. The optimism of the century's first decade was diminished.

Another change affected the churches and their influence in society. Soldiers who had grown used to less stringent moral standards in their lives overseas were reluctant to sacrifice their "liberated" style to the austere requirements of the churches at home. Women, living independent of men because of the war in many cases, were developing a new sense of themselves as competent workers, a sense which had begun with their entry into the work force around the turn of the century. War simply accelerated this process.

> The war provided an occasion for a number of beliefs about women to be questioned. Pre-war prejudices held that women were totally unfit for some jobs. During the war, women were admitted to almost every trade and performed successfully in spite of shortened training periods. [16]

It is generally agreed that women won the Dominion vote in 1917 because of their contribution to the war effort. Canada, at least, could no longer deny that women were anything but primary citizens, even if they were not yet legal "persons". (Women were not judged to be "persons" in Canadian law until 1929.)

An anti-war movement was another aspect of the post-war period that affected the churches. The enthusiasm with which the denominations had supported war, and their active participation in recruitment and propagandizing, came under heavy criticism. Student Volunteer Movements and ecumenical women's groups endorsed the principles of pacifism. Even those churches that had embraced war now turned anti-war, even to the point of lobbying against high school cadet corps.[17]

The question of church union had been postponed by the Presbyterians in 1912 in the hope that they could eventually enter union with the unanimous consent of their congregations. Subsequent votes, however, showed a growing negative faction. At the same time, some of its western churches which had already accomplished unions locally were threatening to leave the Presbyterian Church if union at the national level did not occur.

The issues which split the Presbyterians on union were complicated. Some were suspicious of the political involvement of the Social Gospel Methodists; others objected on theological grounds, particularly on the question of predestination. When their General Assembly voted to unite in 1921, those opposed to union in the Presbyterian Church marshalled their forces for a bitter fight. One congregation's history refers to this period as "a most distressing time" during which some "church pews were empty of regular churchgoers while the women's organizations missed members also."[18] Women were by no means absent from the union debate. Their auxiliaries lobbied fiercely, particularly on behalf of the dissenting Presbyterians. By the time The United Church of Canada came into being in 1925, both sides of union had been fought out in homes, in courts, and in provincial and federal parliaments. Eventually, about two-thirds of the Presbyterian Church entered into the union.

The aftermath of the bitterness is still evident. In one Maritime community, Presbyterian women will not join with United Church women in the ecumenical World Day of Prayer services. Many Presbyterians vowed never to worship in a United Church and have staunchly kept that promise over the years, making concessions only for weddings and funerals. The rupture drove wedges between family members that, in some cases, have never been bridged. In spite of the problems, the women's work went on. Union wasn't even very much of an issue for at least one local Woman's Missionary Society: the only mention was on the cover of its 1925 Minutes book where "Methodist" had been stroked out and "United" written above it.[19]

POST-UNION AND DEPRESSION YEARS

> The women, as we remember and have been told by others, knew their place and mainly kept it. That is, they worked in their homes, took care of their families and supported their men in whatever activities they undertook. But through the stories and from our memories we discern a certain thread. The women taught their children their faith and it was to a great extent through their influence and urging that the men started and supported their churches.[20]

The traditional concept of God had come under attack after World War One, prompting many Christians to question some of their churches' fundamental assumptions about love and justice. In spite of that, the Protestant churches were undergoing some changes which would make them strong, and which would make women stronger within them.

Interest in youths' and children's programming blossomed in the twenties. YMCA and YWCA programs (the YWCA was beginning to address the needs of the young immigrant women it had helped to recruit for domestic labour) flourished, and Tuxis boys, Trail Rangers, Boy Scouts and Girl Guides enjoyed a burgeoning membership across Canada. Perhaps the most important development for the future of women in Canada during this period was the formation of Canadian Girls in

Training (CGIT), an organization which was eventually affiliated with the Woman's Missionary Society. CGIT affected women in two major ways. First, by emphasizing leadership skills and self-sufficiency, the programs it offered taught an entire generation of young women that *they* were capable of being leaders. It is no accident that so many Canadian women in public life today once participated in either CGIT or the YWCA. Second, CGIT and YWCA programs called for new and creative methods of education which would suit both the experience and expectations of adolescent girls and young women. Unlike the Girl Guides which simply adapted boys' programs for girls, the other organizations reflected a female perspective in both program development and implementation.

Canada was hard hit by the Depression, particularly in the prairies where farmers were suffering one of the worst droughts ever experienced there. It was a difficult time for the United Church, still in its infancy as an institution. The first areas to feel the effects of decreased finances were the overseas missions of the church in general. Allocations were reduced by more than half between 1928 and 1935.[21] By contrast, the missions and missionaries supported by the women of the United Church in the WMS were relatively secure. J. W. Grant suggests that the survival of some United Church mission fields can be attributed to the Woman's Missionary Society and that without their support "even greater retrenchment would have been necessary."[22]

Women had taken the reigns too in the area of local outreach at this time of desperate need. Everywhere churchwomen were preparing meals for the hungry, establishing clothing depots or making over clothing for families that could not afford to purchase it, setting up job registries for unemployed men, and offering day-care for those women who could find work. One United Church woman, Anna (Kennedy) Hicks helped to organize a Farmer's Market in Souris, Manitoba so that local farm people would have a place to sell both produce and handiwork once a week.[23] And of course during this period the general fund-raising activities of the women's groups continued and, in some cases, intensified.

The generalized hardship caused by the Depression gave rise to a good deal of thought about the relation of people to money and work. Pensions became an issue for women employed at low wages by the church, and so did equal pay for equal work. Money-based prejudices (racist as well as sexist) began to surface in church policy as people became sensitive to these issues. For example, Canadian medical staff working in India in church-sponsored mission hospitals were eligible for pensions, while Indian nurses (female) were not. Missionary wives who worked hard "...without further compensation than their husbands' salaries",[24] had no pensions whatsoever.

Another issue in this period was birth control. Here, too, a few churchwomen took the lead, recognizing that child-bearing clearly affected women financially as well as physically, making them all the more vulnerable in hard times. Work in this area was nothing short of courageous and did not, at first, receive general support from the church. Dissemination of birth control information and the promotion of sex education were illegal activities then, and were to remain so for several decades. Still, their involvement demonstrates that some churchwomen, at least, were beginning to identify "women's issues" beyond the call for voting rights, and were prepared to address these issues publicly at personal risk to themselves.

The structural role of women in the United Church was being challenged even more directly during the twenties and early thirties by Lydia Gruchy's application for ordination. The question of ordaining her was debated for over a decade at every level of the church.

> despite the fact that she received highest honours of her graduating class and that she had served many long years in some of the roughest and most physically and spiritually demanding areas of Canada...[25]

Gruchy was finally ordained in 1936. Even then, not she but her advocate Dr. E. H. Oliver was credited with the victory: "His knightly and chivalrous attitude and advocacy have finally prevailed." (See Parsons in Section 4 for a further discussion of the Gruchy ordination debate.) Nevertheless, the controversy over women's role seemed to help raise the consciousness of some congregations, for it is during this period that a few churches admitted their first women to session.

WORLD WAR TWO

> Many (service personnel) still keep in touch with families and tell the married sons and daughters (who were tots then) how they romped with them while waiting to board troop ships to go overseas to the battle front.[26]

During the twenties and thirties, the United Church endorsed the principles of pacifism, stating through its General Councils that it held war to be "contrary to the mind of Christ."[27] With Hitler's rise to power and increasing aggression in Europe, however, the church back-peddled somewhat to acknowledge that there was room for disagreement on the issue. Unlike the mood during World War One, there was neither an enthusiasm for battle, nor active participation in recruitment and propagandizing.

Canada's involvement in the war resulted in a shortage of United Church ministers, particularly in the West. In many instances across the country women's organizations carried on the pastoral work. The history of Mount Paul United Church credits its Women's Auxiliary with keeping the Sunday School going and the congregation together during the eight years after 1938 when the congregation was without a minister.[28]

Most women's groups worked with the Red Cross, sewing bandages, knitting caps, socks and scarves, and packing goods that were needed on the front. Personal connections were initiated and maintained by women who wrote regularly to the men and women in overseas service, and many a birthday was cheered by congratulations from churchwomen at home. Friendly hours were established in churches near ports or military bases to provide lonely service men and women with friendship and a sense of community. Families opened their homes to these people, arranged entertainments for them, and even took them for sight-seeing drives at a time when both gasoline and tires were difficult to come by. In at least one community, a choir composed of Navy and Air Force personnel was organized by a United Church woman.[29]

A few United Church women were also working in some of the Japanese relocation camps as teachers and youth organizers. One second-generation Japanese women, Hide Shimizu, was eventually awarded the *Order of Canada* for her work in setting up and supervising the education of thousands of Japanese children in this black period of Canadian history. The United Church had made no protest against Canada's flagrant violations of human rights at the time of the relocation. At the General Council of 1982, forty years after the fact, Vancouver/ Burrard Presbytery circulated a petition deploring this silence.

Ministers were not the only paid workers in short supply during the war years; women were encouraged to enter virtually every part of the labour force to fill the gaps left by conscripted fathers, husbands, brothers, and sons. The federal Government entered into a day-care cost-sharing scheme with the provinces so mothers would be free to work, and "Rosie the Riveter" became a symbol of women's war at home. Their work fatigues, in the propaganda of the day, demonstrated as much patriotism as a soldier's uniform. Churchwomen, if not employed themselves, assisted those who were by offering child-care and/or hot lunches for school-aged children. Spiritual support for the war effort was not lacking either: the Watrous (Saskatchewan) Ladies Aid added *O Canada* to its worship service during the 1940s.[30]

THE POST-WAR YEARS

> In 1946, Mrs. (William) Marvel Cameron was the first woman to be on the Session of the church. This shocked the other churches of the Sault (Ontario), because until this time only men served...[31]

Between 1945 and 1966, the United Church built 1,500 churches and church halls, and 600 manses.[32] Unlike the period of cynicism and disillusionment that followed World War One, the years after World War Two saw a renewed interest in the old Canadian values and in traditional doctrine. Parents who had shown little interest in the church prior to war were sending their children to Sunday School and finding their own way back into church life.

This phenomenon was just one aspect of a collective desire for "normalcy" which was characterized by "an atmosphere of social conformism that was typical of the period."[33] The cold war of the fifties and the new threat of atomic warfare aggravated an anxiety that was already prevalent in a generation of men and women who had lived through hard times during the Depression. The desire for material security seems to have been paralleled by the desire for spiritual security, and the goal of both was social stability. People turned to the church for what seemed to be lacking in other aspects of their lives. Theologically, it was a time during which congregations preferred answers to questions; it was conservative rather than progressive.

During this seemingly quiet period, the lives of women in particular underwent some profound changes. Suburbs were springing up around all Canadian cities and the ideal life for a young family, as portrayed in the popular media and in advertising, was to live in a community of other like-minded young families of a similar income level. An escalating consumer ethic made it psychologically necessary for each household to be self-contained: washer, dryer, at least one car, preferably two.

The trappings of suburban life appeared at first to ease the work of women. Recent studies show, however, that full-time housewives today spend *more* time cleaning, shopping, in child-care activities and on the maintenance and repair of their modern conveniences than they would have spent on cleaning, child-care, and in the actual production of household necessities (clothing, preserves, garden produce) at the turn of the century. The demise of the extended family which incorporated grandparents and unmarried aunts or uncles, meant that the whole burden of housekeeping and parenting fell to one person: the stay-at-home mother. The isolation of the suburban women was further aggravated by the very self-sufficiency of her household. She did not even have an opportunity, in most cases, to carry on adult conversations with her sisters at communal workplaces such as the laundromat.

It was the time of "Father knows best", and the ideal role for women was to maintain the members of the family who operated in the public spheres of work and school. To a great extent this model for family stability was manipulated by both government and advertising. The federally produced propaganda films that had encouraged women to go into non-traditional jobs during the war were replaced with propaganda films showing women returning to the domestic life, giving their jobs back to men. The federal Government also discontinued its day-care cost-sharing program with provincial governments, putting child-care out of the financial reach of most young families so that one parent was forced to remain in the home full-time. School books that in the war years had shown women working outside the home in a variety of occupations were gradually replaced with books showing women as wives and mothers only. At the same time advertising was encouraging a kind of material upward mobility in which status was measured by the visible things one owned (conspicuous consumption) and by the way those things were maintained. The housewife's function was increasingly geared to keeping the family image (which did not necessarily reflect the reality) intact.

Suburbia did not turn out to be paradise after all. During the late forties and fifties all denominations were struggling with a growing demand for family counselling. In spite of statements which recommended mutuality and equality in marriage, the United Church was, in practice, an advocate of the patriarchal family structure. James R. Mutchmor, Secretary of the Board of Evangelism and Social Service, would not hire married women, for instance, because he believed along with other church leaders that their rightful place was in the home.[34]

Women were the most frequent casualties of "the good life," for they had to make the greatest social adjustments. The increase in alcoholism and tranquilizer abuse among suburban housewives should have suggested to churches and other social agencies that women were suffering. Most had all they could wish for materially, but still found their lives to be empty. As a result, women increasingly began to seek paid employment outside the home, particularly when the youngest child had reached school age. The motivation was not so much the money as the need to be with other adults in some sort of continuing relationship.

The same sense of isolation and alienation that sent suburban women into the work force also sent them into churchwomen's organizations and volunteer work. The need for useful activity, for education, for community and for "fellowship" with one's peers was no less acute for them than it had been for their grandmothers and mothers who had founded these groups. All the women's organizations grew and then gradually began to decline as more and more women sought jobs which answered their social needs *and* provided a degree of financial independence which few women had enjoyed before.

The move from urban to suburban churches was accompanied by an increasing lay participation in church leadership. Although the AOTS men's clubs had been founded in the twenties, the women of the church had been better organized for serious study and action. After World War Two, however, the men of the church became interested in Bible study and prayer groups, and in church-based service clubs—so much so that in 1946 the United Church appointed a full-time secretary for men's work, and in 1950 established a Board of Men.

Increased lay activity led to calls for increased lay responsibility. Some positions that had been held only be clergy were taken over by laity and in 1947, the first school for lay church leaders was opened at Naramata, British Columbia. This institution would train many women in Christian

Education and in that way, provide them with a new avenue of entry into the policy-making bodies of the church structure.

During the war years the WMS and WA had cooperated in certain areas of their work to avoid a duplication of activities. Talks of union between the two groups went on more or less continuously from 1948 until their eventual amalgamation in 1962. The social context of these talks, and the general mood of the church, would have an effect on the change in women's organizational relationship to the United Church.

The Formation of the UCW

> We United Church Women in the eighties can almost forget and many of us never knew, the problems, the frustrations, and the worries that were part and parcel of the transition from WA and WMS to the brand-new UCW. An unknown course had to be charted, and we owe much to the ladies who led the way.[35]

The formation of United Church Women occurred in two stages. The first involved the amalgamation of the two existing women's organizations: WMS and WA; and the second was the incorporation of this new entity into the formal structures of the church. Neither process was accomplished simply.

Of the two organizations, the WMS, although smaller in terms of numbers, had the most to lose in the amalgamation. It was financially healthy, organizationally powerful, and had a membership devoted to its goals both at home and abroad. Its publication *The Missionary Monthly*, eagerly awaited across the country, kept its members in constant personal contact with the missionaries and mission fields they supported and provided a bond among churchwomen that was strengthened by a common sense of mission. The Dominion Woman's Association, on the other hand, had only one staff member and virtually no power: its strength had always been at the congregational level. In spite of the difficulties, the union of the WMS and WA was accomplished and the women's work went forward at the national level.

Although many congregations had already formed women's federations (local unions of WMS and WA), others found the amalgamation difficult. Some feared that one or the other aspect of their work and worship would suffer.

> There was dismay and controversy... The women were afraid that the practical side of the work would be overlooked in the zeal for programming by the central office. At this time some women became discouraged and even dropped out, but most remained staunch workers who helped to see this "marriage" of WMS and WA.[36]

51

Another contributor writes that her mother, active in the women's groups in the United Church,

> ...felt for awhile that the devotional aspects were somewhat neglected for more mercenary projects. [37]

Most United Church women, however, suffered the growing pains like their Manitoba sisters, as they "struggled to work together towards a common goal."[38] Some of those growing pains entailed the sorting-out of generational differences.

> Then came the change to United Church Women, a rather difficult adjustment as names for the new units into which it was divided were drawn from a hat. This meant that the group who had worked together for so many years were now intermingled with the younger group, and as one of the suggestions was that first names be used, one can imagine the feelings of women who had never addressed their closest friends by first names now finding themselves addressed as Mary, Goldie, Vinnie, Martha, Lillian, Minnie, etc.[39]

The rationale for the amalgamation of the women's groups was sensible. One organization would be more efficient, reduce the number of meetings most women attended (many participated in both the WMS and WA at the local level), and eliminate any duplication of work. What is *not* so clear, in retrospect, is why discussions always assumed that the amalgamated woman's organization would be incorporated into the structures of the United Church. It could have retained the administrative and financial autonomy that the WMS enjoyed and entered into a new relationship with the church modelled on that of the independent AOTS men's clubs.

The crucial issue determining the nature of the new relations was missions. Two separate missionary agencies—the church and the WMS—meant a duplication of administrative work in many instances, and was especially confusing to those people being served overseas. The Chinese, for example, were convinced from the evidence around them that there was a male United Church of Canada, and a female United Church![40] The benefits to be gained by combining the missionary work were obvious to everyone involved, and the WMS and WA initiated a discussion of women's work in the church with General Council. The stages that followed from those discussions are described by the History Committee of Vancouver South Presbyterial United Church Women in their twentieth anniversary publication, *Recalling Our Heritage: 1962-1982.*

> In the 1950s it became apparent that two women's

52

> *organizations at each level with overlapping memberships were difficult to maintain and both were concerned with the total mission of the church. In 1953 a joint committee of the two organizations asked General Council to set up a Commission on the 'Work of Women in the Church'. This was accomplished, and in 1956 the General Council of The United Church of Canada adopted a report which included the approval in principle of the formation of 'one organization for the women of The United Church of Canada in the Congregation and at Presbytery, Conference and National levels, the aim of which would be to enlist all the women of the United Church for the total mission of the church, and to conserve all the value in the present women's organizations.' This included a commitment to the continued raising of funds, the allocation formerly subscribed to by the Woman's Missionary Society. These funds would now be administered by the national mission boards of the church who would underwrite the mission work in Canada and overseas.*
>
> *Provisional committees were set up at different levels of the church with assistance from Presbytery and Conference officers. The committees were concerned not only with structure, but also with values to be conserved.*
>
> *At the 19th General Council in September 1960 in Edmonton, Alberta, a unanimous vote of approval was given to the new organization, UNITED CHURCH WOMEN. January 1, 1962 was set as the date of inauguration.* [41]

Massive educating went on at every church level in the transition period between 1960 and 1962, but many WA and WMS women still felt no ownership of the new organization. It was, in their view, something imposed on them by "head office".

> *...in 1962 instruction came from The United Church of Canada that the institution called United Church Women was to be formed, incorporating both the Woman's Missionary Society and Ladies Aid—but how?* [42]
>
> *In 1962 The United Church of Canada decided to amalgamate all women's groups under the name of United Church Women.* [43]
>
> *In 1961 The United Church of Canada foresaw the United Church Women, a new organization, being more effective, so ended the era of the WMS.* [44]
>
> *In 1962 the "powers that be" decreed that women of the United Church be reorganized into an association to be called the United Church Women.* [45]
>
> *While we...were happy and busy in our different interest groups, the powers that be in the East formulated a plan for*

organization to include all women of the congregation...[46]

In 1962 General Council in Toronto brought about the amalgamation of these two groups.

The sense of loss felt by these women, although natural enough with the demise of any beloved organization, was not unfounded. The autonomous women's organizations, particularly the WMS, had provided them with a sense of their *own* accomplishment and a sense of their own competence *as women* that the wider church had not. They had been the framework for a sisterhood within the church, from which the members drew nourishment both as women and as participants in the community of Christ. Integration into the structures of a persistently male-dominant institution was, in many ways, a denial of those very needs that had given rise to churchwomen's groups in the first place.

There was much talk about "partnership" and women being involved in "the total mission of the church" during the formation of the UCW. The favourite metaphor for the amalgamation of the woman's organizations with the church was church union. And since this "union" would ensure the placement of women in offices at all levels of the church, it did seem to be a step towards sexual equality. There were still many congregations in which women were not permitted to hold office.

The ideal of "partnership" between men and women in the church was optimistic and talk of "union", suggesting that the combining institutions were of equal status in this process, was misleading. In spite of the talk surrounding the event, the larger institution (the church) was swallowing the smaller (the woman's organizations) in a process of co-optation that had already been seen in the Presbyterian and Methodist Churches in the United States, and that was going on simultaneously in the Anglican Church of Canada. In each case the churches had taken control of work and finances built up by women, without granting them an effective voice in the disposition of the assets they had handed over, or in the continued maintenance of the ongoing work. The people involved in the negotiations had good intentions and believed that a partnership was a real and imminent possibility. What they misjudged, however, was the mood of the times and the ability of an essentially patriarchal structure to neutralize the threat of a growing feminine presence.

The "mood" of the country and of the church in the fifties was conservative. Women were being encouraged to leave the work force and return to their support role within the home. We have already seen that some executives within the United Church would not hire married women. In 1960 an eminent churchman was able to express the following without any embarrassment:

> *The husband is the head of the family, according to the scriptures, and the wife is the heart. On all matters the wife ought to express her opinion and insist that it be*

54

considered. But when a decision has to be voiced to the outside world, the man is the spokesman.[47]

In spite of the fact that women had been *ordained* in the United Church since 1936, the 1963 *United Church of Canada Observer* Reference Edition carried the following information:

The church has many opportunities for trained women to work in Canada and overseas, in Christian education, social service, teaching, nursing, evangelism, and other educational fields.[48]

"Partnership" of the Father-knows-best variety—the kind of partnership being held up as the ideal in the world at large—was an illusion, since it involved a situation of dominance and subordination. At least one contributor understood that the new UCW approximated the status of a dependent wife when she wrote that "...the UCW could be called the 'chatelaine' of the church at that time." A "chattel", the word which gives us "chatelaine", is a piece of property, not a partner.

The United Church gained a great deal with the incorporation of the woman's organization, especially in terms of finances. The money formerly directed to the WMS would now be given to the finance committee of each congregation to be forwarded, along with general church givings, to the new Board of Missions. (Since most congregations combine their contributions in this way, the Division of Mission in Canada does not know how much of its support comes from the local UCW. Fortunately, the Presbyterial and Conference UCW keep track of their members' contributions.) Annual dues paid by each member of a local UCW were for Presbytery and Conference expenses, and local needs were accommodated in much the same way as they had been under the WA.

As far as the church structure goes, partnership was an unlikely possibility at the outset. The General Council, at which "a unanimous vote of approval was given to the new organization, UNITED CHURCH WOMEN", consisted of 315 men and 72 women—a ratio of more than four to one. Of the non-ministerial commissioners there were 121 men, 64 women. (All but two of the 185 ministerial commissioners were men.) Although the commission that had looked at the integration of home mission work recommended "adequate representation of women on all the boards and courts of the church and their related committees",[49] it also recommended that the new Board of Home Missions should have "fourteen ministerial and non-ministerial members, four of whom shall be non-ministerial women."[50] Since the ministerial members would almost certainly be men, the adequacy of "the representation of women" on this particular board is debatable. Similarly, the Commission on the Integration of the Overseas Work of the Woman's Missionary Society and the Board of Overseas Missions advised that the integrated Board should have one-third ministerial members and two-thirds non-ministerial, half of whom should be women.[51] Women, in practical terms, would have one-third the vote and one-third the voice.

Whether measured in terms of gains or losses, the union of the woman's organization with the church was accomplished with varying degrees of receptivity around the country. Perhaps one minister, speaking at the inaugural UCW meeting at a local congregation, sensed some trepidation when he advised his listeners that three things must be taken into the new union: prayer, patience and perseverence.[52] Another contributor reports that the first UCW meeting at her church ended with a rousing chorus of "Rise Up O Men of God" (which some churchwomen sing hearily as "Wise Up O Men of God".)[53] The task for women in the remainder of the 1960s was to forge a new identity within the structures of their church. No longer responsible for CGIT, Explorers, Mission Bands and Nursery Departments, they began to look towards Christian Education Committees and other areas of church work. Churches that had been reluctant to admit women to Session now found them on committees as representatives of UCW, thus opening the way for women generally. The increase in mission givings suggests that women were in fact interested in "the total mission of the church", even if their voice in the determination of that mission was minimal.

A group of women in London, Ontario, reflecting on their role in the church, played with the letters of UCW and found that in their own case they could stand for United Catering Women, United Caring Women, United Cleaning Women, United Changing Women and United Christian Women.[54] Women from another London congregation describe themselves in the following ways:

> *We are wives, mothers, daughters, sisters, friends, acquaintances. We cover every facet of human relationship and family tie. Some of us are new members of the congregation. Others follow a pattern laid down by our mothers, grandmothers and great-grandmothers.*
>
> *We come from every walk of life and level of society.*
>
> *We attend church and Bible Study, go to UCW meetings, lead craft and youth groups, teach Sunday School and sing in the choir. We serve on the Official Board. We give banquets and hold bazaars. We pack bales and give aid to missionaries. We visit the sick and shut-ins.*
>
> *Like any large family we sometimes disagree about how things should be done. After all, we are human.*
>
> *Our faith in God and belief in Jesus have bound us together in a sisterhood. We share fun and fellowship, love and concern. Our faith is strengthened through prayer and Bible Study. We seek to broaden our horizons from ourselves to our families, our congregation, our community, our country and our world.*

*We are daughters of God. We are united
churchwomen.*[55]

The twentieth anniversary of the formation of UCW provided many women with an opportunity to reflect on their collective role in the church. For some, the sense of loss remains.

*I myself wonder if we are as productive—as strong in
the faith—as useful in the UCW as we were in the WMS.
I would remember more of our meetings then than I would
in the twenty years of UCW.*[56]

Others are more positive about the effects of the transition from WA and WMS to UCW.

*The UCW was born at a time when women were
already being recognized as worthy of sharing in the
decisions of church committees, and were being included in
their membership, so that separate roles of church service
seemed no longer necessary. But I do believe the
amalgamation proved very beneficial. Each group shared
the other's spiritual and/or practical resources.*[57]

However the UCW is currently regarded by its members, the organization was certainly a child of its time and reflects the values, concerns and sexual politics of the late fifties and early sixties. That it has worked in other times is a tribute to the women committed to this expression of sisterhood.

The Seventies: Liberation Theology and Christian Feminism

*Somehow we who are involved in this movement must
come to terms with our faith and with our feminism and
trust that the church which we love can accept both.*[58]

The sixties and early seventies were years of social discontent throughout North America and in most of western Europe. The assassination of John and Robert Kennedy and civil rights activist, Martin Luther King, had stunned a generation of young people who were already at loggerheads with the materialistic and conservative values of their depression-raised parents. A new secular humanism took root as affluent men and women began to struggle with the facts of poverty and injustice which surrounded them and upon which, to a certain extent, their own affluence depended. The ideological conflict was not as extreme in Canada as in the United States, mostly because the Canadian style of politics is negotiation and compromise rather than confrontation and polarization.

Many young adults of the period, raised in an era of plenty, felt that the older generation had sacrificed any chance of personal fulfillment for job security and social stability. Some "dropped out" of conventional society into the various sub-cultures—hippy villages or communes—to identify and practise a "new" set of social values. (There were actually centuries-old models for the type of lifestyles established in this period.) Some others, usually the well-educated, went to work as secular missionaries for activist organizations such as the Company of Young Canadians (CYC) or Canadian University Services Overseas (CUSO). Even those who did conform to the prevailing social norms were not as driven as their parents had been to provide their own children with every possible advantage that money could buy. The quality of personal relationships counted for more than the accumulation of "things" in such circles, and the "flower children" of the period sang, wrote, and preached about love and peace.

The changes affecting society were also being felt in the churches. Some congregations encouraged the new expressions of worship—folk masses, liturgical dances. Others, unable to accommodate the new mood of the times, became even more committed to the current establishment values. Aspects of the Social Gospel movement surfaced again to provide a familiar framework for "liberation theology." The *threat* of this Christ-centred understanding of Christianity lay in its view that the church does not necessarily represent the kingdom of God but, as a human institution, is as subject to demonic influences as any other institution.

The rebellious youth of the sixties carried a keen sense of justice and fair play into maturity. The lessons learned from the American civil rights movements, and the spirit of positive activism engendered by such capable religious leaders as Martin Luther King (his "I have a dream…" speech will surely be regarded as the most magnificent invocation of Christian humanist values of the decade) became part of the value system out of which millions of people conducted their everyday affairs. These new humanists would challenge rather than tolerate most forms of elitism, whether grounded in racism, sexism or social class.

Secular feminism was just one aspect of the wider concern with social justice. Women who had been involved in human rights in other areas began to see that they too were politically and economically disadvantaged. Unlike other forms of discrimination, however, sexism was often invisible simply because values which emphasized the notion that women were inferior to men were so entrenched in the Canadian worldview. Sensitive people who would shudder in embarrassment to hear a black man referred to as "boy", for example, would find nothing wrong in calling a mature women a "girl", although the belittling effect is exactly the same in both cases.

The miracle of Christian Feminism in our church is that it exists at all. It would be easier for feminist women and non-patriarchal men to quietly leave an institution that, in practice, does not take seriously their profoundly held religious beliefs. Ann Squire addresses this phenomenon in *Women in the Church.*

> *But still more (women) are moving out of the church altogether. They are no longer rousing up the family on Sunday morning because the church for them is not where the action is. They are more concerned about lobbying on Parliament Hill for equal pay for work of equal value, or campaigning for adequate day-care, or learning how women can cope in a violent society.*
>
> *Oh, some of these women occasionally drift back to church sensing that it may well be something in their early Christian training that alerted them to the social problems of the day, and they want to keep in touch with their roots. But now that their consciousness has been raised they hear in the hymns, the liturgies, the prayers and the sermons those words that exclude female experience. And they notice that some churches still treat women as second-class citizens.*[59]

Ironically, in many cases it was the Christ-teachings around justice and the dignity of the human person that led men and women into the feminist movement. And it is a testimony to the power of Jesus' words and actions that they have shone through centuries of patriarchal ideology which has been called Christianity. The lessons of the Reformation, when Protestant men insisted that priests had no special privilege in either their relation to God or their interpretation of scripture, have not been lost on those involved in the Christian Feminist movement in the church. The male perspective, as expressed through patriarchal theology and philosophy, is not privileged either.

Because feminism affects all of us by raising questions about our very sense of ourselves as men and women, it is a movement that is often misunderstood. The conflicts it raises are not between women and men, although some prefer to see it that way. The opposition is, rather, between patriarchal and non-patriarchal thinking. The former tradition has defined women as secondary, derivative, inferior and defective;[60] the latter acknowledges that men and women are indeed different but that women, and the qualities associated with them, are in no way inferior to men. In theological terms, non-patriarchal people understand that women and men together constitute the image of God. Feminists are *not* anti-male. In fact they would be the first to acknowledge the ways in which patriarchal values have harmed men, particularly in the area of personal relationships. And since we have *all* been socialized to the same cultural values, there are many patriarchal women, not surprisingly, just as there are many men who rejected patriarchy to support the feminist movement both in and out of the church.

Feminists do not want to reverse the situation so that women have the power now held collectively by men. Rather, they would feminize the culture so that it reflects both male and female perspectives, experience and expectations. In doing so, both men and women will be freed from rigid sex-role stereotypes and will be able to integrate the gentle, nurturing aspect of a man, the strong, assertive aspect of a woman. Freedom to realize the best within ourselves is the ultimate liberation.

Christian feminist women in the United Church are working both within and outside of UCW to create an inclusive church, and must be considered a part of today's women's work and worship. Their efforts are not unlike those put forth by the WCTU who, through education and social activism, tried (and are still trying) to bring the kingdom of God a little closer to us. Some also work on behalf of their sisters in rape crisis centres, transition houses for battered women, or in women's resource centres. These activities, too, derive from a tradition of women's hands-on ministry in our church; in the past the WMS and WA were the organizations best prepared to assist those who found themselves in crisis situations.

During the sixties and seventies membership in the UCW declined. In one sense it was a positive phenomenon because more women *were* becoming involved in "the total mission of the church" by serving on Session and other committees. The alienation that had given rise to a parallel woman's structure in the first place was becoming less intense.

On the other hand, many women did not join, or left their local UCW organization because of its emphasis on traditional women's work—the "chatelaine" duties. As one woman put it, "It isn't that we *minded* making coffee, it was that we resented being the ones who *always* had to make the coffee." The account of St. Andrew's United Church, Sudbury, Ontario, suggests that the demise of some of its UCW units also may have been due to the fact that "mission study and worship may not always have been as central as in the former WMS," and that the commitment to mission declined as personal involvement decreased.

> ...the structure of the United Church can seem highly impersonal. When a unit once had specific missionary obligations, it had a greater incentive to fulfill responsibilities than under the present system. It is difficult to generate and sustain enthusiasm for M & S in general, no matter how worthy the individual causes. [61]

Those United Church women who call themselves feminists, and those who do not, all derive their strength from the same tradition of women's work and worship: the WCTU, the missionary societies and the suffrage activists. Feminists in the church owe a debt to the "traditional" woman who,

> ...raised the money, built the sanctuaries, sent the missionaries, laid the foundations on which today's women build. [62]

Indeed, the outstanding leadership abilities, the organizational competence and the financial wizardry of these very women provided the proof
of the power of women working together, and the model for liberated
womanhood.

THE REACTIONARY EIGHTIES

> As I have read some of the "Feminist" literature as put
> out by our church, I feel that the new move to change God,
> and the Father and the Holy Spirit to a male/female
> image...is heresy to Christian doctrine and completely
> incompatible (sic) with the personal relationship of Jesus,
> the Son, as Saviour and Lord with the Holy Spirit (GOD) as
> his Father and Mary as his Mother.[63]

The eighties have been difficult for many Canadians. Record unemployment, high interest rates and a generally unstable business and
industrial community have evoked again some of those conserving values
that arose during the Great Depression.

In hard times women suffer doubly—as citizens subject to the general
social dislocation, and as women subject to the abuses of hurting and
frustrated men who direct their anger inappropriately to their mates and
children. The incidence of woman-battering increases as money becomes
scarcer. Jobs are harder for women to find, and those who are employed
are hurt by percentage wage increases. Women in Canada earn roughly
fifty-two percent of what men earn and a pay raise of six percent (in line
with the federal Government's six and five program, for example) for
someone earning $52.00 is only half as much as a raise of six percent for
someone earning $100.00.

The direction that churchwomen will take in the remainder of this
decade is anybody's guess. There are, however, some signs of a backlash
against the Christian feminist movement in our church. More ministers
are telling me, for instance, that women are the ones who protest the use
of inclusive language in their congregations. Since the basic equality of all
human beings is a principle that derives from Christ himself, it is difficult
to understand the view that the use of inclusive language is "unChristian". It is precisely because women have had no voice in the shaping of
Christian doctrine and liturgy that it is exclusive in the first place. Pat
Clarke, in her United Church of Canada Observer article on the subject,
suggests three major reasons why some churchwomen and men remain
adamantly patriarchal in their point of view.

> An understanding (or misunderstanding) of the Bible as
> demanding that women be silent, subservient and at home.
> Fear of change. Men don't want to give up power;

*women don't want to give up security. As the Rev. Janet
Silman...puts it, 'It's risky to have your eyes opened at 75
and see that your life could have been different.'*

*A deep, irrational fear of women which may go back
unconsiciously to primitive taboos on women as evil,
unclean temptresses.*[64]

In many situations across Canada, women of diverse points of view
are working together in their churches, fostering a dialogue that helps all
to grow together. These are the women who understand that certain of
the issues involved may be open to argument, but that the pain of their
sisters is not. It is profoundly real. One thing about the eighties is certain:
to the extent that their concerns, whether religious or political, are
ignored or trivialized in our congregations, more and more women will be
opting out of the church. And those of us who remain will call this process
"secularization" to say that we were not responsible for their leaving. It is
easy to forget that Christianity is a liberation movement that began with
Christ, not one that ended with him. And the history of the twentieth
century shows us that Canadian women are struggling to find their place
within that movement—both in and outside of the church.

Chapter 4   THE PAST AS A GUIDE TO THE FUTURE

Northrop Frye, perhaps the most eminent clergyman in The United Church of Canada, has said that we walk through life backwards, using the past as a guide to the future. Our understanding of all that has gone before provides a story or context within which we attempt to make some sense of the present. The problem in building on the past, however, is that it has been influenced by various forces. What we call "history" is really only selective interpretation. A native history of Canada would read quite differently from the Canadian histories we are used to reading in our classrooms. It would still be accurate: the difference would be one of perspective. Similarly, woman's role in church and society would be described differently by patriarchal and non-patriarchal thinkers. Neither description would be wrong, but both would be incomplete.

Keeping in mind the difficulties involved, I would like to consider some present trends and policies which affect women in our church and pose some questions about their future. You may not agree with my thinking, but I would ask you to consider it carefully.

THE FEMINIZATION OF OUR WORLDVIEW

> *Creation's Lord, we give you thanks*
> *that this your world is incomplete;*
> *that battle calls our marshalled ranks,*
> *that work awaits our hands and feet;*
>
> *Since what we choose is what we are,*
> *and what we love we yet shall be,*
> *the goal may ever shine afar,—*
> *the will to win it makes us free.*
>
> (The Hymn Book of the Anglican Church of Canada and
> The United Church of Canada, #161.)

The last century has seen an intense feminization of Western culture. More people are less certain about male-centred values and have incorporated into their view of the world some of the ideals associated with a female perspective. In addition, there has been a gradual weakening of commitment to any particular point of view and a tendency to be more flexible and thoughtful in our collective opinions. The feminist movement has not been the *cause* of this change in thinking. Rather, the movement is one of the *results* of a shift in our intellectual environment, brought about with the development of the social sciences during the latter part of the nineteenth century, and with Darwin's evolutionary theory which completely changed our view of people and their place in the scheme of things.

Until the development of sociology, psychology, and evolutionary biology, a human being seemed to be a fairly simple piece of work: a mind and body quite independent of other minds and bodies. We thought that we were in control. This was shattered, however, by the theories which pointed to the many ways in which people, especially children, are influenced by their society. Freudian pyschology, with its theory of an unconscious, undermined the view that humans are exclusively crea- tures governed by reason. The idea that we had evolved from other life- forms placed us in an animal hierarchy, and suggested that we are not necessarily always in control: we are as subject to instinctive impulses as our "lesser" cousins. The theory of evolution also called into question the teaching that we had "dominion" over everything else. This kind of questioning brought forth the wrath of virtually all the churches!

During this same period, sociology and Marxian theory were demon- strating that a society was not made up of a singe group of people, but of several groups which lived together in varying degrees of power and powerlessness. Indeed, the power and advantage of some frequently depended upon the powerless and disadvantage of others. It was also becoming clearer, with the insights of the social sciences, that the value system on which a society was based could actually be harmful to some of its members. Many American slaves, for example, had been socialized to (or had accepted) the values of their masters, even though those values kept them in slavery. As a result, there was a significant movement *against* emancipation among blacks before they were "freed".

In addition to what we were learning about our own Western socie- ties, by bringing the customs and outlook of other cultures to our atten- tion, anthropology was suggesting that our own understanding of the universe was no more "correct" than that of our "distant" relations. That science suggested that in some cases the "primitive" way of seeing things was more profoundly human than our Western ways.

These new ways of thinking challenged the assumptions of Canada's Victorian church establishments, especially the assumptions of the men. Women were already aware that *their* lives were shaped to accommodate the lives of men. They were not as surprised by the concept of socializa- tion as were those who equated their masculinity with the ability to govern their own environment, however large or small. And because most women saw themselves as mothers and preparers of food, they had never been alienated from their "natural" selves in the first place. Darwin's suggestion, then, that physiologically, humans were just another variety of animal, was not as shocking to them as to those philosophers who had imagined themselves spiritual and intellectual beings who had overcome their baser needs and passions. Indeed, women had *always* been charged with irrationality by Western thinkers, so Freud's notion that *all* human beings were governed by a part of their mind which could not be controlled was not nearly so devastating from their perspective!

One general result of these converging ideas was the "God-is-dead" cynicism which became the theological mood of much of the Western world in the twentieth century. In one sense the phenomenon was aptly named: certainly God, defined as all-male, *had been eclipsed*. What wasn't immediately evident was that a new concept of God which embraced both female and male principles, was being born.

Society as well as theology was changing and being feminized. The social services which had been initiated by churchwomen in most instances—feeding, clothing, housing, healing, and educating the disadvantaged —were gradually taken over by governments. The issues of justice surrounding women, and the negative effects of male domination on both women and men, began to be expressed in the courts and in our legislative bodies. Supported by the image-shattering scholarship initiated in the 1900s, women began to seek (and achieve) some social and political status for themselves. The female vote was hard won, however, by women who were thrown in jail or asylums and diagnosed, in many cases, as having that psychological disorder named for women: hysteria (which comes from the Greek word for "uterus"). Ironically, Queen Victoria herself sympathized with the view that women activists were mentally ill and was constantly embarrassed by her sisters' demands for political equality with men. In spite of that, women gradually assumed positions that had previously been closed to them, including the ordained ministry of our own church.

At first the fact that women were in policy-making positions made little difference to the style of an organization or institution. Women had only male models of behaviour before them and simply tried to behave as men might in a similar role. They adapted themselves to situations that had been developed by men for a male lifestyle. As their numbers grew, however, women in some situations began to develop a style of work more compatible with their own perspectives and unique life experiences (such as pregnancy). It soon became evident to these women that *how* we do things, *how* we structure our day, *how* we communicate with each other, *how* we organize and delegate work has been as male-determined as *what* we believe.

This process of intellectual, social, and religious feminization has not been a trivial issue, as some would have us believe. It has been, rather, a spiritual movement that is not going to go away like mini-skirts or beehive hairstyles. Churches and the organizations within the church which refuse to acknowledge the Christ-based principles that form the basis for Christian feminism, will become irrelevant as non-patriarchal women and men (those trying to define non-male-dominated roles for men and women) will seek their fellowship outside of the church. How much better it would be to work toward healing and reconciliation! In order to do so, some of the specific problems facing women of the United Church must be addressed.

THE PROBLEM OF ALIENATION

In the first chapter we saw that churchwomen's organizations came about in the first place because women had virtually no voice within their own denominations. They were alienated from their churches and from each other. There was no shared mission and no sense of sisterhood. Again, in chapter 3, we saw the alienation of many United Church Women which was expressed in the view that the national church imposed an organization upon them that they did not necessarily want. Whether or not that is true is irrelevant; the sense of alienation is real for many women.

Rules and Regulations

> We started out to do things by the new UCW handbook, with the Executive making decisions. This didn't always work too well, as there seemed to be problems of trying to follow written rules when we had always had our own rules as Ladies Aid and WMS![1]

One of the quickest ways to learn how an organization views itself is to wander through the forest of rules and definitions which makes up its constitution. The messages "hidden" there in plain view are very often a surprise to even those most familiar with them. Such is the case with *Guidelines for United Church Women.*

> *The Constitution*
> *...many of our younger women have started or joined new, less-structured groups in the church. These fill a real need for them. They do not think the national United Church Women in our older established churches is for them.*[2]

The first page of the *Guidelines* introduces three major premises which make the problem of alienation worse. Here, "constitution" is defined as "a statement of the fundamental principles which govern an organization" (even though many groups follow the constitution as a

66

guideline only). The preamble then continues, stating that the "following constitution" was approved by the General Council in 1960 and that it can be amended by the General Council *only* (the emphasis is part of the original text). Structurally then, the UCW is not in control of its own rules and regulations, nor of the "fundamental principles" which form its basis. Furthermore, the woman's organization of our church has no legal determination over its relation to The United Church of Canada as a whole, or over the money it contributes.

A legitimate response to this fact might be that our General Council has authority over *many* aspects of church life, and ultimate control over the woman's organization is justifiable. The problem arises because women, and certainly United Church Women, do not easily speak within the male-dominated General Council. If a situation were to arise in which the best interests of the UCW were in conflict with the best interests of the church, the women's organizational voice would be impotent despite women's strength of numbers and their substantial support of the church.

The metaphor which comes to mind in describing the relationship of the UCW to the national church is that of "chatelaine" (as one of the WWW contributors suggested). The UCW is like a working wife who hands her pay cheque over to her husband so that *he* may determine how it may be spent. He will even determine her needs and how much of the money should be returned to her to meet those needs. This may be done in consultation, of course, because we like to think of this relationship as a "partnership". The "Father-knows-best" view of woman's role, so acceptable when the constitution of the UCW was being formulated, continues to govern the organization.

At one level this business of General Council control over the constitution seems a trivial matter. At another level, however, it profoundly affects individual women's sense of themselves as competent and responsible human beings. The essential message in the current arrangement is that the organized women of the church are welcome to contribute all they can by way of time, talent, and money, but cannot be trusted to cooperate in the whole mission of the church as *equal partners*. The "joy-giving self-concept" that was a crucial element of the WMS success is lacking in the UCW for this reason.

Other groups affiliated with the United Church have faced this same situation and realized that an organization's structural relationships affect its individual members. AOTS men's club, for instance, considered becoming part of the United Church in a way similar to the UCW, but finally decided on a more autonomous arrangement. The men's organization remains in control of its own constitution and finances while cooperating in those aspects of United Church work with which it, as an organization, concurs. Even with its limited membership and finances, AOTS has more closely approximated a partnership with The United Church of Canada.

The Name of the Woman's Organization
Should we ask for a change of name? Would this help our image?[3]

The second major concern introduced on the first page of the *Guidelines* has to do with who, exactly, United Church Women are. According to this section they are "women of a congregation who are in agreement with the Purpose and Functions of The United Church Women of The United Church of Canada." And what of those women in a congregation who are *not* in sympathy with the Purpose and Functions, who do not think, for example, that women should be solely responsible for either the flowers in the sanctuary or for the kitchen and its contents (*Guidelines*, page 15), or that women should be doubly charged with financial responsibility for church support—both as women (*Guidelines*, page 2) and as members of the congregation? By constitutional definition, *they* are not United Church Women.

By assuming a name that should apply to all women within our church, the woman's organization has both alienated and co-opted those women who might have been its most creative critics. On the one hand, those who do not think that women, any more than men, should be the fund-raisers and housekeepers are alienated from their organized sisters because they are at odds with the goals. On the other hand, the women of our church who choose not to participate in the UCW are always regarded as potential UCW members since the organization was, at the outset, an attempt to "unite all women of the congregation." The point is, *the women of the United Church are not all alike,* and never have been. A certain self-identification was part of membership in the WMS and WA. Membership in the study-oriented groups *permitted* membership in the more housekeeping-oriented WA. As well, work for the local church *legitimated* the interest and effort expended on the only wholly female endeavour, the WMS. Many women belonged to only one group and that choice had largely to do with the way they saw themselves. The UCW does not permit such choice. In fact as far as the constitution is concerned, *there is no room for diversity among the organized women of the United Church.*

In chapter 1 we saw that meeting, organizing and naming oneselves as an ongoing group is a political act. The naming is both positive and negative—positive in the sense that it establishes the organization as an entity in its own right, and negative in the sense that it separates and sets the group apart from all other groups. Because the name "United Church Women" *can* include all the women of our church, it is practically impossible for women at odds with the UCW organization to establish a political identity of their own. They are simply named as another "unit" and swallowed up by the larger organization. In one instance, some women formed a small group to explore their special concerns as women working within a patriarchal setting. They called themselves the "No-Name Group." Before long they were being pressured to participate in

UCW fund-raising projects, and had been renamed the "Discovery Unit" by the UCW units in their church!

All the women of the church suffer from this business of naming—the UCW membership because it is identified as the *legitimate* United Church women's group and non-UCW women because they are identified, by default, as somehow being outside the circle. The latter group has effectively had *their* church identity stripped from them. Their only alternative is *not* to be one of the United Church Women, a decision which alienates them both from their sisters in faith and from their church.

One observation cannot be avoided at this point. The essential question is: "Who is served by this state of affairs? Who benefits?" In this case, the patriarchal church is served. The "chatelaine" activities for which the UCW is responsible, and the structural dependency of the organization ensure that the organized women will remain in a "wifely" role. Women who wish to organize on a different basis, who are attempting to realize a *true* partnership in the church community, are a threat to the institution. By defining *them* as something *other* than United Church Women, our church is symbolically showing them to the door.

> The Purpose
> *Perhaps the day will come when both men and women will work so closely together that there will be no need for them to be divided.*[4]

The clearest expression of women's alienation from the church is to be found in the Purpose of the Congregational UCW:

> *...to provide a medium through which we may express our loyalty and devotion to Jesus Christ in Christian Witness, Study, Fellowship and Service.*

The message implicit in that statement is that *without the UCW, women do not have such a "medium".* Can women not express their "loyalty and devotion" through the church? What is the medium through which men of the church express *their* faith? Whether intended or not, the "Purpose" of the Congregational UCW, as stated in the Constitution, cements the view that women are something separate and apart from the mainstream of The United Church of Canada.

If the church is unable to stimulate a "joy-giving focus" for the lives of its women, then another kind of churchwoman's organization is as essential today as it was when our mothers and grandmothers were voiceless in *their* congregations. But it must be an organization which is woman-based, and which springs from the real needs of women, not one which is institution-based, coming out of the needs of the institutional church.

69

Pyramids and Circles

The strange thing is, that they like to work, even to organize and manage, but must be led; no one will offer to lead, as President.[5]

The overall organization of the UCW, as set out in the by-laws, is modelled on patriarchy—a pyramid in which the most people have the least power. In the ancient "rule-by-the-father", the pyramid would have the patriarch at the pinnacle, his sons in the next position, and their sons in the next.

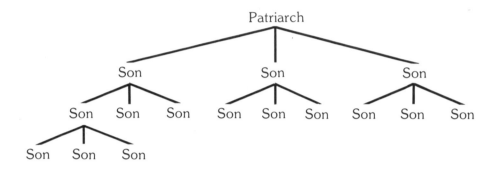

As a system of social organization, patriarchy was extremely efficient. Like so many human institutions, however, it came to view itself as "natural" or "divinely ordained"; philosophies and ideologies which would "prove" patriarchy to be ordained were then developed. Eventually, no other form of organization seemed either plausible or possible. The patriarchal pyramid remains so much part of our Western outlook it has become the organizational model for virtually every social institution— government, military, business, church, and family.

The problems with this kind of organization have only recently been addressed. The major one is that its principles and values have developed out of male society only. *Men* are acknowledged as primary human beings; women are merely the vessels (property) through which men reproduce themselves.[6] The feminine perspective has been either ignored or trivialized. A practical consequence of this state of affairs is the number and frequency of violent attacks upon women.

Another problem is that pyramidal organization establishes hierarchies of both power and status: each stage of the pyramid has authority over all stages beneath it. And regardless of the character of the person who fills the position, each stage carries greater social status than those below. One result of this power and status differentiation is a spirit of competitiveness which develops among those who share the same position on the pyramid. In the diagram, the sons at the second level may eventually end up at war to determine which one of them will assume the mantle of patriarch. Ancient nations solved this problem to some extent by establishing the concept of divine rule, a monarch appointed by God, and primogeniture, a rule by which the eldest son inherits the title, position and property of his father. Neither of these solutions, however, did anything to combat the friction that inevitably arose between brother and brother, son and father. The same sort of structurally imposed frictions can be seen among the top level of any modern institution.

Non-patriarchal women and men have challenged the pyramidal power structures within the church. They have called into question not only the organizational aspects, but also the relation of the minister to congregation. Do those who are ordained take God to the people? Or are they, rather, the catalysts and facilitators who try to discover, along with their constituents, God working through their individual and collective lives? The question is not only theological but also political. Power and status are involved.

It is significant that so many women's groups described themselves as "circles" in the early days of their organization. There is ample evidence that when women are in a position to work out their own ways of organizing themselves, they generally work co-operatively, sharing the administrative burdens, operating out of general agreement. The circle is the perfect metaphor. The concept of "President" and "Vice-president" comes from the pyramid model of organization; a circle acknowledges no head. The "problem of leadership" that has occupied so many pages of the Women, Work and Worship material is no problem at all if we understand that we are all, like Christ, both sheep and shepherd. The most that is needed in a non-patriarchal structure, it seems, is coordination and facilitation—differences in jobs *without* differences in status.

The fact that leaders are not forthcoming in the UCW may not indicate that women feel themselves incapable of leading, but that more women are rejecting the notion that such leadership is necessary. The old structure is just one more way of invalidating their sense of themselves as women. This is not a criticism of the way women have done things in the past: patriarchal organization was a necessary stage in the development of women's groups and was the only model available to us. The first automobiles resembled buggies; decades passed before a style of car evolved with no reference to carriages. Similarly, some women's groups are now assuming a "look" which refers to their own form and function, and not to something which has gone before. Many church and secular groups *other* than women's are learning that there is an alternative to the hierarchical way of doing things.

How we organize affects both what we think and how we feel about ourselves. For example, one or two people speaking from a platform will base their presentation on limited personal experience, statistics and studies conducted by others. On the other hand, one or two people helping a discussion in a circle, encouraging each participant to tell her

71

particular story, will bring forth a far richer understanding of the subject based on experience, and still be able to contribute the "expertise" not covered in the sharing session. The first way of proceeding defines the speaker as "the one who knows", and the participant as "the one who does not know." The second way acknowledges the validity of each person's experience and acknowledges many ways of knowing in addition to academic learning. It *affirms* the person.

The difference between patriarchal (pyramidal) and non-partriarchal (circular) approaches is aptly described in *Your Daughters Shall Prophesy.*

> *Instead of the hierarchical, fragmented, departmentalized, competitive approach derived from university models, wholistic approaches are learner-centred, experience-based, open-access and cooperatively oriented. When students learn only in a setting in which one man (usually the case) is "in charge" and has all the knowledge to be given out as he chooses to those over whom he holds power, they are learning a style of ministry. This style is replicated in the ministry when the one person "in charge" transmits to the church the values represented by hierarchy, fragmentation, and competition. Basic to a feminist understanding of ministry, however, is the assumption that it requires a setting or mutuality in which persons are enabled to value and to name their own experiences, learn from them, and move towards new understandings in the light of their own authority and of cooperative power relations.[7]*

UNITED CHURCH WOMEN AND THE CONGREGATION

The formation of the United Church Women accelerated women's participation in the work of the whole church. Many congregations which had been reluctant to admit women to Session or to have them sit on the administrative committees were now obliged to accept representation from the local UCW. Although such representation was minimal (only one member on the Official Board, for example), it established women as permanent features in the governments of United Church congregations.

UCW representation has also had a negative aspect. In some churches there was (and still is) a tendency to think that *any* woman represented the UCW and to treat *all* the women elected or appointed to the church committees as representatives of the women of the church (i.e. the UCW, since "all women are members of the UCW"), and not as representatives of the congregation as a whole? In emphasizing the "otherness of women", this attitude has worked against the idea of a partnership of women and men in the community of the church.

Another hindrance to integration at the congregational level has to do with the organizational methods of churches and their committees. Most of these are structured on the patriarchal model and use parliamentary procedures which most women find frustrating and tedious. It is not that women cannot learn the procedures—in fact many of them are included in the *Guidelines* ("Conducting the Business Period", page 20). Rather, the elaborate ways devised by men for formal communication seem unnecessarily awkward and heavy-handed. And there have been many instances in which "Roberts' Rules" have prevented, rather than enhanced, the communication process.

Accommodating oneself to such a situation, whether in church committees or outside the church setting, is tiresome business. It is little wonder that women are reluctant to seek office within *any* institution. The solution to this problem so far has been to teach women to follow the patriarchally developed procedures, aggravating a sense of inadequacy among our women.

Women's impatience with the existing ways of doing things is legitimate, and there are alternatives. To its credit, the *Guidelines* include a comprehensive section of "restyling" or "restructuring" the local UCW with this very problem in mind. The suggestion offered there would be useful in developing a more humane approach to general church government as well. When men and women of our congregations have learned to accept, appreciate, and employ the unique qualities that each has to offer, only then will we all be working towards the whole mission of the church. On the other hand, when a group is compelled to adapt itself to the structures and methods of the other, no integration will occur.

MODELS FOR CHANGE
Integration

> *Our young women are very busy women, many working full time, looking after homes and families, and doing what interest them on church committees. It will be interesting to see what they decide to do as time goes on. Some teach Sunday School and lead midweek groups, but so far they are not in the UCW here.*[8]
>
> *We know there will be far-reaching developments in the area of women's freedom and, therefore, responsibilities. What effect will these have on both the family and the church? Where is our ministry to be in our modern world with all its injustices and technological advances? How can we provide challenges for the women of our church?*[9]
>
> *Our church does not have a UCW because our women feel integrated with no need for a separate organization.*[10]

The ideal partnership in the community of the church would be one in which neither partner is structurally, nor numerically superior in matters of administration. Each perspective would be equally valued. According to Women, Work and Worship constributors, integration has already occurred in a few United Church congregations. In these cases the demise of the local UCW should be viewed as a victory for the women and men, not as a loss.

An account from South Gloucester (Montreal and Ottawa Conference) demonstrates just how pleasant life can be when the whole church, rather than just the women, is charged with responsibility for a congregational celebration.

> By 1968 anniversary arrangements were taken as a matter of course. Gone were the endless details the UCW had had to look after. The church treasurer paid the cleaning lady to get the church in readiness. The UCW treasurer paid the florist for a basket of flowers placed quietly in the church. A small Anniversary Committee decided on and invited a guest preacher...and also the visiting choir. Refreshments for the choir were dropped. For some of the ladies of long standing in the church it didn't seem like anniversary without the hustle and bustle of former years.[11]

For the rest, however, I'm sure it was women's liberation of the best sort!

Integration does not eliminate the differences between women and men. There will always be a place in the church for women's fellowship with other women. That sisterhood, however, need not interfere with an integrated approach to church government and policy; it is "in addition to", not "rather than". Some women in our church are experimenting with different models of organization for their groups, and perhaps they offer an indication of things to come.

Project-Oriented Groups

> The young married women of the district are not attracted to the UCW as an organization but we have an excellent working relationship with them. We support their efforts to renovate the Old Hall and make it a real community centre, and we are grateful for their help whenever we tackle a project too big for us to handle.[12]

In some congregations it seems that non-UCW women are organizing around specific tasks. The projects which have involved them range from art displays and study sessions to marshalling community support for women's transition houses. The value of such an approach is that the interests and needs of the women are prior to the organization. This, in itself, generates an enthusiasm that is frequently lacking in the more bureaucratic, ongoing organization of the UCW.

74

A report from British Columbia finds that short-term or ad hoc commitment attracts its younger women, while most of their UCW members are over sixty.[13] The difference is not one of age, but one of lifestyle. Most younger married women are employed outside the home, and many are also active in non-church ministries. These women are less likely to require the sort of social interaction that more isolated wives and older women need on a continuing basis. But the happy satisfaction of having been part of the development, organization and successful implementation of a worthwhile project is attractive enough to outweigh the expenses of time and effort involved.

In addition, cooperative, short-term endeavours can enhance the church community by bringing people together who might otherwise remain unknown to each other. UCW members, on the other hand, tend to work with other UCW members; the projects may change from time to time, but the people engaged in them remain the same.

If we look at some of the psychological rewards that churchwomen's organizations have offered their members in the past (see chapter 1), we can see that the same rewards are being sought today through project-oriented women's groups. They provide a "joy-giving self-concept", a "joy-giving group expression of emotion", "joy-giving work" and a "joy-giving focus for one's life." Such joy is only possible when the task has been elected by the women involved. The practical consequence is a wholehearted commitment to the specific work to which they have been called.

Special Interest Groups

> A group of younger women have formed a group calling
> themselves Young Church Women (YCW). They are inter-
> denominational but their children all go to the Sunday
> School. So far they have not contributed financially...but
> conduct a good Sunday School and hold a monthly
> meeting.[14]

Not all of the special interest groups formed by the women of our church are new. In fact, several of them are composed of women who refused to participate in the amalgamation of 1962. They kept going with their old names and their old ways of doing things.

> It is perhaps indicative of our Eastern Ontario "strength
> of character" that one group, the Ladies Guild, refused
> amalgamation and despite being branded as "rebels"
> continues active and independent to this day.[15]

Such "strength of character", it must be added, is present throughout Canada in the many groups that simply didn't bother themselves too much about the re-structuring going on over their heads. Their groups went on as they had in the past, at the wish of the membership.

Other sorts of interest groups are forming and in some cases, reforming. There has always been a need for the mothers of young children to get together. That phase of woman's life can be lonely, frustrating, and even frightening without the support, guidance, and companionship of other women in a similar situation. The WMS Baby Bands and Mission Bands provided an opportunity for such fellowship, but today there is no specific provision within the UCW organization for the various stages of women's lives. Several women's groups in our congregations are responding to this lack in the UCW. Mothers of infants, of Sunday school-aged children, and of teens, are meeting to share their specific concerns. Other women are forming fitness groups, money-management groups, retirement-planning groups, musical groups, drama groups, consciousness-raising groups, book clubs—the variety is as diverse as the women of our church. The attraction of these special interest groups is that they have established their own purpose and mandate. When the interest is no longer present within the church community, the group can disband with a happy collective memory of the good times that filled a particular need at a particular time. That the organization was not a "forever" proposition in no way affects its value to the members. In this approach too, it is the element of self-determination which inspires commitment. And the "joy-giving" aspects of the shared experience can only enhance the entire church community.

In most cases the newer women's groups co-exist and cooperate with the congregational UCW. However, the congregational UCW is aging (there are some lively exceptions) because of the organization's inability to attract younger women. One thing is certain: if any woman's organization is to continue within The United Church of Canada, it will have to be rethought in terms of *all* the women of the church, in terms of today's understanding of women's and men's roles and, finally, in terms of true partnership.

REFORMATION VERSUS TRANSFORMATION

> *Reformation is a patriarchal concept and it equates power with oppression; transformation is potent yeast putting light into the mix.*[16]

In the Congregation

At the congregational level many women are already rethinking their relationship to the church and are organizing accordingly. Some groups have decided that fellowship and study are reasons enough to meet together as women, and that fund-raising will be done in partnership with the men of the church, or not at all. Others have organized for the specific purpose of making money. The important aspect of this diversity is that today's churchwomen have the choice. No longer do we have to justify our fellowship in terms of its financial productivity: we *are* the church community.

Many congregations depend on the double-giving of women. (See chapter 2.) For that reason, any movement towards financial restructuring will have to originate with the organized women within the congregation. The men of the church, understandably, have little vested interest in assuming a partnership in tasks that have, until recently, been taken on by women.

In her book *Women, Change, and the Church*, Nancy J. Van Scoyoc (a churchwomen's consultant who met with the Conference UCW executive at their National Consultation in September, 1982) formulates some questions that get at the delicate balance between the needs of the institution and the needs of individuals within any congregation.

- *How can housekeeping and other necessary-but-draining jobs be done and activities that nourish and energize people be provided?*
- *In recruiting people for jobs and activities in the church, is the focus on fitting them to the job or starting with their talents and interests and looking for a job or creating one that suits them?*
- *Does over-programming of activities keep individual needs from emerging and being met?*
- *How are clergy responding to women who curtail activities when they seek employment?*
- *How are fellow members (men/women) responding to these women?*
- *Are enough opportunities for small groups made available to fill the need for support and in-depth study or sharing?*
- *Are groups and activities planned with the needs of particular people in mind, such as single or divorced women, older women, career women, or women with small children.*[17]

If we, as women, are responsible members of the church, then we must take some responsibility for shaping the ministry within the community. The moving Spirit cannot speak through us while our mouths are shut.

In the National Church

Re-thinking women's collective relationships within the United Church at the national level is an enormous task that will involve years of discussion and experimentation. However, observations based on conversations across Canada and materials submitted to the Women, Work and Worship project, combined with the past experience of women's groups and certain sociological principles, may provide some suggestions for the future.

One of the major problems women face at Church House is that the establishment there seems to take for granted that women, as a political group within the church, are fully integrated and therefore have neither special needs nor privileges deriving from their womanhood. Until recently, for example, the Division of Ministry Personnel and Education did not monitor ordained women because doing so would have denied their "equal" status with male ministers. In spite of the liberal intentions that gave rise to such a policy, the result was that the national church had no data to compare the placement and earnings of men and women, and had compiled no information specific to women in ministry, such as sexual vulnerability in counselling situations or in remote charges. A study group on Women in Ministry is now in the process of rectifying this situation.

As far as the Division of Mission in Canada is concerned, the UCW is represented on the Ministry with Adults Working Unit, but there is no major grouping that has women as its exclusive mandate. The women have asked for more, and at the 1983 National Consultation, a national UCW Executive was established, with six women representing two conferences, in addition to a president and president-designate.

The truth is, however, women are not wholly integrated and remain, in fact, a disadvantaged majority. One has only to wander through the mazes of Church House to see the ratio of men to women in policy-making positions. For the national church to pretend otherwise only aggravates the situation of women, and constitutes a sort of political dishonesty. If the United Church is serious in its attempts at partnership, then it must provide those intermediate stages that will enable partnership to develop. Structural and doctrinal discrimination do not disappear simply because the national church ceases to acknowledge it. Indeed, women's relation to the church is not just a "women's issue". It is a problem that must be addressed within every committee at every level of our church, for there is where its impact will be felt. The feminine face of God, more clearly reflected in church life, will ultimately cause us to rethink our theologies, our policies, and ourselves.

The Division of Mission in Canada has, for excellent reasons, attempted to avoid a hierarchically organized women's section. It seemed better, if integration were the goal, to integrate the women's concerns with those of the church as a whole. What was missing in that thinking was an honest acknowledgement that in spite of their numbers and financial contribution, women are still marginal participants in most areas of the church. And being marginal they still require a special support structure within the church that can both affirm and assist in the fear, pain, anger, and joy of this birthing process; that can hear and respond to all the women of the church, radical as well as conservative.

The WMS was strong at the *local* level because it had a strong *national* organization which provided a focus for its members. The local UCWs on the other hand, are like spokes on a wheel with no hub; there is nothing that unifies them. A good part of the sisterhood fostered by the WMS was accomplished through its Communications Division. The magazines produced for its members, affiliates, and children put each reader in touch with the whole network. There is no similar glue to bind the churchwomen of British Columbia with the churchwomen of Newfoundland, although they hunger for such contact. This is not to suggest that a new organization of women should be modelled on the WMS, an institution as matriarchal in its way of doing things as the church was patriarchal. We can, however, take some lessons from it.

At the very least, a national organization of the women of the United Church, with a largely administrative function, could effectively bring the concerns of women before the committees of the church. But it would have to represent *all* of the women who are its constituents, and not just those who are presently organized as UCW. The difficulty in effecting such representation is that there is at present only the UCW structure through which to work. Even so, such difficulties have been overcome in some Conferences by Women's Concerns Committees.

The role of the national church staff in such a situation would be to respond primarily to the needs of women as these are determined within their own congregations. Since there is already a trend among non-UCW women to organize around issues, projects or special interests, the national church could provide or suggest resources for this process or, where resources are lacking, develop them. Such an approach would in no way interfere with those local UCW groups who prefer to meet on a continuing basis. Patterns of interests would be quick to emerge, and since the goal of both the church and the women's organization would be to "enable partnership", the use of affirmative action materials (assertiveness training, effective speaking, understanding power) could be encouraged. The United Church is fifteen years behind business, government and educational institutions in this area.

Women of the United Church want to know what others are doing and thinking. The response to the Women, Work and Worship project indicates that there are many creative writers and thinkers among us who, with some coordination, could fill a regular magazine or newsletter. So many of our stories are part of a larger story. When women of the Maritimes packed bales of food and clothing for the prairies during the Great Depression, they didn't know that the salt cod was sometimes mistaken for roofing materials or snowshoes! Such a vehicle for information-sharing among women of our church could also address concerns and celebrate the creation of a sisterhood that has been absent for too long. It could also have a practical aspect—sharing innovative projects that have proven successful, such as the plant sale called a "Slip and Bloomer Tea". There is far more creativity and talent "out there" than could ever be concentrated at church headquarters, and it is a resource we have, for the most part, failed to either appreciate or employ. We can learn best through our own stories, but right now there is little opportunity to share them.

It would be also psychologically and sociologically desirable that, along with a person, women have a place at Church House—a resource centre perhaps, which is available to all, but furnished according to the needs of women; a "room of one's own" in which a woman visiting Toronto could browse for new materials or ideas, or simply to affirm that she is, indeed, a presence within the national church.

The suggestions given above are just a few of the many ideas that have emerged from the Women, Work and Worship materials. They are presented as a starting-point for dialogue. One of the objections to any restructuring—particularly involving staff for women and a resource centre—will be funding. One would do well, in this regard, to remember that the women of the church have *more* than paid their way, and that there *have* been situations in which a staff member has charged specifically with "men's work". Women have always supported the church; now it's time for the church to support its women. The ultimate goal of both a national women's organization and its related staff should be to put themselves out of business. Through education (of the church as well as the women), support and interaction in the courts of the church, both women and men can grow towards partnership and integration.

Reconciliation

All the women of the United Church are United Church women. Far from uniting the women of our congregation, the UCW, by taking the name, has ultimately caused divisions which are artificial to some extent. There are attitudinal difficulties on both sides of the schism, however, and these are expressed in the Women, Work and Worship contribution.

> *...I would like to say a word to the men of the congregation. This is not a Women's Lib movement, even though it may sometimes sound like it this morning.* [18]

The above introduction to a congregational celebration of twenty years of UCW is, in essence, an apology to the men from the women for daring to be competent, effective, and productive human beings. The truth is, what follows *is* a women's liberation story; it does not need an apology. The miracle of our faith is that it has transcended centuries of abuse, bubbling like a potent yeast, to keep bringing the oppressed into the light. Women's liberation is a necessary stage of human liberation.

There can be no shame in reaching the full personhood that God intended. The men of our church will not be devastated by women's competence. Those who *are* threatened will have to embark upon their own journey towards liberation, individually and collectively, as women have. And liberating Christianity will be their strength and guide as well.

The feminization of church and society is a fact. In spite of that, one does not have to be actively engaged in feminist activities, or even agree with all the principles of feminism, to hear the pain of those sisters who have chosen the difficult task of reconciling their feminism with their commitment to the church. Many women have found it easier to leave. In many ways those struggling to transform the church are truer to the spirit of the union—they, too, have committed themselves to the church that can be, not to the church that was.

> ...some of our younger women are ashamed of the work done by WMS, WA and UCW—the "women's work". They behave like young women who leave home and are ashamed of that home... They benefitted by what they learned there but have not matured enough to appreciate their heritage.[19]

It is true that many "liberated" women within our church have turned their backs on the mothers and grandmothers who set the stage for their daughters' successes. Their liberation will not be complete, however, until they have acknowledged the gifts they have received from the past and are able to reflect with pride upon women of such different times and circumstances. Church groups were women's way of liberating themselves in a society which was generally hostile to them, providing little in the way of education, and practically no forum for expressing their talents beyond the home. Those women who first met together in our churches succeeded, miraculously, in achieving joy for their lives. They have bequeathed to us a joy-giving attitude towards the past, if only we'd acknowledge the amazing depth and scope of their work and worship.

The first reconciliation, then, must be among the women of the church. They do not differ much from each other, except in name. We can love and hear and disagree as sisters do if only our church families will provide a caring context. There must also be a reconciliation between the church and the women of the church. And that is not possible until the whole church—the institution and its members—is ready to acknowledge and confess the injustice committed through its structures, its patriarchal doctrines, and its language. The healing is found in the words and deeds of Christ which affirm all people as God's children. The Moving Spirit still moves in them.

There is no appropriate way to end this reflection on women of The United Church of Canada. Our story continues, and we approach new thresholds in work and worship. Together we will breathe new life into the Gospel message, bringing the church a little closer to the kingdom.

In tribute to our mothers who liberated themselves through Christ, we join with Christine Frye in her psalm of a singer.

Lord, accept this song of my heart,
as you accepted earlier the songs of our lips.
You took our bruised and battered spirits
and soothed them with the balm of music;
You took the islands of our isolation
and submerged them in a sea of song.

You took all of us, as we were—
sick or healthy,
anxious or at peace,
sad or celebrating,
or maybe just feeling mediocre—
You took us, Lord;
you turned us loose
to raise our voices and our spirits in the songs
of faith,
of love,
of joy,
of trust,
of prayer and praise.

Lord, it was glorious to sing with you.
Accept now this psalm,
this song of praise and thanks.[20]

Section 2

The Women Who Taught Us

SECTION 2   WOMEN WHO TAUGHT US

Introduction to Section 2

CHAPTER 5   A LADY IN THE PULPIT
The Rev. Lydia Gruchy: First Among (United Church) Women
Five Ministers' Stories
> The Rev. Elda Daniels Struthers
> The Rev. Karen Elizabeth Toole Mitchell
> The Rev. Frances MacLellan
> Ethel Howie
> Stella Burry

Reflections of Two Ordinands—Then and Now
> Ordination
> Marian Soliloquy

A View from the Pew

CHAPTER 6   MINISTERING TO ONE ANOTHER
...Through Overseas Missions
> Ada Sandell
> Anna Roloff

...Through Home Missions
> Gwenyth Hubble
> Florence Bird

...Through Our Churches
> Luella May (Monroe) Young
> Christina Kerr
> Vida Gertrude (Hamilton) Green
> Ethel (MacPherson) MacDonald
> Cecily May (Pike) Penney

...Through Our Lives

Elizabeth Jane (McNevin) Lowe

Margaret (Kee) Dickson

Edna Margaret (Pierce) Sanders

Helen Mary McCurdy

Alice (Gordon) Green

Mabel Louise Dubbin

Grace (Webster) MacKinnon

Sophia Naomi Evangeline (Swift) Greene

Mildred Fahrni

Introduction to Section 2

> *When I received the first request for information about me and a sharing of my story, I was delighted to think that some people actually thought my experience might be worth relating. But too soon the excitement faded, when I realized that I didn't have much of a story to tell, for how could anyone understand or even want to understand the journey of someone who has absolutely no goals, no desires, and no expectations? I let it slide. Like most oppressed people (women in particular) who haven't the tools or the skills to compete in a society where one's worth is a function of their capacity to dominate, I felt that I had nothing to contribute. Then I received the second notice. It was then that I realized that if I were to act responsibly in the hope...of a more 'just' society, I must talk, for it is only through communication that we can come to understand ourselves better and, in the process, become aware of our role in humanizing this society. So here I sit in a cool room in Athens, writing to my sisters so far away, who believe our stories are worth telling. The distance now feels somewhat less. (Sylvia Smith, writing to* The Matrix Collective, *St. Andrew's College, Saskatoon, for* The Matrix Calendar—1984.)

This section consists of stories by and about some of the women who have helped to shape The United Church of Canada. The first of the two chapters which follows provides a woman's view from the pulpit—the concerns, impressions, joys, and sorrows of women who have been called to an ordained professional ministry in our church. The second is an account from the perspective of those who have been called to another kind of ministry—the dedicated lay churchwomen who are the rock on which the church has been built. I hope the stories told there will make the distance between them and us "somewhat less".

There are many stories in the Women, Work and Worship files. Those printed here are representative—tributes not only to the people specifically named, but also to their counterparts in churches across Canada. And there are many stories among us in our own congregations ...if only we'd ask.

Chapter 5   A LADY IN THE PULPIT

A Lady in the Pulpit

Miss Williams, a lady evangelist, occupied the pulpit in the Methodist Church on Sunday evening. She took as her text, St. Matthew 4, 3rd verse: "And when the tempter came to him, he said, 'if thou be the Son of God, command that these stones be made bread.'" In a very explicit and able manner she showed that God intended all His children to be tested. She counselled her hearers not to yield to temptation. With a little more force in delivery, Miss Williams' discourses would be very interesting. She will again have charge of the service the Sunday after next.

(Newsclipping from Beeton World, June 1900. Reprinted in Trinity United Church, Beeton: 1878-1978, p. 56, written by Herb Platt. Included in WWW, Toronto, #7, submitted by Muriel Reynolds.)

The Rev. Lydia Gruchy: First Among (United Church) Women

This is the story of Lydia Gruchy who, through hard work and persistence, made it possible for women to be ordained in The United Church of Canada. Lydia Gruchy was a graduate of the University of Saskatchewan. On her graduation she decided to replace her brother who had died as he was about to enter his work in theology.

Though she did brilliant work in her studies, when she graduated in theology she was not accepted for ordination, but was permitted to work on a field of six appointments in Northern Saskatchewan.

Dr. John Nicoll, the Superintendent of Missions in that area, wrote in his report of her work there: "Miss Gruchy travels roads that are terrible; she drives her own car; she is appreciated by her people; both old and young respond to her leadership."

She had begun asking for ordination when the General Council of The United Church of Canada met in 1926, and continued to do so at every following General Council. One of the years that Nellie McClung attended General Council she was very disappointed that Lydia Gruchy was not permitted ordination. She said afterward: "It was not the men who refused her permission; it was the women of the WMS who voted against it."

It was not until 1936 that the General Council agreed to her becoming the Rev. Lydia Gruchy. She became the first woman to be ordained in The United Church of Canada, her ordination taking place in St. Andrew's United Church, Moose Jaw, in 1936. Miss Gruchy is presently living in British Columbia.

Dr. John Nicoll, who worked hard for her ordination, said: "We hope we may live long enough to say with Galileo not only that the earth does move, but that Christian thought in the United Church does move too."

(Written by Queen Linton for Maritime Conference United Church Women, News-letter, Fall 1982).

FIVE MINISTERS' STORIES

The Rev. Elda Daniels Struthers

I was born in a Methodist parsonage on June 5, 1906 in Colpoy's Bay, Ontario, where my parents had gone as bride and groom in 1904. Father bought a little property twelve miles away at Oliphant on what has come to be known as Preachers' Point and our family has summered there ever since, and developed a great love for the Bruce Peninsula. We love its gray limestone rocks, its white sand and clear water, its rare wildflowers, birds, and sunsets. We were brought up to appreciate the beauty of nature and the wonder and majesty of the Creator-God. Moreover, blessed with the joys of friendship and the warmth of parental love, we early knew God's love.

As far back as I can remember I knew who I was—I was the minister's eldest daughter and so held a unique place in the church in each village or town to which we moved. The church, of course, was always the centre of our life, or rather our activities revolved around the dual centres of church and home, to which school was added as time went on. Mother and Father were a team—mother helped with every aspect of church life and father helped with work at home.

My interest in the outreach of the church to faraway countries and people began in Mission Band very early and was fed on stories told around our dinnertable by father's missionary classmates on furlough from China and Japan. When I was only nine years old father took me with him to "The Northern Summer School" in Wiarton, which he helped to found. The program was geared to young people but the thrust of the "Forward Movement for Missions" must have got through to me because I told him on the train going home that I decided to be missionary. When I was eleven, "Uncle Crossley" of the Crossley-Hunter Evangelistic Team lived in our home for a month while holding services in Tara Methodist Church. It was then that I made a definite decision to give my life to Christ.

After attending high schools in Elora and Hamilton, I wanted very much to go to university, but father said he could not afford to send two sons and two daughters to university on the small salary he was making. While we each had an equal right to higher education it was more essential for the boys to have it. They needed to be able to support families later on, whereas we girls would likely get married and be supported (not pursuing careers). Little did he guess that later both brothers would turn down this chance while my sister and I ended up with the degrees!

I went to Hamilton Normal School and taught Grades One to Four in Hamilton for eight years, from 1925 to 1933. For several of those years I planned on getting married, but the Depression did me the favour of giving me time to think, and I decided that there was not enough mutual interest and compatibility to make a satisfactory marriage. So I reverted to my earlier plan of studying to become a missionary. I went to my father's alma mater—Victoria College—and drank up knowledge as a thirsty person drinks water. After all the giving out I had done while teaching, the well needed refilling.

It was not until I became lost in the crowd on the University of Toronto campus in 1932 that I knew what it was like to be a sort of non-entity. This feeling was heightened at Emmanuel College in 1943-1944 where I was the only woman in a class of twenty-five men, and my sex was ignored completely. Being naturally shy, I found it an uncomfortable climate—everything had been set up for men (even the seats and chester-fields were too high and too deep) and I was out of my element. In argument I could usually hold my own, but felt like a stubborn minority of one at times. At other times there was good camaraderie, and they would kid me about "Daring to be a Daniel". I said the feminine version of that old hymn was "Dare to *Stay* a Daniel", and they asked what I was trying to do—double-dare myself?

The decision to become an ordained minister involved a deep inner struggle. To better my qualifications for work on the overseas mission field was one thing, but to actually become ordained was another. The conflict arose because of the image I had grown up with: father—the little man with the benign smile and persuasive manner behind the pulpit; mother, the ideal helpmate—the minister's wife. I suppose I had unconsciously hoped all those years to become a minister's wife but the suitable opportunity had not presented itself. How could I now cross the sex-line and become a minister myself, being a woman? Would it be proper for me to play what had always been considered a man's role?

After much prayer and soul-searching I decided I ought to try it. Since the church gave its professional leaders the highest training and qualifications, I needed this equipment for the difficult and demanding role of the missionary.

90

While I was participating in a quiet communion service in a small chapel in Melrose Church, Hamilton, preparatory to ordination on June 2, 1944, I heard the strains of the Wedding March drifting in from the sanctuary—a reminder of the role I was *not* assuming. Looking down at my *Book of Common Order,* I found that the place was marked by my mother's wedding handkerchief edged with Grandmother Daniels' handmade lace! I was the twelfth woman to be ordained by The United Church of Canada.

By carrying through on the factors that led to my ordination, I got ahead of my story! From 1933 to 1936 I completed the course in Pass Arts, having financed myself on money saved from school-teaching, and borrowing from home for the senior year. (Incidentally, it took five years to pay off that loan.) In my senior year I lived at the old United Church Training School on St. Clair Avenue and combined part of that course with my Arts subjects so I could reach the overseas field before I was thirty, the age-limit for beginning foreign language study. The matter of where I should serve overseas was discussed with Dr. Ruth Taylor, Hugh D. Taylor and Dr. Winnifred Thomas. We decided on Korea, and I was appointed by the Woman's Missionary Society.

On August 15, 1936 I left Canada and arrived one month later in the Sungjin mission station in North Ham, Kyung Province, Korea. Before I could even begin on my work assignment of evangelistic work with women and girls I had to embark on the long and arduous task of language study. It involved much of interest, challenge and satisfaction as well as being a tedious discipline every day, all day, for two and a half years! Fortunately I liked language and literary studies and considered it a privilege to learn about another culture and get to know people of another race from my own. I found the Korean people warm and responsive to friendly overtures, and I still treasure many of them as my friends today. Korea has often been called "the darling of the mission fields" because of the wholehearted response of its people to the Christian Gospel.

Before World War Two when Korea was all one country, it was difficult for a newcomer to get a toehold because the Japanese rule was becoming more and more oppressive. Along with American women missionaries I helped to work out a program for teenage girls in Korea, using some CGIT principles. We did not dare launch this, for a new program introduced by westerners would have been suspect. So the leader's manuals, etc., were carried in our hand-luggage, and the program introduced a little at a time, as occasion permitted, into already existing church organizations.

Bible Institutes for training lay people had been in existence for some years. I worked out plans for a Junior Bible Institute with a broader program attractive to young girls, but at the last minute this had to be cancelled. These difficulties were because of political factors, not the fact that I was a woman! Life was even more restricted for the male missionaries. I did manage to get five Girls' Clubs started in five places near the northern border of Korea, struggled through teaching Paul's missionary journeys from the Book of Acts in a month-long women's Bible Institute in Hoiryung, and did some choir work. That was about all I could manage in two years before being called home by the Canadian Government because of the outbreak of World War Two. In my day we were instructed not to engage in political activity. Today many missionaries seem to feel called upon to demonstrate their "faith-in-action" by identifying closely with their Korean associates in political-social activities.

After the war, in 1947, I was invited by Dr. Helen Kim to join the staff of Ewha Woman's University in Seoul, South Korea. I served as Professor of Christian Education there for twelve years: 1947-50, 1953-57, 1958-63. Ewha is a showpiece of what Christianity has done for the cause of women's education. From the smallest of all possible beginnings—one missionary's wife teaching one little girl in her bedroom—it grew into the first primary school for girls, to the first girls' high school, then to the first college for women. It is now a university of eight thousand students—the largest women's university in the world. For years the only women leaders anywhere in Korean church and society were Ewha-trained, and it still has an excellent rating.

It was thrilling to be part of this great institution, to enjoy association with staff members (men and women) and students, and to meet the challenge of each day. I had a succession of very good secretaries (in some cases grads of the Social Work or Christian Studies Departments gaining experience and language for further studies abroad). They helped me prepare lectures in the Korean language and mark essays and exam papers. In the end, I compiled a book of Worship Resource Materials which contained the most important songs, poetry, stories, meditations that I had translated from the heritage of western Christendom plus all that I could gather of original Korean devotional material. I usually taught English when asked to do so, and broadcasted basic English lessons for three years over HLKY, the Christian Radio Station, but I considered my main subject to be "Principles and Methods of Christian Education" in addition to some Bible Study and Worship courses.

At Ewha there were daily chapel and weekly Sunday services, and special programs at Thanksgiving, Christmas and Easter, often involving dramatization. Then once a year at the conclusion of Religious Emphasis Week there were great Baptism services, with as many as 1,021 being baptized at one time. I must give the several university chaplains credit for giving me an equal place beside themselves on these occasions. I remember one year when I personally interviewed and baptized more than 100 students. So my dream of baptizing in the name of the Father and the Son and the Holy Spirit came true! I felt that the theological training I had completed on furlough was put to good use and that there was no discrimination against me in this woman's institution of higher learning.

Church Work in Korea

It was not as easy for a woman minister to be recognized in Korean church circles. I remember one time when I was not given a seat at General Assembly on the grounds that "there is no such thing as a woman minister in the Presbyterian Church in Korea." But I did work with the church both denominationally and interdenominationally on many committees, and preached by invitation from time to time. Some years I was associated with the supervising pastor of our Kyungi Presbytery and visited the churches with him as time permitted.

One thing that made it difficult to work with Koreans was and is their factionalism. We went through some harrowing times because of splits in the church and ended up aligned with the most liberal branch of it called "The Presbyterian Church in the Republic of Korea", the PROK. (By Canadian standards they are very conservative.)

I remember that one time when Dr. Ruth Taylor was Secretary for Korea, she came out to meet the PROK and only men turned out. She refused to meet with them until they included representatives of the Women's Evangelistic Society and other women to make up at least one-third of the committee. After some years they did ordain three women elders, but men are still in the decision-making and money-handling offices of the church, with women playing supportive, servant roles. Women missionaries, however, are recognized according to their qualifications. They spoke to, or of me, as "moksa" (minister) and I gained the reputation of being "the benediction-saying woman minister."

I think that one of the important effects of the liberating influence of Christianity in Korea is the higher status it gives to women than that accorded by the Confucian ethic, whose five relationships form the basic structure of their society. In that sense practically everything we westerners did worked toward the liberation of women and, to a lesser degree, men.

There isn't time to tell much about the youth Caravan program I introduced into Korea before it began in Canada. The Caravaners were all women students to begin with, but the men students clamoured to get into it, so very cautiously we tried this. As no difficulties arose it continued to be a co-ed project for a number of years, even after I left Korea. The Caravan program involved taking the wealth of education and the gospel message of love and sharing it with those less fortunate in remote rural villages or islands. I also tried to instill the ideal of Christian Service into the newly organized Social Work Department at Ewha; it was rewarding to be invited back to Ewha on its Eighty-fifth Anniversary to meet with the alumnae and discover that in most cases these women had been not only good housemakers, but had also done real stints of service for church and/or community. I was proud of them; it made my efforts, such as they were, worthwhile.

Looking back over my missionary career, I see some discouraging "plateaux" in language study, some lonesome spots and a variety of difficulties to be overcome, but I never doubted that that was my calling or regretted having gone to work in Korea. Perhaps the thing that was the most difficult for Oriental people to understand and accept was the concept of the *single* missionary. They had been accustomed for four thousand or so years to a society based on the unit of the extended family, and they were perplexed at our individualism. How many sons did I have? None? Then who would look after me in my old age?

When, in 1957, I married Dr. Ernest B. Struthers, a medical missionary formerly of China, and returned to Korea for a full five-year term, they rejoiced with me in the companionship I had found and took quite an interest in our marriage and our home.

Church Work in Canada

Since I could not work in Korea during World War Two, I was placed in Canada. From January 1941 to June 1942 I was Superintendent of the Oriental Home in Victoria, B.C., an orphanage for twenty-six Chinese and Japanese-Canadian orphans. This was more like a parental role than a teacher's role, in that I was responsible for the children after, not during, school hours. I just used common sense plus a lot of love.

From 1944 to 1946 I worked in Newcastle, Alberta, a coal-mining village on the outskirts of Drumheller. There were hardly any adults in the "mission" church, as none of the miners attended. Some of their wives did and they sent the children. Typical of the spirit of a mining town was the feeling that they would just be there temporarily until they made enough money to move on. So there was no community spirit and little incentive to prepare and preach a weekly sermon, but I kept at it. I suppose it was good practice. Although there was very little intellectual stimulation, the Sunday School and midweek children's groups, and Bible teaching in the schools held challenge. I found it difficult to identify with the people on that assignment, and really didn't like it.

During the Korean War from the end of my furlough in 1951 to the summer of 1953, I was invited to be Associate Minister at Westdale United Church, Hamilton in the McMaster University area. This proved to be an ideal position. The work was divided between a senior minister (male) and myself. I was in charge of the large and flourishing CE program and preached one Sunday morning and two evenings each month. Some seventy teachers of primary and secondary schools as well as the university were members of our church, so there was a good deal of trained leadership on which to draw.

The Church School kept growing in all departments, as did the midweek Explorers, Mission Band, CGIT, Junior Congregation. As well, there was a large number of able women in the women's organizations. Westdale had never had a woman minister before, but both men and women accepted me and I spent a very happy two years there before returning to Korea.

After retiring from Korea at fifty-eight, I worked half-time for about seven years, letter-writing and doing editorial work at church head-quarters; speaking and preaching on the outreach of the church. Three years later, I was able to get on the staff of Victoria College as a tutor in the World Religions Course in the Combined Departments of Religious Studies of the University of Toronto. Having lived twenty-seven years in the Orient, I had a feeling for and some knowledge of the non-Christian religions there. I had the fun of taking lectures with the students and then leading discussions with small groups of them afterwards. It meant a great deal of reading as well as a great deal of essay-marking, but I learned a lot and enjoyed being back in a classroom setting.

I began and ended in the teaching profession, Ewha and Victoria being the highlights. The pastoral work at Westdale stands out clearly and happily.

Since retirement I've worked on three ecumenical committees as a volunteer: The World Development Service and Relief Committee of General Council, the Canadian Institute of Religion and Gerontology, and the Jewish-Christian Dialogue between Eglinton United Church (of which I am a member) and Holy Blossom Temple. In addition, I helped my late husband write and publish his autobiography and now hope to continue with a bit of writing for myself. God has blessed me in so many ways—thanks be to God!

(WWW, Elda Daniels Struthers file)

The Rev. Karen Elizabeth Toole Mitchell

I was born in Winnipeg on August 10, 1947, the youngest of three children, and my childhood and adolescent years were spent in Winnipeg. When I was six the family moved from a relatively middle-income area to the North End of the city (the inner-city, slums of Winnipeg). The move was necessitated by family financial difficulties when a grand-mother had to be placed in a nursing home, and the house had to be sold to raise the money.

The formative years there were spent in the North End in what would now be considered poverty. We were not hungry though, nor were we ever on welfare. My father was a coach-cleaner for the CNR and worked all his life. The socio-economic conditions of the North End certainly led to a particular lifestyle. The quality of schools was questionable and those years were difficult, as I seemed to go from the lowest levels to the highest (D to A). We had virtually no contact with churches, although we were nominally Anglican. Some of our clothes came from the Salvation Army Thrift Shops.

At the age of fifteen I first encountered grief and death when my brother, who was twelve years older than I, was killed in a trucking accident. Soon after that (approximately two years) I began to attend a United Church. Gradually I became more involved in that church and eventually became a Youth Worker and church secretary for All Peoples Missions. Throughout this time my religious questions were being formed and although I had no real answers, the quest had begun. At twenty-one I joined the United Church, recognizing that there were still many struggles and questions but committed to that quest and believing the struggle was worthwhile. Earlier that same year my sister had been killed, and out of the depression that followed I felt the urge to dedicate my life to helping and serving others who were caught in the traps that this life lays for all of us.

At twenty-one I also entered university as a mature student, and received my Arts degree from the University of Winnipeg three years later. Then I went on to theology at Atlantic School of Theology and graduated in 1975 with my Master of Divinity. In 1974, I had married Peter Mitchell, also a student in theology.

After ordination we were settled in Newfoundland, and I was the first ordained woman to serve a pastoral charge in that province. After a year I returned to inner-city Halifax and Brunswick Street Church as associate minister, a position I held for two years. In 1979 our first child was born, and I began a shared pastorate in Maitland with my husband. In 1980 we were called to Trinity-St. Stephens in Amherst. In 1981, the second child was born. At present we are still in Amherst, serving in a shared pastorate as a clergy couple with the Rev. Eldon Gunn.

The roots of faith are firmly based in my childhood. We did not attend church, but my mother was a strong person with a great faith. The injustice, pain and hurt of my childhood years, the loss of a brother and sister, the concern of working at building and sharing my beliefs all have led me to this place and this time.

(WWW, Maritime-Nova Scotia, #5, Item 4, submitted by Evelyn Price.)

The Rev. Frances MacLellan

I came into the professional ministry from nine years of teaching in Ontario, where I was always a member of congregations though at different levels of activity. This was to me as natural as breathing because I had been brought up in a home where the lives of both my mother and father included taking responsibility for the life of the church. My mother found time and strength to be both a homebody and president, at different times, of the Woman's Association and the WMS, as well as taking her Christian witness into a number of community organizations.

While I was teaching in my third school I was literally summoned to offer myself for professional ministry through the words of my minister one Sunday: "God needs men and women in his service." I had never even heard of a woman minister before that. How many times I was to hear that same remark from men, women and children even of the United

Church over the next thirty-odd years, from the West to the Atlantic seaboard!

Since my parents were then living in Nova Scotia, I applied for admission into what was then Pine Hill Divinity Hall in Halifax and was accepted as the first woman to live in residence (and the *only* woman to live there before it was demolished). During that time I had opportunities to preach around the area and prove there are female ministers. In conservative Cape Breton where I supplied for a Sunday, an elderly gentleman, holding my coat for me after the service, remarked, "We didn't know whether we were going to like having a lassie, but you're all right."

For my first mission field experience I was sent to southern Saskatchewan where the same apprehension preceded me, I learned later. The community's shock was well expressed by a young Roman Catholic who was sitting on a vantage point overlooking the manse during lunch. I had got into the car of a teacher sent to fetch me for lunch when this young lad asked, "Who was that just got into Mr. Dahonuik's car?" "That," replied another of the United Church, "is our minister." Said the first, "I could have sworn it was a woman!" However, at the end of the summer they asked if they could submit a strong application to have me for their student the next year, and at the end of that summer an old bachelor gave me what, I'm sure, was his highest commendation: "It's going to take a big man to fill your shoes."

In 1953, I was ordained by the Maritime Conference for work in Alberta Conference, for I had strong feelings that I was not particularly wanted at home. The Rev. Hilda Johnson, missionary in India, had been the first woman to graduate from Pine Hill and the first female ordinand of the Conference. The fact that she did the accelerated course offered during the war, however, made me able to claim the same primacy for the regular course. The Rev. Wilena Brown who studied at Emmanuel was ordained with me.

I was settled in the Bow Slope Pastoral Charge, "because I had no children to drown in the water in the manse cellar." After serving in that widespread five-point charge for four years I accepted a call to the Foremost Charge, still torn in pieces by an unfortunate clash of outlooks, where it was possible for me to drive eighty miles going to and from a meeting.

One really never knows what contribution one has made to a Charge. However, I and they could see that the places where we worshipped, sometimes public halls, had been beautified during my time there. Also, through constant exhortation (would they call it nagging?) I helped both charges take on full responsibility for themselves as they became self-supporting charges. I do know that the greatest contribution I made to Foremost was to become ill for an extended period. When I came back to them, they had done all the things they should have done over many years. The taxiing service for me which the men of Foremost had organized among all the men of the town (attenders or not) did more to heal the breach that had been there before than anything I could have done.

In 1962, because of the illness of my father, I sought a charge in the Maritimes so that I might give my mother the moral support she needed. When I received a call to Barrington, N.S., I was told that I was the first woman called into the Maritime Conference (and, I believe, in the Conference as well). Here at last was a reversal of the sad situation in which a young woman of the Maritimes, serving summer field there, was given, back in the fifties, not support but such negative treatment that she gathered it was no place for a woman to serve.

In 1974, returning from a two-year study leave in England, I accepted a call to St. John's, Halifax, as senior, indeed the only minister of one of Halifax's largest churches. Here for the first time I found I was not alone, as the Rev. Ellen Wilson was already serving as associate minister in Bethany. Yet there were still those repeated, astonished remarks, "You're the first woman minister I've ever seen." It reminded me of the experience I had had in England when, through an ex-nun friend, I was invited to speak to a group of Roman Catholic women who were organized to fight the policy of their hierarchy toward the position of women in their church. This experience opened my eyes to many privileges and responsibilities we have, both women and men, in The United Church of Canada.

Last July when I was coming up to the date I had chosen for retirement, one of the dear older women of St. John's delighted my heart when she remarked, after bemoaning my going, "I don't know how we are ever going to get used to having a man."

Besides this sort of "pioneering", it is difficult to say what one's contribution has been. In the Maritimes, I like to think that it may have been providing, on more than one occasion, "mothering" to complement the "fathering" of the male clergy. One man, not of my congregation and so unknown to me, said to me after the funeral of his beloved mother, "I was terribly upset before the funeral service began, but when you came into the pulpit I felt comforted and at peace."

I hope I made some contribution in the courts of the church as Chairperson of South Alberta Presbytery, and Commissioner to the General Council when it met in Windsor, Ontario. That same year I was nominated as president of Alberta Conference and died a thousand deaths as my name hung on until the Conference finally came to its senses and elected Dr. Preston MacLeod, then of Calgary.

After my return to the Maritimes I was made convenor of the Conference Committee of Colleges and Students, as the prestigious body deciding on the elegibility of candidates to be ordained was then called. This position also put me on the national committee. Then, in 1969, I was elected as the first woman president of the Maritime Conference. This really brought the church into the press for a few days, so much so that when I was flying to Toronto to attend the presidents' conference the

98

man sitting next to me turned and remarked rather sheepishly, "I dreamt about you last night." I could scarcely refrain from asking for details, but my better nature won out.

I am delighted to know that a project like this is being undertaken. I only wish the male part of the church had initiated it. Recognition comes hard, as I well know.

(WWW, Maritime—N.S., #1, submitted by Rev. Frances MacLellan.)

Ethel Howie

My first involvement with the church was as a member of first the Junior Choir and later the Senior Choir. As a teen, in 1926, I was able to assist in the leading of a fine young people's group in The United Church of Canada.

Shortly after returning from my honeymoon in 1930, I was surprised to have a church committee call on me to inquire if I would teach a girls' Sunday School class. On Sunday I found myself with a class of CGIT which would be meeting midweek as well as on Sundays! From that first experience grew my interest in youth groups and I was later, over the years, concerned with and leading Explorers, CGIT, Tyros, UCW, choirs, church camps, Christian Education groups, Bible Study groups and Religion classes in public schools.

In 1956 my husband, William Howie, was a delegate to General Council in Windsor, Ontario. While he was there he was approached to consider offering himself as a lay worker for the United Church. Subsequently, we moved our family from Manitoba to Waskatenau, a small town in rural Alberta, and served in that area.

My husband passed away suddenly in 1960 after just three years of full-time church work which he loved and served in so faithfully. The local board and Edmonton Presbytery contacted me and requested that I continue the work. I responded positively and spent five more years in the locale, serving a four-point charge and having full licensing privileges. In 1965 I was called to a charge in Milo, Alberta, and there I remained until my retirement in 1975.

One amusing incident occurred during the period when people were all discussing the "new morality". One elderly, senile gentleman thought that sounded like a great idea so he proceeded to hire a taxi to drive him from Calgary to my home—his intent was to move in with the "lonely lady preacher"! Everyone in the district was excited, except me!

At one wedding I was puzzled at the congregation's hearty laughter while the bride and groom were kneeling at the altar. I later learned that a trickster had painted HE on the sole of one of the bridegroom's shiny new shoes, and LP on the other.

It has been my privilege to be actively involved in many areas of the

Lord's work, quite apart from my regular pastoral duties. I have chaired the World Outreach Division of the Edmonton, Foothills and Yellowhead Presbyteries, and served four years as the Alberta Conference Representative on the National Board in Toronto. This aspect of my work was most stimulating as I met many missionaries and was able to involve myself in Mission Festival presentations. I still remain very keen in this endeavour of church life.

I was twice elected as a delegate from Alberta Conference to General Council and enjoyed the fellowship and learning experience offered at the sessions. In addition, I have been Chairperson of both the Foothills and the Yellowhead Presbyteries. At the present time I am a member of the Ministry Personnel and Education Division of the Alberta UCW Conference. I attend all meetings of Yellowhead Presbytery, am involved in the local Lamont Charge UCW, and generally assist wherever I am needed.

In 1975 I formally retired from the active work at Alberta Conference but have discovered that I have really been "retreaded". Consequently I have assisted with services at Andrew, Waskatenau, Radway, Lamont, Fort Saskatchewan and Partridge Hill. It is a source of joy for me to be able to help out in this way.

Like all lives, mine has had its grand moments as well as its time of loneliness and despair. However, the joyous times far overcame the low periods and I feel I have been well blessed. The flourishing relationships I share with so many cherished friends is reward enough in this life.

Recently I attended a Homecoming in Manitoba and one of my former CGIT girls said to me, "Something you taught us must have sunk in because we are all involved in the church in some way." I replied, "Not my doing—we plant the seed and God gives the increase."

(WWW, Alberta #11, submitted by LaVon Holgate and Mary Thomas.)

Stella Burry

We would be remiss indeed if this section about ministers within the United Church did not mention deaconesses, for it is within the diaconal ministry that many women have found their calling in professional ministry. Today, members of the diaconal ministry are hospital chaplains, educators, editors, inner-city workers, overseas missionaries, congregational workers. Indeed, some feel that they are on the "cutting edge" of ministry, free to work outside what they consider to be the more confining bounds of the ordained ministry of word and sacrament.

Stella Burry was one of the first deaconesses in The United Church of Canada. The Methodist Home and Training School opened in Toronto in the 1890s, and when Stella Burry attended it in 1922, she described it as having a good strong program. Her major was social work, and during the Depression of the thirties, she spent much of her time visiting families:

"Some of those people had lost their homes and they were living in one room in the downtown houses. We did a lot of counselling."

Stella is probably best known for her work in Newfoundland, for she moved to St. John's in 1938 and continued her work there. "I can't begin to tell you all the things I tried to do. When there's a need, you'll get into it with both feet. I knew I had to minister to the poor, but I had time to give to the young people and the churches; we got a camp going...As I look back now, I say to myself, 'Now, how did I ever do that?'"

REFLECTIONS OF TWO ORDINANDS—THEN AND NOW

Ordination

They knelt on trembling knees
With trembling hearts,
While all the weight of centuries of hands
Was laid upon their heads:
The hands of Peter and of John,
Of Augustine and Athanasius,
Columba, Huss and Livingstone...
And countless more of unknown, simple ones;
The priests of God.
So many hands, that laboured, blessed and even burnt
In self-abandonment to Christ...
Hands that lifted, rescued, comforted,
Encouraging with strength for strength
The weak and faltering through many centuries of time...
The hands of parents, teachers, friends,
Those lowly, loving priests of Jesus' loving kindness
*   and his truth...*
A thousand, thousand hands, and yet...but two...
The hands of Christ were laid on them.
The human pressure felt was fully His;
The weight, a lifting by His unseen Love.
Men of His earthly body, representing Him and His
In making visible the living miracle of love;
The incredible touch of soul on soul
Stood there in silence, laying on their hands.
Thus those who knelt
Were fired, empowered, emboldened,
Set apart and sent
As ministers and instruments
To mediate in turn
The miracle of love incarnate
In Word and touch and look.

Marjorie Stedman, 1952

(Submitted to The Matrix Collective, St. Andrew's College, Saskatoon, for *The Matrix Calendar—1984*. This project was funded by Women, Work and Worship.)

Marian Soliloquy

Spirit of love
For years we followed you
groupies of your kingdom come.
Clumsily we muse—
So 'love' means 'cross'.
They wound your nakedness
    in linen cloth
and sealed it in a rock
to regulate your death
or set our watches by.
(time-emptied shroud,
disintegrating property,
run-down, atomic,
petrine clock)

The men had read the signs and left—
in and out—
automatons.
We blamed them,
guards and gardeners,
for our emptiness;
keeping something from us
we could tell
weeping,
crying in our beer.

"Mary, dear!
Sweet female counterpart
in love
I am alive through you."
(Highly irregular)

Impetuous we whirled round
to clasp and claim.—
"Don't hold me so!"

Abashed
we ran to tell the men
to share our news
to help them be
till Love turned in its rough disguise.

People pass remarks
and measure with their eyes.
How long has it been?
Forty days and forty nights?
Forty years or weeks or winks?

"God-in-man"
that clichéd word
the cord that carried life is obsolete
Feel the rushing wind, the livening flame
Loving Spirit, come.

Kathryn Thornton, 1980

(Submitted to The Matrix Collective, St. Andrew's College, Saskatoon, for *The Matrix Calendar—1984*. This project was funded by Women, Work and Worship.)

A VIEW FROM THE PEW

Three dedicated women, the Rev. Frances MacLellan, Miss Janie Noftle and the Rev. Florence Wilkinson, took part in the changes and growth in our charge over the years of their ministry.

In Alberta, the Rolling Hills Pastoral Charge of The United Church of Canada boasts with pride of having been served by three lady ministers for fifteen years except for a period of eleven months. In 1954 the charge was known as the Bow Slope Pastoral Charge, with four preaching-points spread forty miles apart. Rolling Hills had morning services, Bow City and Scandia had afternoon services rotating every other Sunday, and Rainier had evening services as that was the location of the manse.

The Rev. Frances MacLellan, a native of Nova Scotia, studied theology after having been a high school teacher in Port Hope, Ontario. In January, 1954, she came to Bow Slope Charge and was one of two ordained women in Alberta at that time. One of the first tasks she undertook was to organize, or re-organize, a Woman's Association at each point. Bow City had a WMS with which Rainer was affiliated, but Rolling Hills and Scandia chose not be affiliated but sent in donations. Each point became a member of the South Alberta Presbytery WA.

Miss MacLellan carried out her work in Bow City, Rainer and Scandia with joint Bible Studies and communicant classes. She also continued the active Rainer Youth Group started under the Rev. Don Fraser; carried out some social work; and arranged for an annual preaching mission. There was usually an open-air Church Service held in the Scandia Community for the whole Charge once during the summer. It was during this ministry that the Bow Slope Charge went off Home Mission support and became self-supporting.

The first marriage the Rev. MacLellan performed was for Albert and Joan Lester in 1953. Since leaving the charge it has been her habit to send an anniversary card to each of the couples she has married, and wish them Godspeed.

On her way to Rolling Hills each Sunday, she used to stop and pick up one of the housewives and her two daughters for church. One particular

103

Sunday she was visiting with the husband while waiting and, in the course of the conversation, mentioned that she had married one of his acquaintances the previous day in Rainer. He very sincerely congratulated her and it wasn't until later in the day that he found out that she had performed the ceremony!

When Frances MacLellan left Bow Slope Charge in 1957 she accepted a call to the Foremost Charge. Since then we read that she had accepted the office of President of the Maritime Conference for a year.

In September of 1958, Miss Janie Noftle, a native of Newfoundland, came to the Bow Slope Pastoral Charge as Lay Supply. To save so much travel, a manse was purchased in Rolling Hills and the Rainer manse was sold. A manse committee was set up with representatives from each congregation. During this same fall a church building from Surprise, Saskatchewan, was moved to Scandia and services began there the following spring.

In September of 1960, Miss Noftle organized a Sunday School at Scandia. Up until this time the children had been attending the Salem Lutheran Sunday School. Much of Janie's work was with the young people and the elderly. She organized Hi C's and many activities of interest to them, and tried to attend all of the WA meetings. She drove a little Volkswagen "bug" and it was a familiar sight to see her huddling down the road accompanied by her poodle "Curly" and a load of young people off to a Rally, a hay-ride or carolling. At other times she would be accompanied by elderly ladies off to Brooks, where she would help them with their shopping or business problems.

Miss Noftle accepted a call from Burnaby, B.C., in July 1961 as Christian Education Coordinator. For many years we heard from her each Christmas.

The Rev. Florence Wilkinson, a native of Courtland, Ontario, came to the Rolling Hills Charge (formerly Bow Slope Charge) in September 1961. When the New Curriculum designed for the United Church was introduced in 1963, Miss Wilkinson found time to promote this material at the presbytery level as well as within the Sunday Schools of her own congregations. The New Curriculum Adult Study Books were used in classes during the winter months for men and women of the charge.

Florence was the main force behind the building of the Bow Slope Church. She spent countless hours meeting with the building committee, pushing and encouraging, designing, preparing food for hungry men, and even painting and laying linoleum in addition to numerous other jobs. In addition to her local duties, the Rev. Wilkinson found time for presbytery responsibilities, was Camp Director at Elkwater, and was instrumental in establishing a library for the camp. She was, for a time, Supervising Pastor for Vauxhall.

Church work was first in her life but she also took an active place in the community. She participated in the Rolling Hills Home and School Association, transported girls regularly to Medicine Hat for their music lessons, and invited families into her home for a home-cooked meal and an evening of fellowship. How we used to enjoy a special treat when brother Rev. Vic or sister Audrey came to visit. They would sing a duet with Florence at the service Sunday mornings and Rev. Vic would give the sermon. Even though we never met Uncle Will, we received a wealth of knowledge from his related experiences and his books.

The Rev. Wilkinson left our charge in 1968 for Kitimat, B.C. She came back to Alberta Conference and eventually became Conference President for a year. She keeps in touch with an odd visit and a newsy Christmas letter

All three of these women, although different, were very dedicated and efficient. Miss MacLellan and Miss Wilkinson were especially good organizers of time, effort, and the business of the church. The work they carried on has been felt in South Alberta Presbytery, the local communities and in the congregations of our charge. The Bible Study, Choir, and social events carried out on a charge basis built a good relationship between the congregations and kept us up-to-date with the changes and outreach of the church at a time when change in all phases of life were occurring very rapidly.

The effect of three lady ministers is difficult to measure. The men used to say, "When there is a man minister again, I'll come to church". But there has been no change thus far. The children began to think that church was for mothers and their children. One Sunday, when there was pulpit exchange and our congregation was visited by a man minister, it was noted by one of the Sunday School teachers that a little boy remarked to his class mates; "Did you see Jesus come to our church today?"

(WWW, Alberta, #10, submitted by LaVon Holgate and Mary Thomas.)

Chapter 6   MINISTERING TO ONE ANOTHER

...THROUGH OVERSEAS MISSIONS

Ada Sandell, Medical Missionary

Ada Sandell was born in Kidderminister, England, in 1896, to a family of seventeen children. Her father worked for a textile company. Because business was becoming very slack in England, he immigrated to Canada in 1906, and settled with two sons and two daughters in Magog, Quebec. They were employed by the Dominion Textile Company there. Because of poor health, however, Ada's father was unable to forward money to her mother and the remainder of the family back home. Ada's sisters and brothers went to work in the cotton mills and their mother took a job in a steam laundry, leaving Ada to care for the youngest three children. To add to their difficulties, Ada developed a spot on her lung and was ordered to rest, but after a year of care was pronounced well enough to return to school. Finally, in October 1910, the rest of the family set sail for Canada and, after a very stormy trip, arrived in Magog.

Ada, along with her sister and brother, also got jobs with Dominion Textiles while their mother kept house. Three years after their arrival, Ada's father passed away and her mother became a widow for the second time.

When a sister close to her was stricken with typhoid fever, Ada felt she could not go on if Kate did not recover. She crept into a corner away from the rest of the family to pray. Her sister recovered and they had many happy years together; Ada felt her prayers had been answered.

When Ada was twenty-one her four brothers enlisted and went off to war. Two of them were killed in action. At about this time Ada had been attending services at the Methodist Church. At one meeting she heard the Rev. Mr. McEwen, a missionary from Brazil, speak. The missionary challenged the young people to take the message of the love and saving power of Jesus Christ to the millions of people who had never heard his name. Ada felt he was pointing at her. When she spoke to Mr. McEwen, however, she had many doubts, for she did not have the education necessary to take the training. But the fiery minister from Brazil told her she was only making excuses and assured her that if God were calling her

106

to the mission field, then he would show her the way. He did.

Ada prayed and talked to the minister of her church. She had only standard seven (the equivalent of Grade Ten), but found that she could go into nurses' training with that background. Her application to Dr. Fred Stephenson, missionary secretary for the Methodist Church, was accepted and Ada became a missionary candidate. The fulfillment of her dream began at Lamont Mission Hospital (Alberta) in 1919, and after delays because of illness, her training was completed in 1923. Her mission field would be China.

Ada took preparatory missionary training at the Methodist National Training School, graduating in 1924. As it was deemed unwise at the time to send new missionaries to China, she was asked to serve in home Mission work while waiting for an overseas posting. She went to Copper Cliff, Ontario, where she worked for two years with Miss P. O. Follet among the Italian workers at the copper smelter. It would prove valuable experience, although Ada wasn't too keen to be involved in social work.

Seven years after she had volunteered for service, Ada arrived in Shanghai (1926). The missionaries were not able to go up the river to their mission at Szechwan until they had bought supplies and secured passage and permission from both the Chinese and British authorities. During their wait, Ada and Florence Lee, both newcomers to China, took advantage of free time to study Chinese.

As they travelled up river, rumours of unrest greeted them. When they arrived at Ichang, about a hundred miles from Shanghai, they found the harbour plugged with ships that had been ordered to go no further. Their ship, the Shansi, received the same order. More than a week later Ada, Florence and the others in the missionary party were given permission to go ashore. They could room on the third floor of a huge rambling house where elderly missionaries of the China Inland Mission were living. Once again Ada and her companions found a teacher for language study, hoping they would soon be able to go on to Szechwan.

After a week the British Consul ordered them back to Shanghai and their ship made the perilous return through gunfire. Discouraged, Ada wrote to the Woman's Missionary Society Board, asking to be transferred to a country where she could be of service with fewer interruptions. Their stay in Shanghai was not long, however, for Chiang Kai-shek and his army came up from the south to drive the Communist forces into one of the northern provinces. The Mission Board sent women and children home as fast as they could get passage for them, and Ada's group fled to the centre of the city and took rooms at the YWCA. After a week Ada received permission to proceed to Korea. The United Church of Canada had been in existence for two years and Korea was one of their places of work.

Dr. and Mrs. Frank Allen and Dr. and Mrs. H. Williams were also going to Korea to help with the medical work since they could not return to West China. Ada accompanied them, arriving in Hamhung, North

Korea, on April 4, 1927. Finally, after two evacuations and two years in home mission work, Ada was ready to start her work as a nurse.

The forty-five-bed hospital to which Ada was appointed was started by Dr. Kate MacMillan, but was now under the capable superintendency of Dr. Florence Murray, about to leave on furlough. When Dr. Murray returned in 1928, Ada began the difficult task of starting a school for nurses. Education for girls was very unusual in Korea and the only knowledge of nursing the Koreans had was the Japanese style of nursing they saw in the government hospitals. The nurses there were servants to the doctors, and parents of Korean girls did not care to see their daughters in that role. Patients were cared for by the members of their families who stayed with them. They bought bedding, pots and pans, charcoal braziers and charcoal, and camped at the hospital for the period of confinement. Ada did not call this "nursing", but the patients were fed and kept clean.

There were obstacles to the new nursing school right from the beginning. Parents did not want to see their daughters in that profession, and families did not wish to leave their relatives unguarded in the hospital. There were stories that the foreigners used the eyes of Korean patients in their medicine. However, Ada sent notices to the four Presbyterian Churches in Hamhung, announcing the beginning of a training school.

One of the first two applicants did not last long, but soon there were three more. One of those felt she had more education than the others and left. There remained three girls for the first class. Language remained a barrier and it was not easy teaching girls who had never before experienced the nursing profession. Visiting hours, night duty and other Western conventions all had to be worked out with the novices. At last, in 1932, the first nurses passed the required examinations and graduated. Another class of five had been accepted in 1930; the nursing school was in operation. Ada was due furlough and the graduates would be working at the hospital in her absence.

Ada was gradually learning Korean customs through her experiences, usually when she was travelling. She learned the importance of respect for the elderly and, as a single woman, she was soon to find out the reaction of elderly Korean men to her unusual marital status. They could not believe that anyone would remain unmarried; it was so important for every woman to have a son. Age also had more significance in the Orient. There was a different language for the honorable elderly, low-class citizens and children. To mix them was a great sin. Ada also found marriage customs extraordinary, especially as the unions were arranged by parents. The fact that the women of Korea were treated as second-class citizens made it difficult at first for Ada to make any inroads into the practice of Western medicine. The men thought all women should be their servants.

Although Ada was first of all a nurse, she was also concerned about the spiritual well-being of the people around her and took seriously the need for the women evangelist and hospital chaplain. They were always available to care for the patients' and their families' deeper needs. Many of her nurses came to Christ and witnessed to others throughout their entire lives. Their strong faith was manifested during the evacuations caused by the wars.

During the years between 1941 and 1947, Ada was in Canada. Because of the bombing of Pearl Harbour by the Japanese in 1941, she was not allowed to return to Korea. From 1941 to 1945 she was Superintendent of Nurses at the Lamont Hospital where she had taken her training. Finally, in 1947, Dr. Murray and Ada were given permission by the Woman's Missionary Society to return to Korea. They were joined by Elda Daniels and the three of them haunted shipping companies in San Francisco for five weeks until they secured passage on the hospital ship, Hope. Since the ship had few cabins they travelled together in a forty bed ward. They were happy to travel any way at all.

Early in July they arrived in war-torn Seoul which was overcrowded with refugees from North Korea as well as repatriates from China and Japan. Because South Korea was occupied by United Nation's forces, mostly American, there were many families of the military occupying what were formerly Japanese residences. To receive permission to enter Seoul it was necessary to have an invitation from some organization. Dr. Helen Kim of Ewha Women's University invited Dr. Murray and Ada to work in a women's hospital affiliated with the university. The work of getting the hospital in operation was immense. Dr. Murray joined the doctors in organizing the treatment of the sick, and Ada stepped into the nursing department.

Ruth Taylor and Dr. Gallagher of the Board of World Outreach (Canada) made a visit to Korea early in 1948. At this time Ada was invited to join the nursing staff at Severance Hospital which was badly in need of repair. It had always had the reputation of being on a par with Peking Medical University, and had been the first hospital to train nurses. It was also the first medical college in Korea.

During the absence of the missionary personnel, things had changed considerably. Because Japan was at war (Korea was part of the Japanese Empire), anything that suggested American or Canadian control was forbidden. The name "Severance" had been changed during the occupation to "Asabi Hospital" (meaning "morning sun"), and all the departments were headed by Japanese. Ada found there had been very little medical work done, and anything that could be taken away to be used for war purposes had been removed: doorknobs, radiators, pipes and electric fixtures. There was no running water except that which ran from leaks in the roof, and equipment was scarce. The Korean doctors and nurses who had fled to the country during the take-over began to return after the Japanese left. By 1948 they were beginning to restore Severance to working order.

Ada was the only Western nurse at Severance for some time. There were many problems, not the least of which was the attitude of the

Superintendent of nurses. She opposed everything Ada and the other staff tried to accomplish. Although a very capable and charming person, she had married several years before, and it was finally revealed that her husband was a Communist. He had been working on her to undo all that Ada and the others had achieved.

Just as the hospital was functioning again (1950), the Korean War broke out. Ada and a friend had gone to the Korean worship service and were conscious of an air of excitement. But not having heard the news before they left for church, they wondered why people were hurrying here and there, in all directions. On their arrival home they turned on the radio to hear:

> North Korean forces attacked South Korea at Kaesung early this morning and are pushing their way into South Korea. American and Korean armies are on the alert.

Later in the afternoon the sound of firing could be heard as the Communist army made its way towards Seoul. Before long they received the information that all women and children, including Canadians, were to be ready to leave for Inchon Harbour immediately. As Ada led her last Bible class with the nurses, she used the fourth chapter of St. John's gospel and the hymn, "Be not dismayed, whatever betide, God will take care of you".

Six hundred and forty-two American and Canadian women and children were evacuated to Japan on a Norwegian freighter which normally had room for twelve passengers. There were four women in labour and several invalids who needed care and Dr. Murray was the only doctor on board. Six nurses, including Ada, took turns watching the patients. Mattresses and blankets as well as cases of food and milk had been put on board by the army. After two nights and two days, they arrived at Fukuoka Camp where they were billeted before being relocated to various places. The Canadians were sent to Tokyo, and Dr. Murray was instructed to take her furlough. Ada spent the summer at Nojiri and, after several unsuccessful attempts to return to Korea, was advised to take her furlough as well. This was her fourth furlough and her fourth evacuation.

Ada returned to Korea in September of 1951 to dig herself in on Koje Island. She used the term "dig herself in" following an introduction in Canada when a young girl said that Ada had been "excavated" from Korea. Hundreds of refugees from North Korea were on the island and among them were many of Ada's friends from Hamhung. She had not seen some of them for eleven years but they were lined up on the roadsides to greet her.

One Korean woman who had been with the missionaries for many years reminded the others how she always knew the Communists were telling lies when they said the Canadians had forgotten them and would never do anything more for them. Now, here was Ada as living proof that they were wrong. She made Ada feel that Christian mission work was worthwhile after all.

Although the work in the school of nursing occupied most of Ada's waking time and thoughts, she had other duties as well. Since she was the only resident missionary on the island, each Sunday she would visit one of the eighteen refugee groups who met in tents. They sat on the bare earth or on straw bags, but every effort was made to make the tents look clean and worshipful. Ada often thought that some of the things done for the glory of God would have made the more august men of the cloth in Canada smile. But the churches were filled every Sunday morning and evening. Whenever Ada visited one of the churches she was asked to preach, so she was always prepared. Fortunately she was able to use the same sermon over and over, and only her chauffeur knew.

Another chapter of Ada's life closed with another furlough when the United Church Koje "station" closed. A new one opened in Iri, Chulla Puk Do, a city with a population of 89,000, and Ada was stationed there in 1957.

With an Iri nurse, Ada set up a tuberculosis clinic at her residence. From there she gave out TB drugs provided by the local health unit, by Church World Service and from the United Church grant for relief work. They also set up well-baby clinics at a number of churches in the district. They weighed the babies, gave powered milk where necessary, and relief clothing which was coming in considerable quantities. Ada also taught public health, attempting to awaken people to the danger of transferable TB, and to overcome some of the fear and ignorance of leprosy. Very often people would hide their symptons until it was too late to prevent disfigurement.

Ada made an important contribution to the church in Iri. Iri was in a large area where many churches had broken away from the Presbyterian Church in Korea, and joined the Presbyterian Church in the Republic of Korea (PROK), and there were hard feelings, anger and resentment over the split. A sympathetic ear was needed. Ada spent many hours in conversation with the church leaders, listening and helping these men understand how the United Church worked with the Korean Church.

Ada went to a different church each Sunday, often in the morning and evenings, and on Wednesday evenings as well. She was usually expected to preach and did so willingly. Although she had no training as a preacher, she had an excellent command of the Korean language and never failed to give a good message. By the time of her retirement in 1962 there were few, if any, of the 150 or more churches of the three presbyteries she had not visited.

When Ada first went to Iri, the Presbyterian Church in the Republic of Korea was considered by churches of other denominations to be heretical because of the split. While there was a "ministerial association" in Iri, PROK ministers were not welcome. The monthly evening united service which moved from church to church also excluded the PROK people. This problem was solved, in part, by Ada's successful efforts in getting cooperation among various denominations for a United World Day of Prayer service. This was accomplished through Ada's early acquaintance in North Korea with a woman who had come to lead a week's services in an "Old Assembly" church. Ada attended several of the meetings and got the leader from North Korea to persuade the women of that church to organize a committee and include her and some PROK women. It worked, and Iri is one of the few places outside of Seoul where World Day of Prayer is still held regularly as an interdenominational service.

Because of her experience in Korea, her ability with the language and her involvement with the church and church leaders, Ada was made a member of the Joint Committee of Missionaries and Korean Church Leaders, a group which handled all the issues of cooperation between The United Church of Canada and the Presbyterian Church in the Republic of Korea. An important part of this work was the administration of budget requests and distributing the funds received from Toronto. The meetings of the committee were often stormy, and Ada's sense of humour and ability to draw a laugh when things were tense often helped to smooth ruffled feelings.

One of the greatest tributes ever paid to Ada was at the time of her sixtieth birthday, or "hwankap", as the Koreans called it. Ada's years had been evenly divided between the east and the west and between north and south in Korea. Her birthday fell in the year of the monkey. For the first time in sixty years the year of the monkey corresponded with the third year in the ten-year cycle, so horoscopically a perfect circle had been formed, and those who were born at the beginning of the cycle, sixty years before, celebrated the completion of a perfect life-span. It was indeed a time for celebration and the greatest feast day in anyone's life. Ada's party was held in Severance Hospital in Seoul.

It was a wonderful day with many fine tributes to her faithful labours in unseen places; to her great heart; to her friendship with the Korean people; to her stress on quality, not quantity; to her beautiful black hair and dark eyes; to her contribution as a friend, a leader, a teacher, a missionary and a nurse. With her thanks to the many who had helped her celebrate her sixtieth birthday in a way she had never expected, she said she too wished she could stay another thirty years with her friends in Korea.

In 1962 Ada retired to Magog, Quebec. She is now residing in a Home for Senior Citizens in Richmond, Quebec, near her three sisters. She also keeps in touch with her Korean friends who remain so dear to her.

Irene Findlay

(This account of Ada Sandell was assisted with Local Research Funding from the Women, Work and Worship project.)

Anna Roloff

(Anna Roloff is a heroine to our newest sisters in the United Church, the women of the Evangelical United Brethren, who became part of our church in 1968. She was a missionary to China for fifteen years, until cancer claimed her in 1924. The following tribute was written by her friend, Mrs. J. H. Bauernfeind, for the Memorial Service held in Kitchener, Ontario, November 23, 1924. "If God calls me home, I'll be waiting for you" were among Miss Roloff's last words as she bid her friend farewell three days before her death.)

A Tribute

"If God Calls Me Home, I'll Be Waiting For You."
Her days had been numbered, and Heaven was in view;
No tears at departing, no sighs of regret,
But victory and joy as her Saviour she met.
We called her a heroine, as all know who heard
That she braved dangers to carry the Word
To China's benighted,—she loved them so well,
No burden too heavy "the Story" to tell.
Most gladly she gave fifteen years of her life,
To live among people where evil is rife;
The women of Shenchow, they loved her, and knew
Her passion for souls— 'twas so fervent and true.
Her Master and Leader was showing the way,
Her constant Companion, tho' trying the day
A wonderful faith as she journeyed with Him!
Such friendship no crosses or tasks could bedim.
Yet, 'twas not all sunshine, for oftentimes pain
And weariness seized her, and, under the strain
Of giving for others her strength day by day,
She felt need of respite, and coming away,
She hoped to find healing, if God should ordain
To grant her return to her labours again.
But the Lord of the harvest was calling her Home,
His "well done" how sweet as he bade her to come!
We say as we sorrow, "Her work is not done,"
But He who is wiser and calls one by one
Doth measure our lives by our deeds, not our years.
What need then to question? What need then for fears?
On our banner of Missions a star once so blue
Has turned to pure white, and for her comes in view
A glory resplendent from yonder bright shore,
Where suffering and dangers are past evermore.
Young women, arouse you! O, who'll take her place?
May soon come the answer: "We will, by His grace."
The years all too quickly are passing away,
The Master needs workers, He calls you today.
"If God calls me Home, I'll be waiting for you."

Ah! Sisters, they're waiting, till our tasks are through.
The greetings Beyond when our Saviour we meet
Will make Heaven's happiness full and complete.

(From *Anna Roloff, In Loving Memory,* included in WWW, Hamilton, #10, Item 6, submitted by Helen Hall.)

...THROUGH HOME MISSIONS

Gwenyth Hubble

"Rarest and Most Excellent Woman" (an inscription to
Gwenyth Hubble by her friend, Laura Pelton)

One sign of Gwenyth Hubble's lasting contribution to The United Church of Canada is this: the writer, a Roman Catholic, reminiscing about a Baptist for a United Church book.

Gwenyth's passion for ecumenism (she often described herself as an 'ecu-maniac") resulted from her consummate faith in God, and his Word, Jesus Christ, in whose service she spent her life. "Passion" and "spent" are the key words here. To many people she literally fleshed-out the true disciple "who loses her life for Jesus' sake and for the sake of the gospel..." She lived and died in total commitment to God and to those who knew her as minister, teacher and friend.

Just before her death, Gwenyth made a comment to Dr. Harriet Christie that graphically illustrates the fusion of her love for God and people.

> *You know, I have been thinking that now my life is over*
> *and all I can do has been done, I will spend the remainder of*
> *my time in contemplating God. There isn't anything more I*
> *can do about the past, and I look with gratitude and joy to*
> *the future. Therefore I thought I would let my mind dwell on*
> *God. But, you know, I found I couldn't think about God*
> *without thinking about people. Every time I tried to think*
> *about God and my relationship to friends, I found I couldn't*
> *hold them apart.*

Gwenyth's devotion to her British Baptist roots, to scripture, to young people (through teaching high school and working with the Student Christian Movement), to mission and to missionary training (she always regretted that her health prevented her from active missionary work; however, at Selly Oak, Birmingham, her fifteen years as principal of an ecumenical training centre for women helped to fulfill that ambition), to the world-wide church (during her years with the World Council of

Churches), expressed itself in a brief but indelible, unforgettable blaze of glory on the Canadian scene. The metaphor of a comet seems apt here.

The first "sighting" of this comet was an announcement of the (then) Ecumenical Institute of Canada, dated November 3, 1965:

> *A Notice for Your Interest!*
> *Our First Extension Course!*
>   *...Miss Hubble has agreed to take a ten-week course in Bible Study for us.*

A book, a person, a need, an idea, an institute all came together in January 1966 in what seems, in retrospect, an example of the biblical "kairos".

Gwenyth's close friend, Laura Pelton, in recalling this initial period, paid special tribute to Dr. Katherine Hockin who did "a splendid job in laying the foundation for what came to be of such significance to so many people". The original group which met at the Institute numbered twenty-three women from various denominations, including twelve United Church people. By 1972, when Gwenyth died, thirty five courses had been taught in various areas in Metropolitan Toronto. At least ten United Churches had hosted these courses and the total registration came to more than fifteen hundred "students". (United Church women formed the largest single group of participants.)

Harriet Christie summed up the reasons for the phenomenal growth.

> *...In the work (Gwenyth) did in Bible Study and in her relationship with those in the groups, she helped many people to have both a renewed sense of faith, a renewed awareness of the relevance of the Bible for their own dignity and worth...Her scholarship, her depth of faith and her personal spirit made her an interesting combination of openness to the contemporary world and yet so sure of her faith that what was happening in contemporary society did not seem to bother her.*

Her confident, serene faith was contagious.

Gradually, other leaders took their place in this growing ecumenical enterprise. It continues to flourish, to be a sign of her fruitful efforts and source of deepening faith, fresh insights and also a time for the forging of friendships.

A second area of influence was her contribution as "Visiting Lecturer" from 1966 to 1970 at Toronto's Covenant College. First known as the "United Church Training School", Covenant College united with the "Anglican Women's Training College" in 1969 to become the "Centre for Christian Studies". As the calendars stated, Covenant College was "the education centre of The United Church of Canada for the training of men and women for all types of professional work in the church, with the exception of the ministry of the Word and Sacraments."

Gwenyth taught introductory survey courses in New Testament, the Gospel of John, and the Epistles of St. Paul. When the first combined convocation and graduation service was held at St. Andrew's United Church, she gave the address to the graduating class. During her time as lecturer at Covenant College, she showed the same care, concern and commitment that had been characteristic of her ministry from the beginning.

Through her involvement with the Canadian Council of Churches, the United Church was also enriched. In 1966 the Council requested its Faith and Order Commission to undertake a national study on "The Biblical and Theological Understanding of Sexuality and Family Life". The plan needed an organizing and coordinating secretary, and Gwenyth was appointed to this position in March, 1967. Two years later, the report was published, and it is a thorough, detailed, thoughtful presentation of the results of this study.

In a letter written at that time, Gwenyth mentioned its completion and wondered, "Will it create a stir or will its publication pass unnoticed? Dear knows!" In Dr. Floyd's opinion, it broke "some interesting new ground theologically, and...it is one of the most effective pieces of work which the Faith and Order Commission has done within recent years."

Perhaps Gwenyth's impact was felt the most keenly among three particular groups of people, the first of whom were women. She was the first English Baptist woman to be ordained; she and over twenty male classmates became ministers in 1939. Pioneers never have an easy time of it and this was especially true for her. To have her work with the Student Christian Movement recognized as a valid pastoral ministry took some years and much persistence in the face of rather tough resistance. (A man ministered at this time in much the same circumstances and was recognized almost immediately.)

Experiences such as this honed her sense of honesty, perseverance and fair play. Those who knew her in Canada encountered a strong, gentle, compassionate yet challenging, perceptive and wise Christian woman. She was quite frank and open about her shortcomings and spoke of her struggles to overcome them, especially those she thought might prevent her from being effective. In doing so, she communicated courage and confidence to her associates.

Gwenyth was among those whom society calls handicapped. Lame from birth with a congenital hip problem, she led a fuller, more active, mobile life than most of her contemporaries. Because of her various jobs and assignments, she travelled a great deal, often in varying degrees of discomfort and pain. This travelling continued even when she was semi-retired. Her determination to take her full place among the peace, justice and unity developers was impressive. To this end she accepted many invitations to attend conferences, often taking a leading role, even when she joined another special group: those suffering from cancer.

In some ways the manner of her dying witnessed to the fact of Christ even more than the manner of her living. With no self-pity and with full faith in the future, she undertook to reflect on and share with her friends and associates (including the staff at the hospital) what it meant to experience cancer and to be dying.

The blaze of glory that she was remained bright and brillant to the end. Gwenyth reflected the glory of God because she was, and is, a woman fully alive. The last word belongs to a United Church woman, Laurel Burgess, who with her husband has worked for the church for many years. Laurel knew Gwenyth as a teacher in scripture and friend, and has a sense of the scope of her influence.

> *Gwenyth Hubble, to me, was a warmhearted, dedicated woman. She had an exceptional gift for teaching, helping not only young, new missionaries but all who were in her group, to see and understand a living Bible.*
>
> *I will always remember her clear descriptions as she interpreted the meaning of each Bible passage. There will always be a warm spot in my heart for Gwenyth Hubble, because she laid a firm foundation for the Ecumenical Bible Study Groups in Metropolitan Toronto.*

(Written and submitted by Mary Landry.)

Florence Bird

I first came to know Miss Bird through the Japanese United Church in Vancouver, B.C., where she taught Sunday School and led the CGIT group. I presume she had spent many years in Japan as a missionary, since she spoke Japanese fluently. She was not just a teacher or leader, but a "friend" to us all. The Japanese community in those days was closely knit. Our parents having come from Japan, did not know the Canadian way of life and there was much to learn. As we approached our teen years there was much conflict in the ways of thinking between our parents and ourselves, with our parents trying to raise us according to the Japanese standard and culture. We were learning and trying to conform to the ways of our Canadian friends. Miss Bird understood this, seeing the point of view from both sides, and helped us by letting us discuss our problems with her.

The Japanese children attended two schools: elementary or high school during the day, followed by attendance at a Japanese language school. This left very little or no time for outside activities during the week. On Saturday afternoons we looked forward to Saturday School at our church where we had worship service, singing, stories, then a lesson in crafts—embroidery, knitting, sewing, etc. On Sundays we attended church in the morning and again in the evening. Once a month there was CGIT. As you can see, life revolved around the school and the church for us. What would we have done without the missionaries who served us year after year, without ever giving up? We learned in those early years the importance of sharing, of serving others, and of love for another. Miss Bird never lectured us, but taught us so much through her own attitudes and the caring way she worked with us.

With the outbreak of World War Two, the Japanese people were uprooted from their homes in the coastal areas of British Columbia and relocated in the interior of the province, or to Alberta on the sugar-beet farms. Miss Bird left Vancouver and moved to Toronto, once again ready to help the Japanese people who were gradually moving to the East in order to resettle. I, for one, received her full support. When I wrote to her from Slocan, B.C. (one of the evacuation centres), telling her of my desire to relocate to Toronto, she immediately obtained a domestic position for me in a doctor's home. (The Government stipulation was that a young person moving to Ontario must come to a work position.) She met me at the train station, took me out for breakfast, and then to the YWCA for a few days' stay. Since I had arrived on a Saturday, she took me to Metropolitan United Church the next morning. For the next few months I worked as a domestic, keeping in touch with Miss Bird on my days off. From there I moved on to my regular line of work in an office.

Many of the young Japanese people received Miss Bird's help in various ways during the difficult times soon after moving to Toronto. She was instrumental in gathering some of the former Mission Circle members and others to meet regularly at the Metropolitan United Church. This was a time when we were strangers in a big city, and a meeting such as this was a great comfort and support for us. She has touched the hearts of many people throughout her work with the church and she will be long remembered.

(WWW, Toronto, #18, Item 2, written and submitted by Fumiko Ioi.)

...THROUGH OUR CHURCHES

Luella May (Monroe) Young

...Luella had many special friends, not only in her own church, but in other denominations. She and Father Black shared the coaching on the local hockey team. She once arranged a wedding service for a young couple, a Jewish boy and a United Church girl who wanted to be married and who had to overcome the barriers of a mixed marriage with the two families seemingly at odds as to just how it could come to be. A local Anglican clergyman "tied the knot" at the suggestion of Luella, and the wedding was performed in the local museum which Luella had transformed into a lovely Victoria home.

Luella lives on in our church and community for those of us who were fortunate to have known her. She had the insight to look beyond the moment, and perhaps she was bit of a dreamer, but she had the special ability and determination to make things happen. When the church needed new carpet, and there was no money to pay for it, she sat down with pencil and paper and noted all the individuals who had ties with the old village church and proceeded to contact them and sure enough funds came in for the carpet. One of the last contributions she and her husband made to the local church was the installation of the new light fixtures for the sanctuary. She carefully selected them to fit the decor of the sanctuary, and they perpetuate a living monument to her life....

(WWW, Bay of Quinte, #10, written and submitted by Joan E. Chalovich.)

Christina Kerr

...Into her eighties she was still "one of the youngest people I've known." Whether on the floor with the children, considering new ideas, or in Session meetings seeking new solutions to old problems, she was never stuffy, never self-important, never tied down by precedent. (This youthful approach was reflected in her appearance; a favorite model in local fashion shows, she loved to wear bright colours and wore hats with a special flair.)

She was involved with all aspects of the local United Church, giving generously of her time, her talents, her energy, and her "widow's mite." In the early fifties she challenged the congregation to a building program. Having shared her vision of the old church packed to the doors and falling about our ears, she announced she was starting a building fund. Her pension had been increased $10.00 a month and "I'm getting along without it, so that $10.00 a month goes into the special fund." (The church was built!) To supplement the pension she took in boarders, making a home for a succession of young women. Still she made light of any personal difficulties, always seemed to have time with the lonely or the homesick, or the young manse wives coping with their own special problems. In quiet, unassuming fashion she gave and gave—money to help needy youngsters go to camp or leaders to Naramata, a full set of dishes for the church, flowers from her garden, friendship and, above all, the example of her faith: "With God all things are possible."

Kerr was generous in her praise, discriminating in her criticism. A choir member recalls she would be first with praise for an anthem or duet, but would mention on occasion, "I think you need more practice on the tone."

She had a special relationship with several of the young ministers who came to their first pastoral charge. From the pew she requested one to "speak up, we can't hear you." Another recalls "Christina Kerr is one of the two greatest personalities I have met...time to listen, support and lead a young minister into making the decisions without demanding or interfering...critical, with a generous, forgiving heart (and) a sense of humour."

...Laid to rest in 1974, Christina Kerr is alive in a memory that is fresh and green to those who loved her. A fitting obituary could be these words from the wife of one of those young ministers: "As I get older I would like to remember Christina Kerr by emulating somewhat her thoughtful and refreshing approach to life—always seeking for meaning in what might appear meaningless, and really listening to others in a quiet, unassuming way, towards better understanding."

(WWW, British Columbia, #10, written and submitted by Nora McEwen.)

Vida Gertrude (Hamilton) Green

...Not only has Vida supported her own church, she has provided music in Catholic, Anglican and Baptist Churches for weddings, funerals and special services. One Sunday morning she played for the Anglican Easter Service and then walked across the street to play for her own church service. In addition, she has sung with the choirs of the Anglican and Baptist churches as well as the United. If she was ever asked to help out, Vida was never known to refuse...

Now that Vida is going on eighty-two years of age, she must be slowing down, you guess. Wrong! She is still our church organist; she always attends UCW. She is secretary of the manse committee; she is convenor of Citizenship in the Women's Institute; she continues to be secretary of the Eastern Star (her goal is twenty years); and she's always willing to help any and all in any way she can.

Her love for the church and her community has touched and influenced many lives. She is a loving, living, humble example of a Christian woman that most of us would find impossible to equal.

(WWW, Maritime—New Brunswick, #6, written and submitted by Lorena Green.)

Ethel (MacPherson) MacDonald

...She began teaching Boy's Bible Class in 1947 and retired in 1972. When she retired from teaching, the congregation honoured her with a dinner that was attended by a great many of her former pupils and their wives. She was presented with a bronze plaque inscribed with all the names of the 195 boys that she taught. (She had kept a record book with all the names of each class for the 25 years she taught.)

(WWW, Maritime—Nova Scotia, #8, submitted by Marion MacLean.)

120

Cecily May (Pike) Penney

Cecily moved to Grand Falls in 1932 and in 1937 married William Penney, her late sister's husband. She continued to look after his four children, and they had six more of their own to care for and nurture. Her faithfulness and devotion to the work of the church never faltered. Cecily became a member of Memorial United and began the work of the church as a member of the "Currie Mission Circle" for several years until an organization known as the WMS was formed. The work of this group dealt mainly with missionaries overseas and she received a book every month called *The Missionary Monthly*. She felt as though she knew the missionaries personally. Through the WMS she became involved with presbyterials and conferences, acting as secretary of the Grand Falls/ Twillingate Presbyterial and later as president. Cecily felt honoured and privileged to be elected a delegate to the "Dominion Board" in Toronto. While there she attended Bloor Street Church where the Rev. Ken House was minister (a Newfoundlander). She also attended Timothy Eaton Church where another Newfoundlander, the Rev. Herb Pottle, was a minister. She had the pleasure of enjoying a social hour at Mr. Pottle's home. She recalls that this experience was exciting and gave her a challenge to carry on the work of the church.

In 1958, the last year of the WMS, the Presbyterial Executive held at Botwood honoured Cecily with a Life Membership. For years the WMS and WA worked together; in 1962 they united in one Board of Women known as the UCW. Cecily felt, at the time, that this wasn't a step forward, but never became discouraged from continuing on the work of the church. She became president of Grand Falls Presbyterial UCW and after boundary changes, became the first president of the Terra Nova Presbyterial for a four-year term. She held the office of vice-president on the UCW Conference for four years, also serving on committees of the Newfoundland Conference. She was a delegate to the Board of Women in 1966 and in 1968 was delegate to a Consultation of Presbyterial Presidents...

Mrs. Penney's philosophy of life could well be summed up in the words of the following poem (author unknown), written on a page of her UCW Handbook and often quoted by her late husband.

> One ship drives east and another west,
> With the self-same winds that blow.
> 'Tis the set of the sails
> And not the gales
> Which tells us the way to go.

121

Like the winds of the sea are the ways of fate
As we journey along through life,
'Tis the set of a soul
That decides its goal
And not the calm or the strife.

(From "Cecily May Penney", written by Edna Elliot for Memorial UCW, Grand Falls. Included in WWW, Newfoundland, #2, submitted by Gertrude Locke.)

...THROUGH OUR LIVES

Elizabeth Jane (McNevin) Lowe

Elizabeth Jane Lowe was the third eldest in a family of eleven, one of the three babies born in the police barracks in Prince Albert during the Riel Rebellion. That night all the white settlers were ordered to go to the barracks as it was the only safe place to be. The settlers lost almost everything they owned to the Métis...

Elizabeth reminisces about her early childhood days when she and her sisters and brothers walked three-and one-half miles to school, winter and summer, and of the fear they felt when they often met big Indian chiefs, in all their impressive regalia, riding their horses. But these people always passed, smiling at them, never harming them...

Elizabeth is known to her friends and family as "Gram" Lowe and enjoys visits from all of them. She enjoys good health for her age of 97 years and 8 months, and still never tires of reading.

(WWW, Saskatchewan, #25, submitted by Margaret Groat.)

Margaret (Kee) Dickson

...I remember the summer when I was about eight. I shared a bedroom with my grandparents at their summer cottage. A curtain across the room gave privacy, but not silence. In my cozy bed I could hear the preparations of my grandparents at bedtime. Each night I would hear the rustle of clothing and the soft murmurings beyond the curtain, followed by a soft thud as my grandparents dropped to their knees in prayer. I didn't catch the words, but I sensed the beauty of what I was experiencing. I would lie there awed by their devotion and touched in some quiet way in my soul. That quiet awareness of God continued to grow in my life...

(From "The Faith Journey of Margaret (Kee) Dickson", written by Margaret (Kee) Dickson. Included in WWW, Saskatchewan, #17, submitted by Kathleen A. Ellison.)

Edna Margaret (Pierce) Sanders

...Edna's latest contributions to the life of the church and to human-kind came when she suffered from cancer and died after an eight-month illness. She felt that memories, thoughts, and feelings should be recorded in print, that vast quanitities of valuable knowledge are lost when people die and the source of information is gone. Over the years she wrote intermittently and, before her terminal illness, decided to begin her writing seriously. With the onset of cancer, she realized her need to hurry with her project, one she could not complete.

Thus, Edna wrote when she could, always with encouragement from her family especially from her husband. When she no longer had strength to write, she dictated her thoughts to Gordon for him to record. Together, they planned the arrangement of three unpublished books of Edna's work: *Some Events in My Life: A Ragged Chronicle, Reflections* (made up of prose, poetry, and music) and *Reflections on Feelings*.

Edna worked with Gordon to plan her funeral services. How beautiful they were! Solos with music and lyrics by Edna, and one of her poems evidenced once again the great work of this magnificent woman...

(From "Edna Margaret (Pierce) Sanders: Her Life and Work in The United Church of Canada". Included in WWW, Alberta, #12, written and submitted by Helen L. Pierce.)

Helen Mary McCurdy

Last spring (1982) I chanced to attend a meeting at the Windsor Elms, where I now live. The meeting was chaired by Shirley Davy from the United Church National Office, Toronto. The subject of the meeting was "women's place in the church, and the individual contributions that have been made, and are being made". My thoughts went to Miss Helen McCurdy, for perhaps I knew her better than most of my generation. She was a dear friend of my mother. They were both teachers and attended the same church, and as well were members of its Woman's Missionary Society. I felt that some recognition of Miss McCurdy should be made and will make an effort to do just that.

I was born in January, 1910, the third child of Elizabeth Parker Kerr and Captain William T. Crossley of Windsor N.S. When I was seventeen months old, after walking two weeks, I contracted the dreaded Infantile Paralysis and for days could not move, not even my head, and was carried about on a pillow. At that time any form of treatment was unknown, so Mother and Dr. J. W. Reid carried on as best they could. I was later taken to the Mayo Clinic, Rochester, Minn. where they were advised to take me home and bring me up like a normal child. They also recommended an orthopedic surgeon in Boston who was doing pioneer work in Infantile Paralysis. Thus began my yearly trips to Dr. Bradford, which left little time for actual school. I attended classes for a few weeks in September and then went off for treatment until Christmas; school until March, and then Boston again.

During this perod I picked up Diptheratic Paralysis, which made life a little more complicated. (By this time I was wearing two long braces, a back brace, and I used crutches.) In October 1920, I entered the famous Children's Hospital in Boston, where both hips and both knees were operated on and I was in a cast from my armpits to my toes, until Christmas. The surgery enabled me to discard my back brace, but I was not to attend school for two years and had to have a daily two-hour rest each afternoon. At the end of two years I became a pupil of Miss McCurdy. At this time I did not realize what a privilege it was. When I look back at those years with her I appreciate so much the English classes and her appreciation of literature which have been so valuable to me.

Miss McCurdy had been obliged to retire from the Academy because of her mother's failing health. Young people today do not give up their work to look after ill parents, but in Miss McCurdy's day there was no help, such as government pensions, allowances, or homes for the elderly. The only course open to Miss McCurdy was to do what she could in her own home. She already had two boarders and a couple of pupils. Betty Reid was a girl of my age and a victim of Spastic Polio, and a daughter of our family doctor. The other pupil, a boy, also a doctor's son, had severe attacks of asthma, and was younger than we were. His sudden gasping for breath was rather frightening, but Miss McCurdy would open his collar, produce a glass of water, and calmly proceed with our lesson.

She was a wonderful teacher and she and Mother decided that English, Arithmetic, Grammar, and Geography were the subjects most useful to me. I feel that their choice was a good one. In 1927 I said goodbye to this form of study and entered Edgehill School for Girls, next to my home. Because of Miss McCurdy's dedicated teaching I was able to enter Form V and spent three very happy years at the school.

By now Miss McCurdy was greatly worried at the lack of young women going into the Missionary Society and Ladies Aid. After much thought, in January 1937 she invited a group to her home and organized the first WMS Helpers Group. The purpose was to be fourfold—worship, study, fellowship and service. Thus began the Associate Helpers Circle with Miss McCurdy as Honorary President and Connie Crossley, President. Meetings were held twice a month and consisted of a devotional, study, and social period, during which we would sew and knit. In October 1937 we held our first church supper, which consisted of baked beans, potato scallop, pickles, homemade bread, rolls, sweets and tea. For this we charged 25¢ and children 15¢ each! We made the satisfactory sum of $88.01. This supper became an annual event and a major source of income.

During World War One we met four times a month; in two of these evenings we worked for the Red Cross and did other projects. We continued our donations to the WMS and our mission boxes. Other

124

projects in the first twenty-five years of our existence included a new gown for our minister, drapes for the choir loft, repairs to the church's stained-glass windows, repairs to the roof, and substantial yearly donations to the general church fund when we were requested to help balance the budget. We also provided layettes to the local Children's Aid Society and sent a monthly cheer box to a small boy who was incurably ill.

Helen McCurdy was honoured at the twentieth anniversary of the Helpers Group.

> First in our thought and hearts is Miss Helen McCurdy our Honorary President. Without her zeal and devotion to the Missionary cause and her interest in all phases of church life, there would be no Associated Helpers Circle. In the years since the group which bears her name came into being, she has never failed in her constant encouragement and interest in the Circle, or faith in its members as individuals.

Many of the original Circle members were the nucleus of the present-day UCW of Windsor United Church, and Miss McCurdy's high ideals are still remembered and cherished by them.

(WWW, Maritimes—Nova Scotia, #10, written and submitted by Connie Crossley.)

Alice (Gordon) Green

...In 1948 Alice Gordon married A. C. Green of Alberton. A few years after their marriage, Mr. Green's health began to fail and Mrs. Green helped him with his coal business until he died. For more than ten years she carried on the business alone with assistance from part-time help, driving the truck to deliver the coal and loading and unloading it as well. She was perhaps the only woman on Prince Edward Island to have owned and operated a coal and coke business in this manner.

Early in 1969 she gave up the coal business and returned to the nursing profession. She became nurse supervisor at Maplewood Manor, a senior citizens' home in Alberton. She radiated joy and enthusiasm and this brought cheer and comfort to the residents...

(WWW, Maritime—P.E.I., #5, Item 18, submitted by Mrs. Henry Moyse.)

Mabel Louise Dubbin

...What and how Mabel Louise Dubbin worked to improve health and social conditions in the area is a story in itself. Suffice to say that she laboured for thirty-two years as a District V.O.N. nurse and is reported to have brought at least five thousand babies into the world.

For twenty years Mabel Dubbin taught Sunday School to a class of teenaged girls and young women in Victoria Methodist Church and would have continued, but Victoria and St. James Presbyterian united to become Trinity United Church and Victoria was closed and sold. Plays, concerts, garden parties and other entertainments were regular annual features of Victoria Church congregation and Miss Dubbin could always be counted on to participate. As an actress she was second to none.

The Community House, built in 1923 by the Presbyterian Church, came under the United Church at the time of Union in 1925 and was a hive of activity for old and young alike. It wasn't long before Mabel Louise Dubbin was making good use of it with her Mothers' Study Club and Well Baby Clinic. The Mothers' Club became too large and had to be divided into two groups, one a Senior and the other a Junior. Very interesting is the fact that there were two rules which had to be followed: first, no gossiping, and second, no discussion on the topic of religion because of the various faiths of the mothers.

The program was indeed varied. At every meeting a delectable and economical dish was prepared and later served. Lively discussions on such subjects as "Should a husband have to get his own breakfast?" elicited a great deal of fun. There were singsongs, handwork such as tea cloths, children's clothes, etc., made from sugar-bags. Sometimes the groups were allowed the use of the gym floor and with Miss Dubbin as phys-ed instructress, a half-hour on the floor marching, swinging clubs, skipping, helped the mothers forget, even if for a brief time, their problems and troubles...

(From "Mabel Louise Dubbin", written by Elsie Percy. Included in WWW, Maritime—Nova Scotia, #9, submitted by Jessie MacLeod.)

Grace (Webster) MacKinnon

...In every church where my father was called to do the Lord's work, she was always by his side, truly an assistant minister, taking part in nearly every department. In addition to this, her home was also the church office where a good many wedding ceremonies and baptisms took place—a very busy place indeed! Ministers' salaries were meagre in the early days and she, at times, took in boarders besides teaching both piano and voice.

While my parents were in Inverness, there were many people at their door, asking my father to lay his hands on them, believing that since he was the seventh son and my mother the seventh daughter, they possessed healing powers.

During their sojourn in Lunenburg, the United Church came into being and my father, being in favour of this event, did not wish to remain in that locality any longer as his church wanted to stay Presbyterian. The local Methodist Church asked him to stay as its first United Church minister, but he felt there might be bad feelings in the community so he found a new church in Bridgetown where their good deeds and gospel teaching continued for several years.

In 1927 they moved to Halifax which was a big challenge, with the extra responsibility of trying to educate three children.

My mother was a real example of true discipleship and faithful steward-ship. She worked with young and old, from Junior Sunday School classes and Mission Bands to organizing women's groups, directing choirs and plays, and visiting the poor and sick, not only church members but others in the community. She took great pleasure in writing and composing beautiful poetry about the wonders of God and extolling his praises.

I personally think she felt a devoted loyalty to the old Woman's Missionary Society and Ladies Aid groups and was never too keen in later years when the United Church Women was formed and the larger groups were divided into more individual smaller units. I believe she felt for awhile that the devotional aspects were somewhat neglected for more mercenary projects....

(WWW, Maritime—Nova Scotia, #12b, written by Lilian (MacKinnon) Piercey and submitted by Rev. Frances MacLellan.)

Sophia Naomi Evangeline (Swift) Greene

...Grandma had her own driving mare named Daisy, known to all around as The Missionary Nag. This pet mare sometimes jumped across puddles, but Grandma had no fear as she travelled about hitched to the two-wheeled gig, collecting the mite boxes from the women of the Woman's Missionary Society. One of the children went along to run into the houses. Usually everyone at home came out to the gig to have a chat. Deaf as she was, she was always welcome. When all the boxes were brought in, she would have a gathering of ladies come to open them up and count the money. Grandma knew the hard sacrifice some made to give and she was seen to whisper a prayer over a widow's mite quite often. She remained treasurer for twenty-five years and made her daughters and granddaughters life members at a very early age. Along with this was implanted the love and joy in serving in the church....

(From "Grandma Greene's Legacy", included in WWW, London, #7 written and submitted by Betty McConnell.)

How Do We Get That Way? (Mildred Fahrni)

When someone says to you, "You never change", it may be considered as a compliment, but to me it seems a very questionable one. I feel we should all change and grow and mature while we maintain our faculties. This is not to say that early influences are no longer effective in one's life, but that they continue to be a part of the whole.

I was fortunate in being born into a home where both parents were committed to Christian principles, and tried to maintain them in their own lives. They also applied them to their community and international views. My first fifteen years were spent in Manitoba, moving every four years from town to town where my father was sent by the Conference of the Methodist church. As income was limited, life was relatively simple. We coped with immediate needs by growing our food, cutting our fuel, getting our water from a pump and making our own clothing as most of our neighbours did. There was a sense of community and sharing as we cooperated in many of these activities, and we were concerned with each other's needs and tried to share in meeting them. These, as well as the scriptural injunctions, were probably the basis of my socialist beliefs.

Schooling widened the circle of concern and gave increasing insight into the causes of the discrepancies in income in our own and other areas. University opened up more understanding and I remember particularly the influence of Dr. Boggs, affectionately called Teddy, of the University of British Columbia, through his course "Capitalism, Socialism and Communism". He not only gave us theory as we delved into Karl Marx and other proponents, but he took us to IWW (International Workers of the World, also known as "Wobblies") meetings and encouraged us to speak to gatherings and share in discussion. This was a very vital part of my growing conviction that the *laissez-faire* (every-man-for-himself) approach was contrary to Christian principles.

My understanding of the ethics of Christianity was strengthened in this period through attending seminars with Dr. Sharman and being subjected to his searching questions of "Jesus in the Records."

Years followed when teacher-training and teaching demanded most of my time and thought. The next important period was later when doing post-graduate work in Bryn Mawr, Philadelphia. I was assigned to a practicum in the industrial area where unemployment was widespread and I came to realize my "Bandaids" of helping people adjust could not solve the basic causes of their problem which were the result of industrialists moving their premises to areas where labour laws were less demanding and child labour was available.

Further insights came when I spent the next six months in the East End of London, in Kingsley Hall, where Muriel Lester had tried to build a community centre providing for the social and educational needs of the area without the disadvantages of the alcohol sold in the pubs. Again I realized that the unjust free enterprise system had reduced a large portion of the population to a meagre income while a few luxuriated in the results of their labour. During this period I had the most significant contact of my life when Mahatma Gandhi came and lived with us during the four months he attended the Round Table Conference with the British Government.

During the next six months I attended the London School of Economics where I heard lectures by Harold Laskie and Beatrice and Sidney Webbs, as well as others of the Fabian group. There were occasional events with George Bernard Shaw. Fortified by theory as well as practical evidence, I was now prepared to join the Socialists who were bent on changing the world in our time.

Before returning to Canada I took a short tour with other international students to the Soviet Union and was excited by the vibrant youth who were already involved in changing their country from the dominance of a wealthy hierarchy to a socialist society. I was deeply affected by their enthusiasm and commitment.

Returning to Vancouver I faced the personal adjustment of the thirties and worked under the YWCA with "Unemployed Women and Girls", again realizing that I could not solve the problems of the victims of an unjust economic system. Now it was time to become active in trying to change the system. What ambition! A group of us set up study groups discussing such books as Shaw's, *A Woman's Guide to Socialism*.

After some months we decided that it was time to act and, with others, we formed the "Reconstruction Party." Across Canada at this time things were happening in the labour and farmer groups. After representatives met in Calgary in 1932, a conference was called to bring the groups together and form a new party. The following year I attended the Foundation meeting of the Co-operative Commonwealth Federation (CCF) which was formed in Regina. The Manifesto started by stating, "From each according to his ability, to each according to his need". Inspired by J. S. Woodsworth, who became the leader, we returned to dissolve the Reconstruction Party and work in the new party, using every opportunity to take advantage of any platform and even run in the federal election a few months later.

Political expertise was limited, but most of us were evangelists working to bring about radical change...and convinced that we could. Here my religious conviction and social activities were in harmony, and I was supported by such fine leaders as M. J. Coldwell, Tommy Douglas, Connell, David Lewis and others.

Realizing that the public had to be aroused and educated, we set up Summer Schools over a number of years, at Deep Cove, Gabriola, etc., and went on lecture tours throughout the province. Time has proved that the task is not as simple as some of us thought, and must be continued. As time has gone on, and it has become evident that the capitalist system inevitably leads to war, we are more than ever convinced of the necessity of change. Not only the insanity of a world seemingly bent on self-destruction, but because of my religious convictions that "violence breeds violence" and that the way of love and non-violence is the only way to save the world, I continue in my eighties to share where I can through the Fellowship of Reconciliation, the Coalition for World Disarmament, and other Peace groups, to try and bring about the changes necessary to reverse the present policies and build a world where "there is no occasion for war".

(Written by Mildred Fahrni.)

Section 3

Patchwork Pieces

SECTION 3   PATCHWORK PIECES

Chapter 7   WOMEN, WORK AND WORSHIP

Women Do...

Women Laugh...

Women Tell Their Stories...

Women Reflect...

Patchwork Pieces

What's in a Quilt?

You look at my quilt with a quizzical eye,
Remark on its beauty and ask—
If it's worth all the time and work that it took
To complete such a painstaking task.

'Twas a labour of love, I try to explain—
A means to express what I feel
And preserve for the future some small part of me
That everyday life may conceal.

Into its patches I've stitched all the thoughts,
The dreams, the struggles, the fights,
The gladness, the sadness, the joy and the pain,
And the search for beauty and rights.

It's a simple quilt, really, just pieced out of scraps
In a pattern I worked out one day.
I sorted and pondered before I began,
And finally arranged it this way.

Some are gifted with words or with paints to express
The beauty they wish to portray.
My scraps and my needle are canvas and book;
I'm artist and author that way.

(Author unknown. WWW, London, #1, Item 7, p. 9, submitted by Kay Brodie.)

Like "patchwork pieces", the materials in this section are leftovers—
bits and pieces that, taken together, tell us something about who we are
and convey the richness and diversity of contributions to the Women,
Work and Worship project.

Chapter 7 WOMEN, WORK AND WORSHIP

WOMEN DO...

April 25, 1889—This is the long looked-for day—*the election for Repeal of the Scott Act.* There was an all-day prayer meeting in The Presbyterian Church for the women; the ministers took charge at different parts of the day, in turn. Such earnest prayers were offered that the right might win, that it might be right to keep *the Scott Act as being so much better than high licence,* but it has been ordered otherwise, and the Act was repealed by about 1000 majority but *we do not intend being discouraged but only work the harder for Prohibition.*

May 14, 1889—After tea I went up to meet Miss McKenzie, and she and I went around until dark with a petition to get new signers, asking the *commissioners not to license the two saloons.*

October 5, 1893—Mother went down to the Parsonage this evening to a meeting of the ladies of the church. They intend petitioning the Trustees not to try to fix up the old church but pull down and build a new one.

October 6, 1893—Ladies met tonight again in the church with the Official Board, to present their petition to have a congregational meeting, but it was voted on and overthrown. Have decided to decorate the old church.

(From the diary of Lillian M.G. Coates (1869-1936). Included in WWW, Bay of Quinte, #4, submitted by Jean Sheridan.)

London, June 20th, 1913

Dear Winnie;

You certainly did send me a long newsy letter and I was so glad to get it.

Yes, a Ladies Aid or anything you have a mind to call it would be a fine thing. The way to go at it would be this. Have it announced that such a society is to be organized. Then at the meeting for organizing, appoint a provisional secretary and chairman. Then elect by ballot a president, secretary, and a treasurer. The first ballot you can make what they call a nominating ballot. That is, you can take a number of the names that get

136

the highest number of votes and vote on them. Of course, the person getting over half of the votes is elected and you proceed with the next office. Your executive (that is, your officers) can appoint any committees you please for different work—for instance, a programme committee if you wish. The heads of these committees belong to your executive. The use of your executive is to save time in your meeting. The executive can meet and plan things, then these plans or decisions are brought in to the general meeting and read as minutes of the executive and voted on, one at a time, or you can do all your business in the general meeting; but sometimes it saves time and trouble to do it the other way. Anything decided upon by the executive must be voted on in the general meeting to be legal.

The Order of Business is usually:
1. Hymn
2. Prayer
3. Bible reading or chapter reading
4. Hymn
5. Minutes of last meeting
6. Report of treasurer
7. Receiving of new members and fees
8. Taking up any old business left over from the last meeting
9. Taking up any new business
10. The education, literary, or social part of your meeting
11. Closing excerises.

The foregoing order of business would do for almost any church society you might organize. I hope I have made it all plain. Your idea of mothers meeting and nursery, etc., is fine. Anything that would be a help in the everyday life of the women. Even sewing meetings where you could teach some of the poor women who do not know how to sew, lending patterns, anything helpful. I think it would be a beautiful work and most Christian. You know the texts about the cup of cold water and bearing one another's burdens. Your society could be all of that. Of course, you will meet lots of discouragements and possibly disagreeable women but if you try to remember that "we are workers together with God", it will make it look different....

Your loving sister,
Maud.

(Excerpts from a letter written by Mrs. Maud White to her sister, Mrs. Winnifred Stewart, in Saskatchewan. Included in WWW, London, #9, submitted by their niece, Marion Anderson.)

Colpitts WMS was organized July 1924 by the late Mrs. A. G. Parking of Petitcodiac, with seven charter members....These monthly meetings were looked upon with great enthusiasm, especially by the member having the next meeting. A meal was prepared and cooked on a wood-burning stove and the wooden floors scrubbed the hard way. The ruffled curtains were washed, starched and ironed. The stove had an extra coat of stove polish and was buffed until one was at the point of exhaustion. The pre-school children were always in attendance. It was not difficult to get transportation in the summer, but a different story in the winter. We needed a team of horses, an able-bodied man and a few shovels on hand....

(WWW, Maritime—New Brunswick, #10, Item 6, written by Inez Calpetts, submitted by Gwen MacRae.)

My Recollections of Mount Paul United Church—1928-1978

...My sister...and I scrubbed the church floors on our hands and knees as we did not like mops. When my sister left, Mary McGregor introduced me to the mop and for years this was how the church was cleaned. Later on the floors were oiled—a messy job. As we could not afford a janitor, we cleaned the church without charge. Some of the L.A. ladies would gather at the church when there was wood to saw and pile into the basement. How we laughed and had fun doing this chore, with no grumbling.

...Social gatherings were held in the home of Mr. and Mrs. N. Morton as the Rev. Wilson did not approve of dancing in the church hall...These were very happy times when everyone let down their hair, so to speak, and enjoyed themselves. When we held our first dance in the hall someone asked Mrs. Wilson to dance and, boy, did the Reverend lay down the law to his wife. He was like a little bantam rooster as Mrs. Wilson was taller than he was....

(From The Golden Years: Mount Paul United Church, 1928-1978. Included in WWW, British Columbia, #8, submitted by Mabel Burnett.)

The Fowl Supper (Some women preferred to call them "foul" suppers!)

...These suppers became an annual affair. In those days the water wagon came around twice a week to unmodern locations. Second Street was in this position. Mrs. Middleton, who lived close to the church, supplied one water barrel, and another was also obtained from another WA member, then the request went in to the Waterworks to obtain the water. The WA members worked a week before the suppers, and a week afterwards to clear everything away. They said it was great fun and rewarding, even if they were working under adverse conditions. Besides the two barrels of water in the basement, there was also a big old black cook stove. Potatoes were boiled there, and a few tables were set up for work space. Dishwashing water was obtained from kettles on the stove or from a small tank at the side of the stove. Dishwashing was then relegated to one corner of the basement with a table and two large dishpans. Most of the vegetables such as turnips and carrots were cooked in the homes and brought over. Canned peas were heated on the stove. Turkeys were baked at one of the city bakeries. The ladies made the gravy. The husbands of the ladies obtained saw-horses and planks or boards which they set up in the church upstairs. They also borrowed plates, cups and saucers and cutlery from Grace Church. The ladies brought platters, creams and sugars, salt and pepper shakers, bowls for gravy, and vegetable dishes from their own homes. It was quite an effort on the part of these ladies and their husbands since no one had cars for transportation. Trucks brought the dishes from Grace Church and the makings of many of the tables. Between 300-400 people crowded into a little church for at least four sittings. As one WA member stated, "we were noted for our good feeds."

(WWW, Saskatchewan, #24, submitted by Joyce M. McManus.)

The Bake Sale

...There were only a small number of ladies in the old church so before a bake sale each one had to do a lot of baking. Mabel liked to make cakes and Eileen made pastries. Eileen would take time from her tart-making to phone Mabel to see how she was coming along. Mabel would say: "I'm doing the spice now." She mixed the white cakes first, then the spice, and ended with chocolate without having to wash the bowl!

(WWW, Toronto, #4, submitted by Leonora E. Wilson.)

Sour Dough Starter

    2 cups flour
    2 tbsp. sugar
    1 tsp. salt
    2 cups warm water

Mix in large bowl and let stand covered at room temperature for 2 days. This becomes a spongy mass and has a yeasty aroma. Refrigerate in a large covered bowl and feed after each usage with:

    1 cup flour
    1 cup milk
    ¼ cup sugar

Leave for 24 hours before using again. (This may be frozen if you tire of it.)

Cora's Biscuits (1½ dozen, large)

    2 cups sour dough
    2 cups flour
    2/3 cups salad oil
    1 tsp. soda
    4 tsp. baking powder
    salt

Knead, roll lightly to ½ inch thick. Bake at 425 F., 10-12 minutes.

Raw Chili Sauce

18 large tomatoes, 2 sweet red peppers, 4 cups celery, 2 green peppers, 7 large onions, 2 cups white vinegar, ½ cup salt, 1 oz. mustard seed, 6 cups white sugar, celery seed.

Peel tomatoes, cut in small chunks (or grind). Cut celery fine. Put onions through chopper. Mix together with chopped peppers. Sprinkle with salt. Let stand all day, put in collander and let drain all night. Put in kettle and add sugar, vinegar, mustard and celery seed. Stir periodically for 4 hours. Put in jars. Do not fill quite full, and seal.

Green Tomato Raspberry Jam

5 cups green tomatoes, put through chopper or blender
5 cups sugar

Cook together till mush, about 10-12 minutes. Add a teaspoon lemon juice and move off heat. Stir in 1 large raspberry jello. Let set a few minutes, stirring occasionally so fruit doesn't settle at top of jar. Put into jars and seal while hot.

Grape Jelly from Beet Juice

3 cups beet juice
1 package grape Kool-Aid
1 package (3 oz.) grape jello
1 package Certo crystals

Boil 7 minutes. Add 4 cups sugar, boil 2 minutes. Jar and wax.

Greta's Great Carrot Cake

3 cups flour
2 tsp. baking powder
2 tsp. baking soda
1 tsp. cinnamon
4 eggs
2 cups sugar
1 1/3 cups salad oil
3 cups finely grated carrots
1 cup chopped walnuts (optional)

Combine first 4 ingredients and mix with fork. Beat eggs until light and lemon-coloured. Gradually add sugar, beating all the time. Add vanilla, beating on low speed. Blend in dry ingredients. Stir in grated carrots. Put in 12-cup (10"-tubular) pan or 2 loaf pans. Bake at 300 F. for 1 hour and 15 min. in tube pan. Unmould and cool.

Rhubarb Crunch

½ cup melted butter
1 cup flour
¾ cup rolled oats

¾ cup brown sugar
1 tsp. cinnamon
½ tsp. salt
4 cups chopped rhubarb
¾ cup sugar (½ cup will work here too)
2 tbsp. cornstarch
1 cup boiling water
1 tsp. vanilla

In medium saucepan, melt butter and cool a bit. Work in flour, oats, brown sugar, cinnamon and salt until crumbly. Press half in 8 x 9 baking dish. Cover with rhubarb. In small saucepan mix sugar and cornstarch, then add boiling water and stir and cook until thick. Remove from heat and add vanilla. Pour this hot syrup over rhubarb. Now sprinkle and pat remaining crumb mixture over the top. Bake at 325 F. for 50 to 60 minutes. When cooled, cuts nicely into squares for eating with a fork, or cuts into smaller squares for finger-munching.

Now, in 1982, United Church Women in Montreal and Ottawa Conference tell how they **SHARE THEIR SPIRITUAL GIFTS AS THEY,**

Attend church regularly
Prepare and lead worship services
Share their faith in inspirational messages
Lead in prayer

And, AS THEY SERVE AS,

Elders
Stewards
Trustee Board Members
Members of all Church Boards, such as Ministry Personnel and
    Education, Worship, Manse, etc.
Lay Representatives to Presbytery and Conference
Church-Door Greeters
Ushers
Bible Study Leaders
Prayer Group Leaders
Supporters of Kerygma Groups
Organists
Leaders and Members of Choirs
Participants in "Caring Community"
Sunday School Teachers and Superintendents
Christian Education Workers

Leaders of Vacation Bible Schools
Leaders of midweek groups such as CGIT, Messengers, Explorers, Youth Groups, Wolf Cubs, Scouts, Brownies, Guides, Religion-in-Life Award Classes, 4H
Leaders and Promoters of Mission Study throughout the church
Convenors of Stewardship Education

And, AS THEY ORGANIZE,

Telephone Prayer Circles
World Day of Prayer Services
Programs on Mission
Ten Days for World Development
Stewardship and Social Concerns Presentations
Meetings with Speakers and Audiovisual Presentations
Junior Congregations
Church Nurseries
Baby-sitting for Young Mothers
Bible Study Groups
Congregational Fellowship and Coffee Hours
Spring and Fall Thanksgiving Services

THEY USE THEIR TIME, TALENTS AND TREASURE,
to help supply

Funds to help build churches, church halls and manses;
Funds to help repair and maintain church property: furniture, furnishings, water, sewage, electricity, lights, kitchen equipment, lounge furnishings, carpeting, etc;
Funds to help buy organs, pianos, choir gowns and choir music;
Church office equipment Gestetners, etc.
Audiovisual equipment
Funds to pay insurance on churches and manses
Funds to pay manse taxes
Assistance in paying minister's salary
Assistance in paying off mortgages on church property
Grants of money (to take advantage of special discounts, or so debts could be retired without penalty)
Church memorial books
Weekly church bulletins
The United Church Observer to all church families
Copies of *MANDATE,* Upper Room, These Days, etc.
Flowers for the sanctuary and the sick
Hymn Books, Service Books and Bibles
Maintenance equipment (such as vacuum cleaners and lawn mowers)

Free janitorial service

Support for Sunday Schools, midweek and youth groups, vacation schools, etc.

Assistance for church camps (both for maintaining camps and sponsoring campers)

WOMEN SUPPORT

The Mission and Service Fund

Local church projects

Presbytery and Conference projects

Hospital chaplains

Operation Go Home

Montreal City Mission

St. Columba House

Griffith-McConnell Home for the Elderly

Mission to the Deaf (Puerto Rico) by collecting Campbell Soup labels

Foster children

Leprosy Mission and Bible Society (by collecting used stamps, etc.)

Community hospitals, homes for the elderly, retarded and senior citizens

Sheltered workshops

Fellowship of the Least Coin

Amnesty International

Project Ploughshares

Operation Dismantle

Help to churches or families who have lost their buildings by fire

Donations to outside charitable organizations and foundations for various diseases.

THEY REACH OUT IN LOVE TO THE COMMUNITY AS THEY

CANVASS... for Church, Bible Society, Cancer Society, Heart Fund, all manner of medical and charity fund drives.

CLOTHE... the needy, the burned-out, native people, refugees.

DONATE... all manner of gifts, letters, cards, stamps, baking, candy, money, used stamps, books for a university theological library, and so on—ad infinitum.

DRIVE... elderly and handicapped people to church and church meetings and clubs, for meals on wheels, patients to treatment centres, the mentally handicapped and the blind, those who are unable to go shopping or to the bank alone.

OPERATE...	nearly new shops, lunch stands, tearooms, etc.
ORGANIZE...	dinners, lunches, teas, potluck meals; celebrations for birthdays, anniversaries, showers, Christmas events; art, music and craft classes; community friendship coffee parties; plays and entertainments.
PREPARE...	worship services for presenting in homes for the elderly, the retarded, nursing homes, senior citizens' homes, health centres and hospitals.
PROVIDE...	emergency services, meals, transportation, baby-sitting services to stricken families, services aimed at enabling older people to live in their own homes.
SEND AND TAKE...	home-baking, homemade candy, gifts, fruits, cards and letters, to people in all the homes mentioned as well as to sick and shut-in and elderly people in their own homes in the community.
SERVE...	lunches and teas after funerals, and at various community events.
SEW AND KNIT...	afghans and clothing for children, the sick and elderly near and far, for those burned-out, mittens for needy children.
SPONSOR...	refugee families, friendship clubs for senior citizens.
TEACH...	home-cooking to men in a half-way house, crafts to retarded children and adults, young mothers in the community, etc.
VISIT...	children's homes for the retarded and handicapped as well as nursing homes, homes for the elderly, and shut-ins in their own homes. Some also bring elderly people and children to their own homes for visits.
VOLUNTEER...	their services at blood-donor clinics, citizenship courts, hospital auxiliaries, community libraries and all the kinds of homes previously mentioned.

(From Voluntary Church Work: A Life Style for Women. *A project of Montreal and Ottawa Conference United Church Women of The United Church of Canada, 1982. This project was funded by Women, Work and Worship.)*

144

WOMEN LAUGH...

The Ladies Aid

We've put a fine addition on the good old church at home;
It's just the latest kilter, with a gallery and dome;
It seats a thousand people—finest church in all the town;
And when 'twas dedicated, we planked ten thousand down.
That is—we paid five thousand—every deacon did his best—
And the Ladies Aid Society, it promised all the rest.

We've got an organ in the church—very finest in the land,
It's got a hundred pipes or more, its melody is grand.
And when we sit in cushioned pews and hear that organ play,
It carries us to realms of bliss unnumbered miles away.
It cost a cool three thousand, but 'twill stand the hardest test;
We'll pay a thousand on it—the Ladies Aid the rest.

They'll give a hundred socials, cantatas too, and teas;
They'll bake a thousand angel cakes and tons of cream they'll freeze;
They'll beg and scrape, and toil, and sweat for seven years or more,
And then they'll start all o'er again for a carpet on the floor.
No, it isn't just like digging out the money from your vest,
When the Ladies Aid gets busy, and says, "We'll pay the rest."

Of course we're proud of our big church, from pulpit up to spire;
It is the darling of our eyes, the crown of our desire;
But when I see the sisters work to raise the cash which lacks,
I sometimes feel the church is built on women's tired backs;
And sometimes I can't help thinking, when we reach the regions blest,
That men will get the toil and sweat—and the Ladies Aid the rest.

*(Author unknown. Reprinted in Centenary: Princeton United Church, 1880-1980,
p. 42. Included in WWW, London, #8, submitted by Mrs. Murray Forrest.)*

Definition of our Committee:

We, the unwilling, guided by the unknowing,
Are doing the impossible, for the ungrateful,
And having done so much, for so long, with so little—
Are now qualified to do anything with nothing....

(WWW, London, #1, Item 1, p. 4, submitted by Kay Brodie.)

1928—Mrs. Joe Wright recalls that when the Women's Auxilliary decided to install running water in the kitchen of the church, two members of the session, Mr. W. Strangways and Mr. W. Robinson heard about it and attended the next WA meeting to find out more details. They suggested that this was not a good idea, as it might cause problems with frozen pipes in the winter. The ladies made it clear that they were not going to change their minds and the issue was closed. Running water was installed!

(Bert Platt, Trinity United Church: Beeton, 1878-1978, p. 61. Included in WWW, Toronto, #7, submitted by Muriel Reynolds.)

What is a Grandmother? (A nine-year-old's view)

A grandmother is a lady with no children of her own. She likes other people's little boys and girls. A grandfather is a man-grandmother. He goes for walks with the boys and they talk about fishing and stuff like that.

Grandmothers don't have to do anything except to be there. They are old so they shouldn't play hard, or run. It is enough if they drive us to the market, where the pretend horse is, and have a lot of dimes ready. Or if they take us for walks, they should slow down past things like pretty leaves and caterpillars. They should never say "Hurry up."

Usually grandmothers are fat, but not too fat to tie your shoes. They wear glasses and funny underwear. They can take their teeth and gums off. Grandmothers don't have to be smart. Only answer questions like "Why isn't God married?" or "How come dogs chase cats?" Grandmothers don't talk baby talk, like visitors do, because it is hard to understand. When they read to us they don't skip or mind if it is the same story all over again. EVERYBODY SHOULD HAVE A GRANDMOTHER, ESPECIALLY IF THEY DON'T HAVE TELEVISION, BECAUSE THEY ARE THE ONLY GROWN-UPS WHO HAVE TIME.

(WWW, London, #1, Item 4, p. 3, submitted by Kay Brodie.)

Poor Child

College Professor:	Such rawness in a pupil is a shame,
	Lack of preparation in high school's to blame.
High School Teacher:	Good heavens, what crudity; the boy's a fool
	The fault, of course, is the grammar school.
Grammar School Teacher:	From such stupidity may I be spared—
	They send them to me, quite unprepared.
Primary School Teacher:	Kindergarten blockhead...they call that preparation?
	Worse than none, is my estimation.

Kindergarten Teacher:	Such lack of training ne'er did I see;
	What kind of woman must the mother be?
The Mother:	Poor helpless child, he's not to blame—
	His father's folks were just the same.

(WWW, London, #1, Item 4, p. 2, submitted by Kay Brodie.)

To Whom it May Concern

She rose before daylight made crimson the east
For duties that never diminished.
And never the sun when it sank in the west
Looked down upon work that was finished.
She cooked unending processions of meals,
Preserving and canning and baking.
She swept and she dusted, she washed and she scrubbed,
With never a rest for the taking.
A family of children she brought into the world,
Raised them and trained them, and taught them.
She made all their clothes, patched, mended, and darned,
'Til miracles seemed to have wrought them.
She watched by the bedside of sickness and pain;
Her hand cooled the raging of fever —
Carpentered, painted, upholstered and scraped—
And worked just as hard as a beaver.
And yet as a lady of leisure, it seems
The government looks on her situation.
For now, by the rules of the census report—
It enters—NO OCCUPATION.

(Author unknown, WWW, London, #1, Item 4, p. 4, submitted by Kay Brodie.)

The Lord's Little Pig

"Wife," cried the farmer, "come and see
A sight to delight your eyes;
For a litter of six little baby pigs
We've got today in the sty."

And the wife, with a smile, said "Husband dear,
Don't you think you can now afford,
In gratitude for increasing stock,
To give one little pig to the Lord?

"When last they asked us to help the church
You said you had nothing to spare;
But with calves and lambs and pigs coming in,
Don't you think you could now do your share?"

147

"Right," said the farmer, "For all the pigs
Look healthy and likely to live.
And so when they're sold the money for one
To the Lord we'll certainly give.

"For we'll send the six away to the fair,
As soon as they are fat and big;
But we needn't decide beforehand which
Is to be the Lord's little pig."

The piglets grew and flourished, till
The farmer's boy, unskilled
With a crash the heavy gate let fall—
And one little pig was killed.

Then the angry farmer came to the house,
And to his wife he said,
"We'll have NOTHING NOW to give to the church,
For the Lord's little pig is dead."
AH, FRIENDS, BEWARE THAT YOU NEVER TRY
TO GIVE UNTO GOD THE WORST,
AND MOST ESPECIALLY, DO NOT LET
THE LORD'S LITTLE PIG DIE FIRST.

(Author unknown, WWW, London, #1, Item 4, p. 9, submitted by Kay Brodie.)

WOMEN TELL THEIR STORIES...

A Letter Home

(Written by a young woman who emigrated from Kent, England, to Canada in 1892, to help her sister-in-law with her young family. This letter to her mother, written in verse form, was written while the author was travelling across Canada by train.)

Far from old England, the land of my birth,
    Far from Kent County, the dearest on earth.
Dear native shores I have bidden farewell,
    On soil Canadian from henceforth to dwell.

Over the seas by steamer I've come
    Now by the train I am hastening on,
Flying through country so lovely and green
    Lovelier scenery never was seen.

Can this be Sunday? God's sweet day of rest,
    Day of the week that we all love the best,

148

Must I get sermon from green fields and trees?
   Surely God's love is displayed in all these.
Now you are singing in chapel at home
   Much I'm regretting that I cannot come.
But I know you are remembering me in your prayer
   And you to the grace of God's throne I can bear.
Thus far on my journey in safety I've come
   Meeting kind friends wherever I roam.
Shall be in two days, I trust all being well,
   Safe in the home of Jabez and Nell.
I trust that we all shall meet together some day,
   If not in this world, God grant that we may
Meet Father and Albert on yonder bright shore
   And all dwell together when partings are o'er.

(Written by Mary Jane Fagg. Included in WWW, Saskatchewan, #21, Item 2, submitted by Marion Serviss.)

In the Fullness of Time

...The earliest records of our church (1867-1884) give names of women and girls who were confirmed but make no mention of any women who participated in church work. However, in the Minutes of the annual congregational meeting of 1885 we find that a committee of three women had been appointed to collect for the missionaries. This record is the first one that mentions women at work in our church. From that time until duplex envelopes came into use, the money given for missionary work by our congregation was collected by young women who went from house to house explaining the need for missionary work and the money to carry it on. We believe, therefore, that in about 1885 the door of opportunity for Christian women to serve actively in our church began to open.

During the years that passed between 1885 and 1904 we cannot find any record to show women providing any service in the church apart from collecting the missionary money. Nevertheless, the door of opportunity for these women to use their talents further in the service of the Lord opened more widely in 1905.

Before this time the precentor gathered the choir (all men) to the front seats of the church during worship services and led the singing without musical accompaniment. Then, in 1905, the congregation agreed to use the organ that Mrs. Isabel Atkinson had donated to the church. Apparently, neither the precentor nor any other man in the congregation was able to play an organ. For this reason, Annie Hierlihy (Mrs. Daniel MacPherson) was the first organist in Brae Presbyterian (now United) Church and the first woman to direct its choir. At the same time, the superintendent of the Sunday School was unable to find men to teach all classes and two women were asked to give assistance....

Although the women were faithful in their work and worship in the church, they provided little or no leadership in the congregation during the next quarter-century. Then, in 1930, when no man wished to serve as superintendent of the Sunday School, Mrs. Alice MacFadyen was appointed to this office. Mrs. MacFadyen, a devout Christian mother, who had been converted as a young woman, was surprised when she was asked to carry out this task, but felt the request was a call from God. She was the first woman to provide such leadership in our church....

(WWW, Maritime—P.E.I., #5, Item 8, submitted by Mrs. Henry Moyse.)

A History of Women in the Estlin United Church

...We have all the Minute books in our possession—they are revealing, touching and humorous. Membership has varied from the first thirteen, up to forty, down to nine, and we are now fifteen.

In 1921, when Estlin boasted a most beautiful Grange Growers Hall, and where the ladies met each month during the winter, there is a most humorous motion that "we buy our own coal and keep it under lock and key." It sounds as if they were indeed being put upon. Those were the days of opulent lunches (when girth was not the obsession it is today) and on a motion of adjournment, "all were willing, as already tantalizing odors of tea and coffee were drifting in from the kitchen, but this only proved to be the preliminaries to a very dainty repast which attested to the thoughtfulness of the hostess to women's special tastes in particular."

Many of the traditions started back in "the olden days" we still adhere to; we still houseclean the church the day before Mother's Day—I wish I could remember when I am on my knees waxing a floor, or polishing pews, that my Mother did these same tasks—and likely as not did not utter one word of complaint....

...We did try one thing different in that we decided to have a spring luncheon meeting (potluck in nature), hoping to ensnare a few new members. This ruse didn't work at all, but we continued it because we just plain enjoyed it.

(WWW, Saskatchewan, #18, submitted by Mrs. M. McQuoid.)

A Short History of the United Church Women

In January, 1962
Was born the UCW.

Inheriting some great traditions
From Ladies Aids and Women's Missions.

One hundred and sixty-three years ago:
1819—I'm told it's so,
Women in Canada's Eastern parts
Helped in churches with all their hearts,
Because they wanted *all* to hear
The sacred Gospel—loud and clear.
They had no voice in church affairs—
(The *men* thought that the job was theirs);
For 'twas the men who built and planned
To operate churches in this land.
The women gradually learned
Their efforts were no longer spurned.
And as the people settled West,
In B.C. many came to rest.

You know, you'd really have to search
To read about women and the church;
And though they merit much attention—
Of them, there's seldom any mention.
Ministers' wives—great pioneers—
Were frustrated, lonely, had many fears;
And yet, they served and gave their all
Because they, too, had heard the Call.
But what of Ladies Aid, you ask?
They organized; took on the task
Of supporting projects of the men
By raising funds—a bold move then;
In fact, in eighteen sixty-three,
The First Presbyterians gave a "tea"—
A most ambitious evening's "do",
With speeches, songs and instruments too;
One dollar was paid to gain admission:
(Building Fund suffered from malnutrition);
Just short of six hundred fifty dollars were made
By what *seems* to have been the FIRST LADIES AID.

It was in 1881,
WMS Methodists were begun:
As Indians up our B.C. coast
Required help the very most,
They were provided with education,
Christian faith and medication.

Then in 1886,
Came the Congregationalists,
Who organized to meet the needs
Of people home and overseas.
The women in those far-off days
Decided there were funds to raise
So missionaries and supplies
Could reach the fold who otherwise
Were lacking in so many ways—
Receiving help, gave God the praise.
So here at home and 'cross the seas,
The ladies did so much to please.

In 1887 we find
Presbyterian women of one mind:
To establish schools at Barkley Sound—
Students in Indian homes were found.

Exactly 94 years ago,
In 1888, 'twas truly so,
Victoria women—Methodists all,
With sympathy, had heard the Call
To open their first rescue home
For Chinese girls—no more to roam.

Just 19 years from century's end
Began that most exciting trend:
For Congregationalists and Methodists
Placed WMS on all their lists;
Then Presbyterian WMS
Added to the Ladies' success.
For there they were—with modest piety—
Each Woman's Missionary Society.

Decades came and decades went;
The gospel 'round the world was sent
To women and children in foreign lands—
A marvellous way of joining hands.

Later, in 1925,
The United Church had come alive;
The WMS was in full swing,
All doing practically everything;
Supporting missions in coastal places;
Sending missionaries to other races—
The Orient, Africa, Asia too—
The service given just grew and grew.

The Ladies Aids, well-organized
In local churches were recognized;
Gave countless hours in peace and war—
But no one ever kept the score.
The Ladies Aids (I don't know why),
Changed their name as time went by:
So WA's were first begun
In March of 1941;
And WMS and WA
In almost every church held sway.

On Presbytery, Conference, Dominion Board,
The WMS has served our Lord;
Provided training, placement, pension—
(Relieving retired women's tension).
Dominion Council of Women's Association
Became aware of their dedication
In raising millions for many reasons,
Never ceasing throughout the seasons;
Depression, drought and war years, sad,
Found church doors open—to make folk glad;
The WA did all it could
To make life better, happy, good.

It was in 1958—
A memorable, historic date
That WMS and WA
Amalgamated on a special day:
The Women's Federation they became—
The very same ladies, with one brand-new name.
They'd serve the church's total mission—
A truly commendable ambition.
However, it wasn't so very long
Before the new name was all wrong:
Provisional committees had talked and sat,
Devised a new "structure"—and THAT was THAT.
A name in '60 was given approval,
But two years passed before the old one's removal.
AND THEN, in 1962
WAS BORN THE UCW.

*(This is the first part of a history prepared by Mrs. M. Jean Lathwell
of Knox United Church, Vancouver, for the twentieth anniversary
celebration of UCW. Included in WWW, British Columbia, #7, submitted by Lillian Soga.)*

WOMEN REFLECT...

On Bugs and Things

A tiny bug did roam
Upon my garden walk,
For he had left his home
To find a juicy stock.
He had no malice in him,
He only had to eat,
He didn't see the danger
Of the clumsy walking feet.
These steps in line of duty
His tiny form did crush,
They failed to see his beauty,
They only thought of rush.
Others with their meanness
Of life that's filled with strife
Stepped upon him madly
And crushed his little life.
This world has need of pity
For things both great and small,
In country and in city
This need is very tall.
The harmless little creatures
Which get into our way
Might have consideration
If love we would display!

(By Mabel Gamble, from "Granny's Melting Pot". Included in WWW, Alberta, #1, submitted by Ruth Gray.)

Do not let
the capricious mood
of his masculinity
dictate the moment
of your living,
my sister!
Do not allow
yourself to remain
captive in the web
of cultural domination,
overpowering servitude,
my friend!

Listen...
heed the symphony
of voices singing
the songs of liberation,
whipped on the winds
of the world.

Stand up, my sister,
feel the wind!
Feel the force of the gale
sting your lifeless cheeks
to glowing womanhood.

Take the hand of a friend,
my sister,
and look together
into the mirror
of tomorrow.

(Written by Jill Perkins, Singapore, printed in 1982 Cyprus Hills UCW. Rally Report. Included in WWW, Saskatchewan, #2, submitted anonymously.)

Death   Ellen Jean Wood, 1981

(The following poem was a journal entry during the author's last year at St. Andrew's College, Saskatoon, Saskatchewan).

Death comes over me like snow falls over the prairie.
All of a sudden there is no dirt, there is only white snow,
    flake upon flake.
It happens so casually, that I hardly notice that death is
    coming on.
Oh I'm not dying a death from cancer, or heart failure, or a
    medical problem.
I'm dying a death of absolute frustration.
I'm dying a death of over-exposure to a system of education
    that has no regard for life.
I cry.
I cry because I realize the death I'm fighting with; and I'll
    not endure the fight, because you're in power.
You're the ones, you can train me and tell me how to be.
You have the power to fail me, to kill me, to make me break
    under your laws, regulations, courses, your marks.
You can surely kill me over four years, to the point where
    I forget who I am.
You can kill me, but I slowly realize.
I slowly realize, that under the numbness of this place, you
    haven't killed my spirit, God's spirit in me.

I just need to keep that spirit out of your reach, and this
   god-damn system of theological education.
I have to have some confidence in the Spirit that you won't
   numb me beyond this present time.
Some day when you think I'm finished these courses, you'll let me go.
And then slowly at first, the numbness and death I've learned
   from you will go.
And I'll never return to that state again, to your state.
For I know that you will be dead, dead and buried in your
   numbness called theology.
I'm not looking forward to that, or even hoping for that, I
   just know it will happen.
I'll be sad, I'll cry.
I'll cry because of the waste of your life, your function,
   your purpose.
But I'll be comforted because maybe, just maybe the death will
   end with old age, the passing away of the old men.
Maybe a new age will be born
Maybe if someone with a spirit
   comes in,
There can be life
There can be theological education.
And not a slow, constant death inflicted on those who have God's
   spirit;
Maybe, Oh God, maybe I'll see it in my lifetime.

(Submitted to The Matrix Collective, St. Andrew's College, Saskatoon, for The Matrix Calendar—1984. This project was funded by Women, Work and Worship.)

To a Young Friend in Prison

(This poem was written by Mary Austin Endicott after a visit to a young man in Kingston Penitentiary. He had commented on the marvellous design of a snowflake which settled on his sleeve. He wondered if human life really had any plan or meaning.)

There is a design, dear friend,
And its purpose is perfection.
Its form and being are unknown to us,
But nature abounds in miracles like snow.

Late in the Plan came man whose capacity
To suffer or inflict suffering is unique.
He also cares; and the apex of his evolution
Is the process of perfecting his concern.

In terms of history man is very young;
Short aeons ago he lived in trees.
How long till we shall reach the goal;
All for one and one for all.

Who knows? But we are on our way
And moving fast, unevenly and with stumbling.
Now we near a fork in the road,
One way marked Suicide.

In the new age a new man will emerge;
We are not accidents, but symphonies…
All my life led me to that day,
The day you needed a friend most of all.

You are in the tumult of creation;
I in the quiet channels. But we are both in it.
To some degree each guides his little bark
Onward to the sea.

(Included in WWW, Toronto, #12, submitted by Shirly Endicott Small.)

Women, Work and Worship

(These are the last 13 verses of a 25-verse poem.)

What was created in us
Is not ours to keep.
God let it just pass through us
From creation's deep.

And when we think we're useless
Because our kids have gone
He shows us other talents
Our individual dawn.

He shows us how our service
Has helped to make us grow.
There's so much to communicate…
So precious much to know.

So whether we are silent
And quietly do our part,
Or sing, or dance, or draw, or write
Worship comes from the heart.

And though we read in history
The valiant deeds of man…
We know that 'tis her story
That fulfills God's plan.

For it is we must nurture
The human, help him grow.
We share the pain of others
In ways that women know.

Our love can be so tender
Or mighty, mighty tough,
And if our vision widens
We know when it's enough.

Enough stockpiling weapons
To blow each other up.
Enough of teaching little boys
That violence is enough.

Enough fighting for power,
Enough of greed and games.
Enough of legal loopholes,
Enough of short-term aims.

If we would really change things
And build for Life, not war
It's we who have the power
All are looking for.

We have men in their tender years
When values are begun.
And hands that rock the cradle
Can get a whole lot done.

So if the women of the world
North, east and south and west
Would hear again God's word of Peace
Our worship would be blest.

Let us unite our energies
And feel the Spirit Power
That shows us what is ripe for us
In this present hour.

(Written by Lena Klassen of Kelowna, B.C. Included in WWW, Saskatchewan, #23, submitted by Rita M. Klassen.)

Ministry

All: MINISTRY is more a matter of being God-ward than it is of speaking God's words—
   —for who can presume to know what God intends to say, or through what medium, or in what unexpected place God proposes to say it
   —from generation to generation, or from person to person?
A: MINISTRY, therefore, is not theologizing or paternalizing, or ecclesiasticizing;
   it is simply laying one's self open to the exciting, sometimes

comforting, sometimes challenging and demanding, creating and forgiving spirit of God's aliveness within the world and within ourselves.

B: MINISTRY is the unselfconscious God-wardness which a person broadcasts through her being, her working, her playing, her creating, and her caring
—and at places where people's lives impinge on one another in God's vast world—
for it is there that those who know God exercise their ministry;
and the witness of who they are and what motivates their being speaks silently and ministers incidentally along the way.

C: MINISTRY has little to do with building warm, cosy, and exclusive ghettos to "togetherness", where manufactured moments of monolithic "fellowship" support like-minded people in becoming more like-minded—
shut off and safe from the loneliness and the hostilities which they have had a part in creating in the world, and from which they are seeking to escape out of the world.

All: MINISTRY is the process of equipping one another, not to run away, or to hide from life—
but to survive and to overcome, joyously and generously.

A: MINISTRY is not the time and energy-consuming task of pouring holy oil, liberally (or even evangelically)
into the non-working parts of congregational or ecclesiastical machinery,
in the everlasting hope that it may be made to run smoothly.

B: MINISTRY cannot be reduced to the professional function of the incubation of orthodox ideas and ideals,
which fail to hatch into life because too often those who sit on the nests of power have been too afraid to permit the fertilization of those ideas,
or have had feet too cold to enable a birth—let alone a new birth.

C: MINISTRY cannot be entrusted to a ruling rooster or a broody hen.
Nor can it safely be left to the manipulators, the more dangerous and insidious of whom are perhaps not the overtly aggressive or autocratic,
but the covertly quiet gentle persuaders—both of whom seek the same goal—to motivate people not to exercise their own unique ministry, but to support what is prescribed by those who happen to possess the prerogatives of power.

All: MINISTRY is pilgrimage—itinerant, like the apostle Paul who tra-

159

velled from place to place, being neither ordained nor settled into one
location or one theology;

>like Paul, before his letters of practical advice to congregations
>had become hardened by the generations into theological
>systems operative for all time;

>>like Paul, supporting himself by his daily work: risking
>>danger, encouraging his friends in and from prison.

A: MINISTRY is a way of life rather than an institution.

>It pays its own way, and is not supported, inequitably,

>>according to the measuring-stick of the community's
>>affluence, the preacher's popularity, or prejudice towards
>>race or sex.

B: MINISTRY is serving

>—a hand holding a helping spoon at dinner time; a bent back
>scrubbing a shiny floor;

>>an arm outstretched to fold linen or make a bed in a
>>strike-bound home for elderly people who cannot serve
>>themselves.

C: MINISTRY is worship in the new

>—for a growing some, in the words and shapes of now with the
>new songs of new people;

>>celebrating new life: with movement and dance in
>>unexpected places at unconventional times

>—sharing laughter and distress, standing or seated,
>opposite one another briefly

>—before returning their ministry to home, to market-
>place, to office and factory and school, and all the
>meeting-places of community and world.

*(Written by M. Joyce Dickin, taken from EXCHANGE, Spring-Summer Issue, Vol. 1,
No. 3, 1977, pp. 13-14. Included in WWW, Saskatchewan, #4).*

MINUET (OFFERTORY)
by Gwendolyn Richardson

Moderato

(Included in WWW, Alberta, #5, submitted by Beth Tachit.)

MEDITATION

by Gwendolyn Richardson

Organ

Largo

(Pedals)

(Included in WWW, Alberta, #5, submitted by Beth Tachit.)

Section 4

Investigating Women,
Work and Worship

Introduction to Section 4

One of the primary goals of the Women, Work and Worship project was to stimulate research about churchwomen—an area of study that has been virtually ignored in Canada. Realizing that several perspectives would be richer than any single one could be, Women, Work and Worship offered six research grants, hoping to stimulate such investigations.

The response was better than we had anticipated and we finally had to choose from eighteen worthy applicants. The six we decided upon were selected for their relevance to the overall project, for their diversity of subject matter and approach and for their geographical diversity.

The papers range from "conversational" to "scholarly", but each has important information and insights to convey to us. All of the authors are committed, in various ways, to continuing their study of women, work and worship. Their views may not be yours, but they raise valid, and in some cases, disturbing questions for your consideration.

The first three chapters of this section focus on women's place in our tradition. Some of the materials they contain do not compliment the institution of the church. Nevertheless, if we are to understand women's work and worship we must face that tradition head-on, warts and all. To do otherwise would devalue all that our mothers and grandmothers tried to accomplish.

The three authors offer a starting point for *informed* discussion and do not pretend to have easy solutions for the future. There is one thing they would agree upon: whatever our future, it is for certain that it will be grounded in the past. Whether we choose the strands that have liberated, or the strands that have oppressed, will depend in large part on how well we have heard and understood our collective story.

The fourth chapter, "Liberating Christianity", reflects upon traditional male-centred theologies and suggests that just as Christianity liberates us, so can we help liberate Christianity from its perverse patriarchal chains. The church has yet to be established—"what we love we yet shall be"—and *all* Christians must participate in that process if the whole body of Christ would be restored.

The fifth paper considers the role of the minister's wife—a role that has become increasingly complex, as women make lives for themselves outside the home.

The final paper by Marion Pardy brings the Women, Work and Worship project full circle, for it was at Ruth Tillman's funeral that the idea for a book about women in The United Church of Canada was born. Although this paper is about a particular person, we would like it to stand as a tribute to the thousands of women whose ministries in and out of the church has shaped all of us. This book, and this project, is for and about them all.

169

Chapter 8   WOMEN AND POWER IN THE UNITED CHURCH OF CANADA

Shelagh Parsons

SUMMARY

• *At the time of church union in 1925, the church (as was society) was filled with fears about the nature of woman. Church union, with its commitment to "unity with diversity" was to have enormous impact on women's position. Even so, the change from a powerless auxiliary position to one of participation has not been without struggle, nor is it complete.*

The exclusion of women from positions of power within the church has historical and ecclesiastical roots; theology formulated by the early church fathers portrayed women as perpetrators of sin and irrationality, defective males whose sole purpose was procreation. In the late nineteenth and early twentieth centuries, women began to fight some of those attitudes, and thinking about women began to change.

The Woman's Missionary Society (WMS) was the women's organization at the time of church union. In the WMS, women found purpose, a place to grow, and serve. In 1925, the WMS had a million-dollar budget and over 275 women workers doing missionary work overseas and in Canada. In the 1930s, a successor to the Ladies Aid took shape, and in 1940, the Dominion Council Woman's Association (WA) was formed. The difference in the two organizations can be seen by looking at their aim and objectives: the WMS looked to unite all women of the church for the World Mission of Christianity, as well as providing missionary education for children, teenaged girls and young women; the WA saw themselves advancing the "home-building of The United Church of Canada", in a helping relationship to the clergy.

When the WMS and WA amalgamated in 1962 to form the UCW, the immediate effect seemed to be a reduction in women's power, for even though the intent of the amalgamation was to integrate the women into the structures of the church, the financial and other independence of the WMS in particular, was lost; and men continued to out-

number women on church committees and policy groups.

The status of professional women church workers— deaconesses, missionaries, and women clergy has changed throughout the years. Overseas missionary work provided women with professional opportunities unavailable to them at home; women were first certified as doctors because they were prepared to serve abroad or among native people in Canada. Deaconesses were not officially members of presbytery or of the order of ministry until 1964. Although there was some feeling that the training and ministry of the deaconess was inferior to that of the ordained clergy, at the same time, the place within the structure did provide the potential for a greater say within the policy-making bodies of the church.

The struggle over the ordination of women to the ministry of word and sacrament provides another view of women's changing power within the church. Lydia Gruchy's ordination in 1936, after eight years of debate, did not come easily. Although by 1948, fifteen women had been ordained, placements within the congregation were difficult to find. Indeed, the official structures of the church made it even more difficult. At the 1962 General Council, for example, a recommendation was passed which suggested that young married women should not be ordained, and that married women who were pregnant or with young families should be suspended from function until their family responsibilities had been fulfilled. It is interesting to note that those recommendations have not been followed by church leadership!

The struggles for women to take their place within the power structure of the United Church are not over. The UCW does not have the independence of the former WMS, and it has become clear that integration has not dealt adequately with the question of equality in the courts of the church. Integration of deaconesses into the courts of the church has meant a decline in the number of candidates for the diaconal ministry. At the same time, it is being recognized that training for the ordained ministry has little emphasis on Christian education, expecially that of children and youth, or on outreach and mission work. Feminist theology has challenged seminaries and the church at large to begin the process of changing patriarchal attitudes. Although The United Church of Canada has come far in raising the status of women, it still has a long way to go. Respect for diversity cannot be an excuse for tolerating unjust and discriminating attitudes.

—editor

In 1925, women of The United Church of Canada, like all women of the day, lived in a society filled with cultural and historical fears about the nature of woman. The United Church structure reflected these fears, as did the theology inherited from Presbyterianism, Methodism, and Congregationalism. In their relation to both administration and clergy, women were auxiliary to the church courts; decision-making was in the hands of men, except for a few exceptions at the local level. Clergy leadership was entirely male and, as far as can be ascertained, founded on conservative theological positions (such as Thomas Aquinas and St. Augustine) which held the female to be inferior in the order of creation. There were signs of change and a growing strength in the women's auxiliary organizations, but overall, women were powerless in any structural sense.

From its beginning, the guiding principle of The United Church of Canada has been "unity with diversity". At its inauguration ceremony, the church was identified as a "united and uniting church". The biblical focus of the service was Paul's letter to the Ephesians, with specific reference to the "one body with many parts"; this scripture has continued to punctuate significant occasions in church history. The commitment of The United Church of Canada to "unity with diversity" has given rise to two significant tendencies which affect women and their church role. One is an emphasis on dialogue among persons holding different positions and attitudes. The process of dialogue was necessary to church unity, and this way of communicating became the ideal, a switch from more dogmatic and hierarchical ways of doing things. The second has been a tendency for attitudes and beliefs to become more and more individualized. Instead of being identified by narrow and exclusive credal statements, the uniting church focussed on a structure flexible enough to involve its diverse people.

The potential of the "new" church to accommodate a variety of attitudes was to have enormous impact on women's position. Static positions of the past could be challenged because the emphasis was on structure rather than on a uniformity in beliefs and attitudes. Such an emphasis provided women with an opportunity to alter their socially and ecclesiastically prescribed position of structural powerlessness. It also presented opportunities for communication between the sexes and provided a more inclusive setting than previous institutions had allowed.

Women may have influenced this initial development. Challenges were already being made to the traditional concept of the order of creation while union talks were taking place. A few women were fighting for suffrage in the political realm and some lone pioneers, like Sarah Grimke and Elizabeth Cady Stanton, had dared to challenge the notice that women could not interpret the Bible. The Woman's Missionary Societies were growing in strength and demonstrating their competence in overseas mission work. Inroads made by individual women and women's organizations must have had a subtle impact on the quest for unity among the Protestant churches.

Although the principle of "unity with diversity" made change possible, the changes in women's ecclesiastical and administrative status have not occurred without struggle, nor are they complete. Women's roles in the church, whether individual or collective, have moved from the powerless auxiliary position created by historical and cultural fears to a participatory position battling discriminating attitudes. The attempt by women to alter what Rosemary Reuther identifies as "cultural, political and psychological"[1] has only begun.

Attitudes Inherited from Christian History and Tradition

There was once a gospel according to Mary Magdalene which portrays Mary as a disciple of Jesus; it was excluded from the canon as gnostic material in the early years of the Christian Church. There were also women saints. St. Lioba, for example, was a skilled classicist who was "learned not only in Holy Scripture but in the works of the Church Fathers, in canon law and in the decisions of all the Councils."[2] Although her disciples spread throughout the Church of Germany, we hear and know little about her today. In the mid-1370s, St. Catherine of Sienna was instrumental in attempts to return Pope Gregory XI to Rome from his exile in Avignon. She saw this as a necessary step in the reform of the church. "Catherine's work as ambassador, negotiator and reformer is fully recorded in many letters."[3] Yet few persons in church circles would know either her name or St. Lioba's, for they were not deemed as important as St. Augustine, St. Jerome, or St. Thomas.

Christian history has been selective. Patriarchal structures and attitudes put a high premium on male roles and writings, and tended to discount women's contribution to the church. As a result, the history and theology that is our heritage represents male thought and male interpretation. Women, too, have been defined in patriarchal terms and that definition has clouded their understanding of their own nature, their social roles, and their religious experience.

Anthropologists and psychologists suggest that patriarchy is rooted in misogyny—a hatred of women. This hatred is based on fear: fear of women's creative power; fear, retained from infancy, of the omnipotence of the mother; fear of being found lacking as a man, whether in the husband or son relation; and fear of women's ability to form a society exclusive of men. Patriarchy is reflected in Old Testament references to the God of Abraham, Isaac, Jacob, and is reinforced by the interpretation which holds Eve responsible for the "fall". It is also demonstrated in such

173

New Testament passages as 1 Timothy 2: 9-15, 1 Corinthians 11: 4-12. Recent scholarship depicts Jesus as empowering women and challenges interpretations that woman's inferior status is divinely ordained. Yet this remains an important and debatable point for Christians.[4]

The Fathers of the Church continued the view that women are inferior and warrant little or no status in church and community. Accounts of women who had been active in the early Pauline church were removed from official "histories" or denounced as questionable, perhaps in an attempt to legitimate the Christian church by appealing to past Judaic tradition. St. Augustine attributed evil to woman, because he thought she caused the irrational movement of the male member.[5] He equated irrationality with sin, and rationality with divine qualities, and argued that since women made men irrational, they were the perpetrators of sin and also the embodiment of irrationality. The male was rational and divinely oriented while women were of the lower nature, irrational and of the flesh. Jerome held out a fragment of hope for women. He maintained that women, through the mystical life, could transcend their fleshy nature. Virtue was attained by being like men, and denigration of the physical appearance was encouraged to do away with any physical attractiveness. Manly courage and conduct were emphasized.[6] A third perspective is reflected in St. Thomas' anthropology. To him, women's sole purpose was procreation. As a follower of Aristotle he believed that all infants were destined to be males but, through accident or injury during conception or gestation, became female. Thus women were defined as defective males. St. Thomas concluded that the only purpose for this defective male was reproduction because in all other ways— friendship, help, intelligence—men were more suitable.[7] Such patriarchal attitudes are deeply embedded in our thinking. Beliefs of female inferiority, the need to have men in control, and the identification of women with flesh, seduction, and evil are still prominent in imagery, myth, and symbols today.

In the late 1800s and early twentieth century, women began to actively refute some of these misogynistic descriptions of themselves. Women's suffrage movements were organized, and as part of the same phenomenon, women sought to participate in the world through foreign mission societies. In doing so they began defining who they were in terms of their own qualities and experiences. Women in the church, although still relegated to an auxiliary position, had discovered and exercised their personal and collective power through their own organizations and activity. Past definitions and attitudes about what women were and were not capable of began to change.

Woman's Missionary Society and Women's Auxiliary

The Woman's Missionary Societies (WMS) were the women's organizations at the time of union in 1925. It was through them—Congregationalist, Presbyterian and Methodist—that women made their contribution. In them, they found purpose, a place to grow and learn, and developed leadership skills. As Genevieve Carder, former deputy secretary of the Division of Mission in Canada, said in an interview, "Many women, like my mother, seemed to live vicariously through the missionaries for whom they were responsible."[8]

Missionary Society women began to glimpse a vision of what they might accomplish. Their statement to General Council in 1926, on the occasion of the union of the three Societies, shows a burgeoning confidence in their own value, strength and potential.

> We believe it a matter worthy of record to state that this too, was a memorable occasion, second only in importance to the event of June 10, 1925, and the first meeting of the General Council.[9]

The united societies had a million-dollar operating budget and over 275 women workers doing missionary work overseas and in Canada. Jean Forbes, one of these women, captures the spirit of this movement in *Open Windows*, a book she wrote about the WMS. "They bravely did things that had never been done before by means that had never been tried and they did not fail."[10]

References to men and male assistance suggests that there was some male support, but there was also fear that the women's organizations were threatening the established order.

> *The church authorities of 1881 were far-seeing statesmen when they gave to the new society sole responsibility for work under its care. Responsibility created ability, stimulated prayer, gave wings to faith and generated enthusiasm.*[11]

The women, however, did not see themselves as anti-establishment, nor did they wish to claim the movement as such.

> *The Woman's Missionary Society in each of the denominations was created, not to give women a more prominent place in church, nor to promote women's cause, but to meet the need of the church for women's cooperation in the great missionary enterprise."*[12]

Although the societies saw themselves as auxiliary, at some level they must have had a sense of what was occurring. In *Open Windows*, Jean Forbes uses the Lake Louise scene as a metaphor for the Woman's Missionary movement and its relation to the rest of the world.

> *There before us lies the little lake whose waters run the gamut of many colours—blue, green, amethyst, gold and grey—and in the still surface is mirrored the great age-old Victoria Glacier five-and one-half miles away and heavy with its shining embankments of snow and ice, many of*

175

them two hundred feet deep. On either side, the mountains stand like guardian sentinels, watching each other's shadows reflected on the bosom of the lake and pointing with patriarchal fingers upward to the heavens as if to emphasize their supreme infinity.[13]

Then Forbes goes on to describe the WMS members as "good mountain climbers pressing on to achieve their high purpose to make Christ known."[14] By referring to mountains as patriarchal fingers, and the women as mountain climbers, we can see only too clearly the change that was occurring.

Hazel Hefren, in her historical thesis, describes the WMS as matriarchal. "The Society took a great deal of responsibility for the missionaries in a matriarchal way."[15] An interview with Dr. Beatrice Wilson also suggests the WMS was hierarchical and protective. Although it grew in independence and self-definition, the women generally maintained a dependency on structure and authority. It was, however, a structure created by women, supported by women, and administered by women.

A second women's organization took shape in the 1930s as a successor to the "Ladies Aids". Its concerns were focussed locally and its purpose reflected the current social view that woman's proper role was that of wife and mother. The national organization, called the Dominion Council Woman's Association (WA), was formed November 19, 1940. Initially they reported on efforts to furnish manses and provided information in this regard to other groups. Then war-related activities: sewing, knitting, hostessing, and assembling parcels for overseas shipment occupied the organization for several years. The study essential to the WMS was less apparent than the "doing" of the local WA.

The male clergy were overwhelmingly supportive of the new organization, an attitude which was not present in responses to the WMS. Following is the Moderator's reply to the WA report in 1940:

> *We express to her, and through her, to the Association, the supreme satisfaction of the General Council of our church for the report which has been so ably presented. We rejoice in the splendid and sacrificial work of the women of the Dominion, represented through this organization of our church. Every minister's work is sustained and strengthened by the educational, spiritual and especially social maintenance of the church life by the local association. Today, they not only continue these phases of our work, but have taken on the enormous burden of knitting and sewing for war purposes. The tremendous output of finished materials was presented to us in the War Service Report.*[16]

Such accolades, deserved as they were by the WA, were *not* given to the WMS for the tremendous amount of work *they* were doing overseas and in their home missions. In fact we find the WMS asking for assurance of continuing support.

The difference in the two organizations can be seen in their aims and objectives.

Woman's Missionary Society: Aims and Objectives:

> To unite all the women of the church for the World Mission of Christianity.
>
> To provide missionary education for children, teenaged girls, and young women.
>
> To encourage study, prayer, and giving on behalf of Christian Missions at home and abroad.
>
> To share in sending the Gospel and Jesus to every Canadian and to peoples of other lands.
>
> To bring healing and education to those in need.
>
> To aid in the development of the Christian Church in Canada and of the world-wide church of Jesus Christ.
>
> To create bonds of Christian friendship between its members and peoples of other races and other lands.
>
> To enlist the whole membership in united effort for temperance, social welfare and world peace.
>
> To build a fellowship committed to the doing of God's will and to the extension of God's kingdom in the home.[17]

Woman's Association: Aims and Objectives:

> To administer and govern all matters of general policy for advancement, spiritually, educationally, socially and financially of "The Woman's Association" in the home-building of The United Church of Canada.
>
> a) Spiritually—by knowing God and practising his presence. In following always the best guidebook, the Bible, in which are well-defined rules for our guidance and obedience to him, will bring us to our desired goal, supreme love for God and love for our neighbours as ourselves.
>
> b) Educationally—by making a study of the relationship of the Woman's Association to the church, the home, the school, the community and the nation.
>
> c) Socially—by being a friend to all—helping the weak, feeding the hungry, clothing the needy, visiting the sick and, in every possible way, by word or deed, giving encouragement and help to those less fortunate than ourselves.
>
> d) Financially—by the voluntary systematic way of giving or raising of money through individual and group effort. Let

> us always, when planning a program of financial activity,
> be sure it is in keeping with the ideal life of our church.
>
> To give information, to prepare and forward literature
> pertaining to WA work to any Woman's Association of the
> United Church.
>
> a) Information—how to furnish the parsonage...list of
> furnishings.
>
> b) Literature—the following literature has been carefully
> compiled by our women...a devotional folder with creed,
> theme song, constitution and history.
>
> To receive and prepare Association report.
>
> a) Statistics on size, money raised...
>
> b) Women's page in The United Church Observer...
>
> To promote Woman's Associations in congregations...[18]

The WMS clearly had a world vision and mission that was independent of the United Church structure. Their service, defined by the teachings of Jesus, was active—quite different from the passive stance of obedience taken by the WA. The WMS saw itself as an organization with an evangelistic mandate of its own, while the WA saw its members in a helping relationship to the clergy. The two organizations also differed in their financial relation to the church. The WMS raised funds for the wider arena of mission work and were the sole decision-makers when it came to the allocation of those funds; WA monies supported the local church but were generally turned over to finance committees for dispersal. The organizations reflected two different understandings of women's role in both church and society: the one independent and aggressive in world mission, the other serving, sacrificing and passive on the home-front.

At the congregational level, many women belonged to both organizations and shared in both identities, so the amalgamation and integration that took place in 1962 was not as dramatic a change locally as it was nationally. The independent action of the WMS, the decision-making and controls, were absorbed into the new structure. Since the amalgamation took place at the same time as integration into church structures, it is difficult to determine the results of the merging of the two different self-concepts. Structurally, at least at the national level, women ceased to be auxiliary. Their intended involvement on the various division committees was a step toward a new relationship, and the tension between the two women's groups was either minimized or redirected toward the struggle of being part of the total church.

Integration was initiated according to the principle of "unity with diversity", but there seem to have been other motivations as well. A growing awareness of the power of the independent WMS and of the financial indispensability of the WA in many churches quite likely spawned a desire in the patriarchal church for some control over this work. (Similar co-optations of powerful women's organizations had occurred in American Presbyterian and Methodist Churches.) Although the integration agreement allowing for equal representation of men and women, lay and clergy, reflected a movement away from hierarchical government, it reintroduced the potential for inferior female status.

At the congregational level, the women's organizations began to decline. Many women felt that they no longer had a say in mission and education. Communication in these areas, and the matter of local responsibility, were confused. Women workers and missionaries, no longer connected with local groups, lost personal and sometimes financial support. The immediate effect of the structural change, therefore, seemed negative in terms of women's power. Regardless of the official equality granted with integration, women were not *actually* integrated into the structure. Equal representation may have been the ideal but on most committees, women continued to be well out-numbered by men.

Those who sat on the integrated committees: women such as Dr. Beatrice Wilson and Genevieve Carder—were aware that they were breaking new ground. Both Wilson and Carder have stated that they felt pressured by negative stereotypes which portrayed women as irrational, emotional, and without substance. They were quite conscious of their battle to be recognized by predominantly male courts and committees whose membership may well have been nurtured on Jerome's views that women, now part of the governing body, could only achieve *spiritual* equality if they became like men.

Deaconesses, Missionaries, Women Church Workers, and Women Clergy

The roles of deaconesses, missionaries, women church workers, and women clergy also reflect changes in women's status. The training for most missionaries and deaconesses was through the United Church Training School (later to be called Covenant College and then the Centre for Christian Studies). This was not true of women clergy who studied at seminaries with men. Women at the Training School had a variety of educational and occupational backgrounds: nursing, teaching, social, and secretarial work. The live-in setting, with varied courses of study prepared women to serve in social and educational spheres both at home and abroad. Women clergy, on the other hand, had a traditional seminary education with much stronger emphasis on biblical, theological, and historical studies and on the liturgical practices of church life.

Missionaries

Missionaries employed by the WMS had learned, through many years of experience prior to integration, their own capabilities and worth. They had developed support systems to strengthen each other, and the school provided them with the needed skills. Independence from the church courts in the early years had created some tension. In 1930, for example, it is recorded that "the relevant sections of the Basis of Union and of the

Manual defining the duties of the Board of Home Missions and of the Presbytery in relation to Home Mission work and workers do not necessarily include the work and workers of the WMS."[19] After discussion about the need of supervision, the church proposed that WMS work would be within the bounds of presbytery and administered by the Home Mission Committee. This proposal was rejected by the WMS which recommended a reciprocal agreement by which the WMS would continue to direct the work, and that two members would sit on the Home Mission Committee and be corresponding members, along with the Chairman of Home Missions, of the Presbyterial and Conference Branch Executive. Whether or not this full proposal was accepted is unclear. However, the motion was passed that the work be directed within the bounds of presbytery and this would be accomplished by two WMS representatives in the Home Mission Committee. Such negotiation and reluctance to relinquish their control indicates a sense of self-worth and power previously unknown in women's church organizations.

Overseas missionary work provided women with professional opportunities unavailable to them at home. Women were first certified as doctors because they were prepared to serve abroad or among native people and it was on this basis that they were accepted into the Medical Association. There were also opportunities in religious and educational work. Marion Niven, acting principal of the Centre for Christian Studies until June 1982, notes that "the missionaries were allowed to do many things that would never have been tolerated here." As missionaries returned and began filling in for clergy in isolated charges, initiating new missions in difficult areas, they repeatedly proved themselves capable as effective workers for the church.

Deaconesses

Deaconesses saw themselves in a role very different from that of missionaries. Rather than emphasizing evangelistic mission, they wished to serve the needs of people through charity and social aid. There was more emphasis on the imitation of Christ than on converting the heathen; obedience to the order and self-negation as part of the vocational call were more prominent than in the missionary role.

Methodist and Presbyterian deaconesses carried vestiges of the monastic celibate tradition and, unlike male clergy, Presbyterian deaconesses were actually required to take a vow of virginity. This reflected an attitude in the church that a woman must denounce her own sexuality to function in the religious sphere. Even the prescribed dress negated her femininity, reinforcing the Jerome teaching that a woman must be manlike to be spiritual. Women's growing emancipation certainly affected the deaconess movement, and the change was reflected in the continuing controversy over the uniform which was originally designed to hide the flesh. Through the years it was modified until it became optional and, finally, the decision was made that a pin would be designed and worn as a means of identification. This process symbolized an evolving perception among deaconesses that they were women in community with other women, and that the old posture of self-effacement was no longer relevant to their ministry.

The Deaconess Order remained in an auxiliary position until 1964 and, although its members were involved in the work of the church, they were not officially members of presbytery until that time. Then, not only were they given access to the courts of the church, but they were identified as members of the order of ministry. This change in status gave rise to conflict. Many deaconesses understood their role in terms of lay ministry and rejected the elevated status which identified their interests with those of clergy. As well, other women preferred a style of leadership which was non-hierarchical and rejected the association with clergy on that basis.

Simultaneous with the change in the structural status of deaconesses was the growing sense that both their training and ministry were perceived as inferior to that of ordained clergy. Such attitudes made it difficult for many to accept deaconesses as equals in the courts of the church. As discrimination on the grounds of gender became less socially acceptable, the focus shifted to educational and vocational elitism.

> The Deaconess Order provides an opportunity for women who may not be prepared to assume the binding life-long obligation of the ministry in Word and Sacrament or may find it difficult to devote the long period of six or seven years preparation for entrance upon it. The church has allowed this important order of the ministry to suffer neglect. The candidates are trained at a special school and its members can fulfill a wide variety of ministry as missionaries, nurses, social workers, directors of religious education, congregational assistants and institutional chaplaincies. [20]

The second-string status in the order of ministry effectively nullified any power gained by the new structural position of the diaconate. However, the place in the structure *did* provide an arena for dialogue and potential for a stronger voice in the policy-making bodies of the church, and these factors necessarily changed the way a deaconess saw herself. Prior to her inclusion in the courts of the church, she went out prepared to prove herself, not expecting to be considered the equal of an ordained minister. Shelley Finson, now teaching at the Centre for Christian Studies, says of the early '60s, "It was clear you were prepared to assist the minister in a congregation." In the new understanding of her role the deaconess went out prepared to team with, not assist.

Some deaconesses did feel accepted and equal and found support in Presbytery. Others, however, felt excluded because of innuendos about their educational and vocational inferiority. Conflict between the two points of view grew as younger students of the Centre for Christian

Studies began taking their place, *assuming* equality in the courts and prepared to do battle with those who would discriminate against them.

Women Church Workers

The Fellowship of Professional Women Workers was established in 1939. Membership was a mixture of missionaries and deaconesses, as well as lay women employed in congregations. This organization helped to support workers throughout the country by providing social and education opportunities. It also provided an arena in which the concerns of church workers could be aired, as well as a collective voice which could address the courts of the church, of which they were not a part. When deaconesses were admitted to the order of ministry, the organization began to decline.

The association did continue on to merge, eventually, with the Deaconess organization in 1963, forming the Fellowship of Deaconesses and other Women Workers. Then, anticipating a union of the Anglican and United Churches, the Anglican Training School and Covenant College joined to become the Centre for Christian Studies. Consequently, the Fellowship became the Association of Professional Church Workers and included Anglican women in its membership. Since 1964, the organization has been struggling to establish a purpose. Some members withdrew, finding their support in the courts of the church; others remained for the fellowship with women. Splinter groups have focussed on women's issues, but the Association, as a whole, remains unsure of its collective identity.

Inter-Board Committee of Women Workers

The Inter-Board Committee of Women Workers was established in 1928 to recruit women workers for the United Church, to promote the employment of trained women workers, and to initiate and maintain standards for training. The committee was also concerned with salaries and benefits. To some extent deaconesses were connected with this organization but, because they were already affiliated with the WMS, it was unclear whom the board actually served. In 1936, the committee became the official representative body of the Deaconess Order and its name was changed to The Committee on the Deaconess Order and Women Workers.

The new committee required a full-time secretary with a permanent office and in 1938 the Rev. Lydia Gruchy, the first woman ordained in the United Church, was appointed to the position: $2,000 of her $3,000 salary was solicited from the women's organizations, demonstrating their direct link at that time with the women workers. The board mediated between the auxiliary women workers and church structure and took on an advocacy role. It was discontinued when women workers and women's organizations were integrated into the general church structure.

Women Clergy

The struggle over the ordination of women to the ministry of word and sacrament provides another view of women's changing power in the church. This challenge did not come from women, however; in fact, many actively opposed Lydia Gruchy's several applications. Men, rather, advocated the ordination of women—men such as Dr. H. Oliver, principal of St. Andrew's College, and Dr. Pidgeon, the first Moderator of the United Church. Dr. Beatrice Wilson thought that "the credit really due Lydia Gruchy was that she allowed herself to be used for what, essentially, was a just cause."[21]

The introduction to Gruchy's ordination service, which took place in 1936 after eight years of debate, demonstrates that her victory was greeted with mixed emotions at best.

> We have come tonight to mark a step in our church's history—a development which we owe, not to the intransigent demand and agitation of women, but in the first instance, perhaps to our revered and affectionately esteemed Dr. E. H. Oliver. His knightly and chivalrous attitude and advocacy have finally prevailed.[22]

In the speaker's view, woman's proper role was passive and non-agitating. Because Gruchy had "allowed herself to be used" for the greater cause, and had not made demands on her own behalf, many were convinced that she was exceptional and not representative of women generally.

> There is not the slightest possibility of women ever displacing men in this calling—not that that would be a terrible calamity even if it did come. Those who urge this change in our polity do so, no doubt, with the thought that it would only be in most unusual cases, something like Miss Gruchy's, that ordination would ever be asked for or thought of and that the dangers that some people see are never likely to exist anywhere else than in their own imaginations.[23]

Although the ordination changed woman's status in the church, it did not alter discriminatory views. The "unity with diversity" principle also accommodated beliefs in natural inferiority and superiority.

The move to accept women into the clergy may have resulted from the growing strength of the WMS. Women were *not* demanding recognition in the structures of the United Church because they had their own strong organization which was expanding and employing able, well-educated women. Their success was causing anxiety among some of the men. There was no male control over the organization, and prejudice about female administrative compentence, or the lack of it, were being challenged. Principal H. A. Kent articulates this concern in his minority report to the General Council in 1928, against Gruchy's ordination.

> *What the church needs at the present time is not more femininity, but more masculinity. Women's work in the church is carried on with admirable zeal and faithfulness. What are men doing?*[24]

The grudging acceptance of Lydia Gruchy to the ministry of word and sacrament was an accommodation to women's growing strength outside the church structure. But the place created for women within the church emphasized the traditional areas of women's church work—Christian education and nurture—reinforcing past attitudes of woman's natural sphere.

Although by 1948 fifteen women had been ordained, placements were difficult to find. Congregations did not call women ministers. Attitudes about woman's primary vocation as wife and mother put ordained women in a no-win predicament. If married, they were violating either their call to ministry or their commitment to family. There seemed to be an expectation, once again, that ordained women, to be spiritual leaders, must deny their femaleness. The inability to equate them with their male counterparts is obvious.

In 1962, recommendations were put forward which actually suggested that young married women should not be ordained, and that married women who were pregnant or with young families should be suspended from functions until their familial responsibilities had been fulfilled. It was also recommended, in an amendment, that female candiates for ordination should be required to have a physician's medical certificate to indicate their emotional stability. The original recommendation was passed, the amendment was not. A small but significant number asked that their negative votes be recorded.[25]

These recommendations, made at precisely the same time as the women's organizations (WA and WMS) were integrated into the church structure, can be viewed as an attempt to secure the clergy as a male domain, or as an expression of renewed control. They indicate, in either case, that integration was not founded on new attitudes about women. It is interesting that the recommendations were not followed by church leadership in years following. There was a steady increase in women candidates, and a new phenomenon occurred: clergy couples. Clearly there had been a shift in consciousness, especially for women. Ministry and family were no longer mutually exclusive. True partnership in ministry had become a real option in spite of the stereotypes and a not too receptive church.

Policy Statements and Issues Related to Women

Another area in which United Church attitudes can be viewed are the various commissions specifically related to women.

One of the earliest informal policies was the support of education for women. Girls' schools were established across the country by WMS workers, and United Church colleges, such as Victoria, began making efforts to support women in study. Although education was encouraged, it was not the intention to challenge the accepted role of woman. This is evident in an article in the *New Outlook,* June 1925, by Miss E. T. Addison, Dean of Women at Victoria.

> *The education of women is one of the most important and most difficult problems of the day, for women may or may not enter homes of their own, their education may or may not fit them for what ultimately becomes their work, and they have to adapt themselves to ever-changing social order.*[26]

Education was seen to develop a woman, but not alter her basically dependent and adaptive role. In spite of that, higher education resulted in greater self-esteem, skills, and independence, and thus contributed to her emancipation.

The issues of family life and marriage were addressed at various times in the United Church. A report on "The Meaning and Responsibility of Christian Marriage", made to General Council in 1932, is remarkable for its understanding of mutuality in marriage. It refers to past subordination of women and encourages their present emancipation. The report also supports birth control as responsible action, but recommends that it be a decision of individual conscience. Sexual relations are understood as part of the bond, not merely for procreation.[27] Certainly, in 1932, such attitudes were not fully realized in the lives of United Church families; they are, however, an expression of the church's progressive leadership at that time.

There was a similar report in 1946 on "Christian Marriage and Christian Home" which provided an historical and theological rationale. It repudiates St. Augustine and interprets the male/female relation in Genesis as an equal comradeship.[28] The report clearly supported the equality of women and men within the community of the church.

In 1962 a Commission on the Gainful Employment of Married Women presented a unique report. The Commission had done sociological research into the nature and problems of working women and learned that many were sole-support parents earning minimal income. It recommended daycare to aid these mothers. In addition, it made reference to the guilt employed women feel and recommended that the church make an effort to destigmatize the woman working outside the home. The report, with all its emancipated thinking, was passed by the same council that cautioned against the ordination of young, married women!

Another report supported the right of women to make decisions about abortion, although it did not support abortion itself, except in circumstances in which the fetus was abnormal or continued pregnancy endangered the life of the mother. This policy statement, along with the others, demonstrates the United Church's view that women are whole and autonomous persons. The actual practice, of equality, however, has been erratic and inconsistent.

Conclusion:
Effects of the Changes and the Present-day Situation

In 1972 research was done on the United Church Women (WA and WMS amalgamated) to assess the organization, and determine future needs. Membership, in a decline since amalgamation and integration, consisted mostly of married women, aged 45 to 55, who were not employed outside the home.[29] Their role-definition at that time was more in line with the WA's than with WMS. There was a significant increase in the number of women in presbyteries, conferences and General Councils throughout the '70s. Women began to chair committees and assume other leadership roles in church life. It is not surprising that, with many of their potential members involved in leadership elsewhere, the numbers of active United Church Women (UCW) began to dwindle.

The struggles within the UCW have varied. Many of its members feel the organization no longer has the purpose it once had. The independence of the WMS from church structures, for example, had given many a sense of creative power and self-worth without challenging their passive, supportive roles in home and community. The decline of the auxiliary position—separate but equal, in their own view—thrust many back into a dependent status of earlier days. Other avenues within the new structure were not seen as fulfilling. In addition, it soon became clear that the integration had not dealt adequately with the question of equality. Most women had not been trained to fill leadership roles in the wider church, and years of discrimination had made competent women question their own abilities. Then, too, the hierarchical way of doing things was alien to women who, given their own controls, formed circles.

The UCW is now caught like an unemployed worker who has acquired skills that are obsolete. She must retrain for the computer age but doesn't know whether to take hold of her resources and regain her independence, or allow herself to be absorbed and retrained to a role which does not guarantee an equal partnership of deed, word and vision with her male counterpart.

The exodus of men from church, as women replace them on committees and in the courts, is another result of integration. The unity that was intended has not materialized in many cases. Any creative growth in mutuality has been matched by some retrenchment in past discrimination.

The integration of deaconesses and women workers into the courts of the church has resulted in a decline in the number of women presenting themselves for training in those areas. Opportunities in both secular and

186

ordained ministry have held greater attraction. Women, now within the structure, have been invited to prove themselves in the male domain by providing the traditional academic requirements. However, as more women have attended theological colleges they have come to realize that the ministry for which they were being prepared has been, for the most part, male-defined, and has adhered to traditional views of male and female roles. They have found little emphasis on Christian education, especially of children and youth, or on outreach and mission work, areas considered women's domain. The whole church has suffered as women have competed on male terms to gain recognition: important areas of ministry have begun to flounder and men have been unwilling to move into them. In fact, as women have moved into "male" ministries, men have withdrawn in many instances.

The Centre for Christian Studies, having originally come into existence because women were excluded from ministry and auxiliary to the church, has been struggling through the years with a stigma of inferiority. The areas in which it has valuable background and experience— Christian education, social action and outreach—have yet to be recognized by the wider church. The myth that seminary students are prepared as well, or better, in these areas is questionable. *True* integration will see this program of studies accepted as valuable training for areas of ministry that have been neglected.

Deaconesses (later called commissioned or diaconal ministers) are, like the UCW, trying to find their way in the structures of the church. A recent consultation (February 1982) focussed again on their need to be recognized as having a ministry that is valid in its own terms. A slide presentation called "Waiting as Fast as We Can" identifies the valuable contribution of women in this form of ministry, and the need for its continuation. The title adequately identifies the dilemma. The greatest concerns are the perceived inferiority of education and the inability, except by special permission, to perform sacramental rites. Resolution of these problems in favour of those in diaconal ministry may alter the status of the diaconate, but not the underlying discrimination experienced by many women clergy, regardless of their educational qualifications.

Feminist theology has challenged seminaries and the church at large to begin the long process of identifying and changing deep-rooted patriarchal attitudes. Now that they *have* secured a place in the structure, it is time for women to name their own experience, contributing women's insights to shape theology in new ways. It is also time to rid ourselves and society of attitudes and structures that have resulted in a culture exclusive of women's power and influence.

The policies of The United Church of Canada have been visionary and liberating but it is only in their implementation that the church can grow. Internal conflict remains. The policy on the gainful employment of women, passed at the same council as the regressive policies on women ministers, is only one example. The willingness to ordain women, yet the failure to call them, is another. It would appear that the church has failed to educate its people in either its policy and positions or in a theology of equality of women and men.

The Task Force on Sexism is a response to this failure. Its mission is the raising to consciousness in women and men some understanding of the profound divisions between them. It is an attempt to reveal the roots of patriarchy and encourage value changes that will liberate *all* humans. This "freeing" involves a struggle with beliefs and an openness to new theologies. Initially, the Task Force floundered. Leaders believed the best way to handle concerns about sexism was to bring people with diverse beliefs together in dialogue. Awareness began to grow that this was an issue of *justice* and that accommodation to conflicting views was not always possible or desirable.

The United Church of Canada is still in transition and, although there are groups struggling to find an identity within the changes, it has come far in raising the status of women generally. But it still has a long way to go. Along the way it must face its investment in the principle of "unity with diversity". Respect for diversity cannot be an excuse to tolerate unjust and discriminating attitudes. It remains to be seen whether the United Church can respond to this challenge.

Shelagh Parsons

> *Shelagh spent many years as a commissioned minister in The United Church of Canada before being ordained this past year. She is currently working in a team ministry in Edmonton, Alberta.*

Chapter 9

CHRISTIAN FEMINISM IN THE UNITED CHURCH: RESOURCES IN CULTURE AND TRADITION

Randi R. Warne

SUMMARY

- *Christian feminism today presents an almost bewilder ing range of options, from the call to preach to an emphasis on motherhood and maternal values. Feminists differ in how women's problems are defined and solved, but stand united in their rejection of patriarchal conservatism which says that men and women are fundamentally different because of their biological nature and that power and work should be divided accordingly. Women are defined by their capacity to reproduce and are inferior to men.*

  Feminists have reacted to the patriarchal conservative position in a number of ways. Maternal or conservative feminism believes that if women are truly mothers of the race, the world needs women's nurturing influence. Indeed, the structures of power can be transformed by the presence of women within them. Separatist feminism is an extreme position which contends that the differences between the sexes is absolute, and any relationship with men would simply make patriarchal power permanent. Liberal feminists believe that behavioural differences between men and women are caused by social conditioning because men and women are essentially the same. Most believe that motherhood is a service only women can provide, but that responsibility for raising children belongs to both men and women. Marxist feminism says that the division of the world into the public (male) and the private (female) spheres is the direct result of unequal property relations within a capitalist system. When the notion of private property was established, it became important for men to have sons, so that wealth could be passed on. Women became reduced to chattels, their reproductive capacity an important commodity to be both guarded and controlled.

  Radical feminism is perhaps the most misunderstood theory because of its belligerent image. It affirms the view that women's position is biologically determined. Because women can bear children, they have been physically dependent on men who have used this position to exclude them from positions of cultural power and influence. Radical feminists consider that male domination weakens both sexes and the primary objective to be the redistribution of power in all human relationships.

Feminists today have discovered that they have a heritage in women who worked together to bring forth a new vision of humanity. In the nineteenth century, women were seen on the one hand as immoral, untrustworthy, physically frail, and mentally deficient; and on the other as asexual and unworldly, guardians of morality and shining beacons of selfless Christian love.

One of the most influential movements for moral reform was the Woman's Christian Temperance Movement (WCTU), founded in 1873 and led by Frances Willard. The WCTU urged people to give up alcohol and nicotine and adopt a healthy lifestyle. Concern for the next generation led to positions on birth control and divorce that were quite radical for the time. The WCTU and the YWCA became important in the emergence of the Social Gospel movement, as middle-class Christian women worked in slums caused by urbanization and immigration.

Nellie McClung constantly rebutted criticisms of women's activism in the late nineteenth and early twentieth century. McClung believed that social transformation required structural transformation: this meant both suffrage and women's ordination. As long as women could exercise influence only indirectly, the world, as well as the church, would continue to meet men's needs and speak to men's concerns. Part of the structural transformation was to be direct political action, something impossible at that time because women were not yet "persons" and lacked the vote.

McClung's feminism was not well received by the church which continually failed to extend the promise of equality to women, even though by doing so, it was directly departing from Christ's teachings. In addition, the church limited its effectiveness in refusing to draw on one-half of its resources. McClung offered many suggestions about overcoming inequality. In addition to legal change, she supported women's access to all professions. She encouraged marriage, but felt that marriage itself had to change.

For the Christian feminist, the patriarchal conservatism of traditional Christianity is unacceptable. Separatism is likewise unacceptable, as is the Marxist analysis. Liberal

190

feminism allows participation, but uses power to increase women's access to existing systems rather than changing the system itself. Although maternal feminism is attractive, the "special nature" view of women fails to acknowledge the extent to which all experiences have been influenced by the male-dominated culture.

The greatest resource for the development of a transforming and enduring Christian feminism lies in the radical feminist option which calls for a change in perception and rehabilitation, so that God's original intention of cooperation and equality is restored. Those convinced of the revolution of thought required by radical feminism should be encouraged by the example of Nellie McClung.

—editor

The woman's movement, which has been scoffed and jeered at and misunderstood most of all by the people whom it is destined to help, is a spiritual revival of the best instincts of womanhood—the instinct to serve and save the race.

Nellie McClung
In Times Like These, p. 66

The emergence of Christian feminism is a development of vital importance for the United Church. Yet, according to Patricia Clarke's article in *The United Church Observer,* March 1981.[1] Christian feminism presents an almost bewildering range of options, from the "call to preach" to an emphasis on motherhood and maternal values last seen in Victorian times. Such diversity is characteristic of the energy and excitement of the Christian feminist movement and reflects the openness to new perspectives which is one of the United Church's traditional strengths. At the same time, it emphasizes the need for systematic clarification and reflection.

Such reflection is absolutely necessary if the insights of Christian feminism are to endure. Analysis can channel energy towards achievable goals, while reflection can offset the tendency to repeat the errors of the past, and allow us to build upon prior accomplishments. How crucial this is can be seen by an overview of Christian feminism itself. Although this form of women's activism is usually considered to be relatively new, it dates at least from the middle of the last century. It seems that Christian feminists have been "afflicting the comfortable" for generations!

No less important is the clarification of Christian feminism for non-feminists. Like any other political label, "feminism" is a loaded term, carrying with it images that are neither flattering nor accurate. I suspect that many who reject feminism out of hand may be surprised to discover how many of their own concerns are addressed. Even where differences remain irreconcilable, it is still preferable to recognize them for what they are, rather than to construct demonic versions of what they might be.

I. RESOURCES IN CULTURE: FEMINIST FRAMEWORKS[2]

Feminists differ in their assessments of the causes and solutions to the problem of women's lot. They stand united, however, in their rejection of patriarchal conservatism, the position which has prevailed in western culture for millenia. The *patriarchal conservative* believes that men and women are fundamentally different by nature, because of the difference in their biological function. Women are defined by their capacity to reproduce, regardless of any other talents or aspirations they may possess: they are born to be mothers. A properly ordered society recognizes this fact and divides its labour accordingly.[3]

Patriarchal conservatives maintain that male and female spheres of activity can be seen as "separate but equal". More often, however, women's work is seen to be more limited and inferior to men's. Here again biology is the culprit, and a great deal of energy is spent scientifically "proving" women's diminished capacity for abstraction, higher mathematics, spatial relations, and so on. Whether or not these qualities are important or desirable is not questioned, nor is the possible role played by male bias or social conditioning in determining women's performance on these tests.

To the patriarchal conservative, women are either different from, or inferior to men. History becomes the story of men's achievements, for women's role has not been achievement, but reproduction.[4]

Feminist Stances

Feminists have reacted in a number of ways to the patriarchal conservative position outlined above.

Maternal or *conservative feminism* agrees with patriarchal conservatism that fundamental differences between the sexes exist, and that they are biologically based. It disagrees, however, with the traditional limitation of women's place in society. Conservative feminists believe that if women are truly mothers of the race, with all the 'maternal' virtues of compassion, nurture, and self-sacrifice, then the present condition of the world demands the immediate application of women's purifying influence in the public sphere. As mothers, women have a duty to make the world safe for their children.

Men are considered to be what they have always defined themselves: warriors, thinkers, hunters, competitors, and rulers. What maternal feminists question is the worth of these qualities in creating a human world. Liberation means expanding women's influence to offset the destructiveness caused by men, either through direct participation in the structures of government, or through the development of parallel organizations with women's particular interests in mind.

Maternal feminism embodies what is called a "special nature" view of women. Biological difference is given a spiritual dimension: some maternal feminists believe that the structures of power can be transformed by the mere presence of women within them. Maternal feminism was an extremely influential viewpoint at the turn of the century, and gave shape to the Canadian movements for both temperance and suffrage.

In its most extreme form, the "special nature" view of women can lead

193

to a separatist option. *Separatist feminism* contends that the differences between the sexes are not only fundamental, but absolute. The male-dominated world is judged harshly as a violent, corrupt, and exploitative creation, an inevitable product of men's insatiable lust for self-aggrandizement and power.[5] Separatist feminists believe maternal feminists are naive to assume this essential male bloodlust can be reformed through women's positive influence. Rather, any relationship with men, whether social or physical, is seen as perpetuating the power of a patriarchy bent on the destruction of women and the world. Any group capable of developing nuclear weapons that protect buildings and annihilate people is, in this view, not only deranged, but utterly irredeemable.

Believing men will probably destroy the world in this generation, separatists tend not to give much thought to the future propagation of the race. Some attention is paid, however, to scientific and technical means of reproduction such as *in vitro* fertilization and cloning, with parthenogenesis (egg-based reproduction without sperm) considered a future possibility.[6]

Liberal feminism rejects "separate spheres" no matter how they are interpreted. The individual is to be evaluated solely in terms of her/his own worth, independent of any pre-defined roles or expectations. Because motherhood tends to interfere with achievement in the public sphere, many liberal feminists reject outright the demands of women's traditional role. Others believe motherhood should be considered a social service that only women can provide,[7] but that women's unique responsibility ends at giving birth. Both men and women are therefore responsible for child-rearing, although additional help may be purchased (e.g., nannies, privately-run daycare).

Liberal feminists uphold the liberal ideal of free competition in an open marketplace even though they recognize that for women the marketplace is not open when individual women are discriminated against because of their sex. Legislation against such practices is considered sufficient to end them. Education and foolproof reproductive control are additional factors in women's liberation. Once people are taught to see that women and men are essentially the same, and once women can ensure that sameness by overcoming their biology, women will be free to compete with men on an equal basis. Women will be free to pursue goals of their own choosing[8] because behavioral differences between the sexes will be eradicated through the social conditioning which produced them in the first place.

Marxist feminism likewise sees entry into the public sphere as a necessary precondition for women's liberation.[9] The division of the world into public (male) and private (female) spheres is here taken to be the direct result of unequal property relations within a capitalist economic system. According to Engels, people originally dwelt in peaceful, matriarchal, cooperative communities where all goods were held in common. With the development of the notion of private property, it became

194

important for men to establish a patriarchal lineage, so that their worldly wealth might be inherited by legitimate sons. Women's reproductive capacity became a commodity to be fiercely guarded and rigidly controlled. Secluded in the home and fed 'pie-in-the-sky' religion, women were reduced to chattels, providing unpaid emotional and material services to their working husbands in return for meagre financial security.

Marxist theory on women is problematic in several respects. As its focus is economic, it tends to disregard or downplay those aspects of human experience, such as reproduction, not traditionally considered part of the economic sphere. Nevertheless it makes a significant contribution to feminist analysis in its assessment of the nature and function of the family. While its solution to women's subordination (the abolition of private property, the integration of women into public industry, and the establishment of a communist state) is unacceptable to many, its evaluation of the structural impediments to sexual equality in western society remains an unparalleled resource.

Radical Feminism: The "root" solution

The final type of feminism is perhaps the most misunderstood. Radical feminism often conjures up images of belligerent activism and destruction of time-honoured forms of human relationships. Ironically, it may be precisely this radical stance which offers potential support for non-patriarchal conservative values in the long run.

Radical feminism rejects both the liberal contention that liberation is achieved through the gaining of civil and legal rights within the system, and the Marxist assertion that women's liberation will be achieved by wiping out capitalism. Instead, it affirms the conservative view that women's position in society is biologically determined. Because women are the childbearers, they have been dependent upon men for physical survival. Furthermore, men have used this dependence to their own advantage as a basis for excluding women from positions of cultural power and influence. Finally, the very function of mothering has been "privatized", its social significance trivialized, as men have arranged society according to the priorities of their own experience. In a male-dominated world, human issues are reduced to "women's issues", and the cry for equality is heard as the strident complaint of the ill-adjusted.

Radical feminists believe the inequality perpetuated in patriarchal culture has had grave consequences for how we understand our world. The world is split into two fundamentally opposed parts, e.g., "Spirit" and "Nature", good and evil, mind and body, even man and woman. Ephesians 5: 22ff. provides a familiar scriptural example:

> Wives, be subject to your husbands as to the Lord. For the husband is the head of the wife as Christ is the head of the church, his body, and is himself its Saviour.[10]

This theme is taken up later with regard to parents and children, and masters and their slaves. Christ, husbands, parents and masters are related to, but stand over, the church, wives, children and slaves, who must obey them.

For patriarchal conservatives, this pattern represents the right ordering of nature. Radical feminists do not deny the distinctions between the elements of each pair, but they do question such division of power and consider male dominance detrimental to both sexes. The primary object of radical feminism, therefore, is the redistribution and ultimate balancing of power in all human relationships. Race, class, and global economic structures become part of radical feminist analysis, because all forms of domination and subordination are seen as interconnected. In fact, radical feminists consider sexism to be the "root form" of all oppression.[11] It follows that once sexism is eradicated, other inequalities will be resolved as well.

Liberation for all will result from the re-balancing of human society, although the costs of change will be high for those who presently reap the benefits of the system. Although radical feminists expect First World males to oppose sweeping changes that would rectify the imbalance, they do not believe men's natures are fixed. Rather, men might be likened to spoiled adolescents, used to getting things their own way for so long that they cannot accept the fact that maturity requires fairness! To be adult, one must see the other's point of view. Radical feminists have been encouraged in recent years by the support and hard work of men who not only support fairness as an ideal, but embody it in their lives. Despite its apparent anger toward men, radical feminism ultimately embraces human liberation as its goal.

Radical feminists are not convinced of women's manifest maternal destiny in propagating future generations. They do, however, agree with conservative feminists that the bringing forth and nurturing of new life is at least as important as a larger GNP. Putting people before profit, radical feminists would restructure society so that traditional women's concerns (children, food, clothing, shelter) would receive the highest priority. Virtually all radical feminists consider this shift impossible within capitalism. Many envision a kind of small scale cooperative socialism (perhaps like the family farm), as the economic structure most consistent with their values. In any case, radical feminists tend to see their struggle as a lengthy one.

II. RESOURCES WITHIN TRADITION: NELLIE McCLUNG[12]

As we have seen, how the problem is defined determines what solutions are proposed. The clarification of perspective is thus essential for Christian feminists. Of equal importance is the discovery that Christian feminists have a heritage. Even within a tradition which has tended to reflect, as Nellie McClung might say, "the masculine view", women have laboured together to bring forth a new vision of humanity. In the past no less than today, the precise character of that vision was not uniform. Women were chastised for their inconsistency, ridiculed for their presumption, and altogether subjected to the same techniques practised by anti-feminists today.[13]

Stephen Leacock, for example, argued that laws should be enacted to *increase* women's dependency, on the grounds that women were immoral, untrustworthy, physically frail and mentally deficient:

> *For the pursuit of business her head is all wrong. Figures confuse her. She lacks sustained attention and in point of morals the average women is, even for business, too crooked...Women get low wages because low wages are all that they are worth.*[14]

The exceptional woman, who did not live down in the standard of inferiority Leacock described, was considered a freak of nature, a "sport"; any feminist who challenged his assertions became a "meddlesome, a vociferous, intrusive...Awful Woman with Spectacles", rightly burnt in the Middle Ages as a witch.[15] Against this backdrop McClung's achievements are even more outstanding.

Leacock's women-hating outburst expressed the dark side of the stereotype of womanhood which emerged in Victorian times. This "Cult of True Womanhood" signalled a radical departure from woman's traditional image as a carnal, lusty Eve. Where men were once considered to have sole claim to the spiritual realm, materialist Victorian males preferred to think of the lusty arena of business, competition and politics as the "real world". Woman's place was the home, her spiritual duty motherhood.[16] The "good" woman was asexual and unworldly, a guardian of morality and a shining beacon of selfless Christian love. Of this development McClung remarks:

> *Man long ago decided that women's sphere was anything he did not wish to do himself, and as he did not particularly care for the straight and narrow way, he felt free to recommend it to women in general. He did not wish to tie himself too close to home either and still he knew somebody should stay on the job, so he decided the home was woman's sphere.*[17]

Devalued by nineteenth-century science, religion, too, became part of woman's sphere. Its theology was transcendental and its focus individual, with a particular concern for moral (i.e., sexual) purity. In the ideal version of Victorian morals, women's indirect influence in the home would be sufficient to ensure the proper functioning of right relations in the world. By instilling in their children the correct moral virtues, women could control the spiritual destiny of the entire human race. Hence, "the hand that rocks the cradle rules the world".[18]

197

Unfortunately for the Victorian patriarch, it soon became clear to many a Victorian chatelaine that her task was impossible as presently defined.[19] As she had long been told, the world was a wicked place, filled with temptations too great for even the best brought-up boy to withstand. Too, not every child had the benefits of the "true woman's" moral teachings, particularly in the lower, immigrant classes. To fulfill her divinely destined role, therefore, women's mandate for moral mother-hood had to extend to the whole world. Indeed, it was the Victorian ideal of true womanhood, interpreted from women's perspective, which came to dominate women's movements for moral reform.

Women's Reform Movements

One of the most influential of the women's movement for moral reform was the Woman's Christian Temperance Movement, founded in 1873, the year of McClung's birth.[20] Under the dynamic guidance of its long-time leader, Frances Willard, members of the WCTU sought to foster a "religion of the body" to parallel Christ's religion of the soul.[21] Strangely prefiguring current health trends, Willard urged people to give up alcohol and nicotine, and adopt "the scientific gospel of whole wheat flour, a diet largely farcinaceous, simplicity in dress, abundant ventilation, and generous exercise."[22] Knowing as mothers that healthy minds and healthy bodies were inextricably linked, the woman of the WCTU looked forward to:

> the clear-eyed, steady-limbed Christians of the future,
> from whose brain and blood the taint of alcohol and
> nicotine has been eliminated by ages of pure habits and
> noble heredity.[23]

This quotation reflects the beliefs, common at the time, that characteristics acquired by one generation could be passed on genetically to the next. Many Christians reformers, McClung included,[24] came to support eugenics proposals such as the sterilization of drunkards, mental retardates and "moral defectives".[25] In general, however, environmental solution such as education was preferred.

Concern for the next generation's genetic welfare also led to positions on birth control and divorce that were quite radical for the time. McClung herself spoke out publicly in favour of planned parenthood, on the grounds that children were too precious to be brought into the world unwanted.[26] Further, husband and wife were to have a full relationship independent of their responsibilities as parents:

> Marriage is a divine partnership based on mutual love
> and community of interest...the pleasant glowing embers of
> comradeship and loving friendship give out a warmer, more
> lasting, and more comfortable heat than the leaping flames
> of passion, and the happiest marriage is one where the
> husband and wife come to regard each other as the dearest
> friend and the most congenial companion. (p. 33)

(In proposing mutuality as the proper foundation for marriage, McClung made a significant departure from the maternal feminism with which she is usually associated. While she undeniably upheld many maternal feminist beliefs, a careful reading of her work indicates more radical [and significant] elements in her analysis.)

The founding of women's organizations such as the WCTU and the YWCA were important in the emergence of the Canadian Social Gospel movement.[27] Historian Richard Allen suggests that factors such as urbanization and immigration created pressing needs to which Christian women could apply their talent for moral motherhood. Building on their traditional role as "helpmeet", middle-class Christian women entered the slums to educate, "Canadianize" and "Christianize". They were appalled. The extreme poverty and abysmal living conditions faced by Canada's urban immigrant poor shocked many back to their parlours, but even more into political action.

Against the Victorian conservatives who met the rising tide of women's activism with the charge that womanhood was being sullied, McClung proclaimed:

> Inasmuch as we have sat in our comfortable, respectable pews enjoying our own little narrow-guage religion, unmoved by the call of the larger citizenship, and making no effort to reach out and save those in temptation, and making no effort to better the conditions under which other women must live...in God's sight—we are fallen women! And to the church officials, ministers and laymen who have dared to deny to women the means by which they might have done better for the women of the world, I would like to say that I wonder what they will say to that Scotch mother (whose young daughter was forced into prostitution) who lay down happily on her death-bed believing that God would care for her motherless child left to battle with the world...I wonder how they will be able to get away with that old fable about their being afraid of women 'losing their femininity'. I wonder! (p. 78)

The "means" to which McClung refers took at least two forms, suffrage and women's ordination.[28] McClung did not see these primarily in terms of individual women's opportunity for self-fulfillment; she believed that social transformation required structural transformation. So long as women were required to exercise influence only indirectly, the world (no less, the church) would continue to meet men's needs and speak to men's concerns. As it was, "the world, as made by men, is cruelly unjust to women", (p. 76). Her essay, "The Sore Thought", looks ahead to liberation theology, in which she lays out the nameless (because corporate) crimes sanctioned by the "man's world" of business. She asks:

199

> *What about the crime of holding up the market so the*
> *price of bread goes up and poor men's children go hungry?*
> *...The crime which the state commits in allowing such a*
> *condition to prevail is as yet un-named. (p. 90)*

A crucial part of structural transformation was to be direct political action. At the time McClung was writing, women had virtually no rights under the law. Not yet "persons", lacking the vote, they had no control over the conditions of their lives, short of choosing a husband. McClung's novels illustrate women's dilemma. For example, *Purple Springs*, the final volume of the Pearlie Watson trilogy, tells the story of one "Mrs. Gray" who risks social censure by refusing to attest to the legitimacy of her son, James. Pearlie (a woman like McClung) rises to her defence, discovering by the end of the novel both "Mrs. Gray's" husband and the reason for the deception. James' grandfather had disapproved of his son's marriage, and could legally have taken James from his mother—for in 1921, the year *Purple Springs* was written, women could only be legal guardians of bastards. Men could sell their wives' property and use the money for drink, while their children starved, and women had no recourse whatever. McClung saw righting this injustice as a religious necessity, a means by which women could "demonstrate God to the world". "The demand for votes," she contended "is a spiritual movement." (p. 78)

So, too, was the women's movement as a whole.[29] McClung had little patience with the troublesome men who made women's activism necessary, but her scorn was reserved for what she called "the Gentle Lady": "The Gentle Lady has a very personal and local point of view. She looks at the whole world as related to herself." (p. 63) Opposed to suffrage, the gentle ladies invoked the Victorian stereotype of women's frailty ("We are gentle ladies. Protect us. We are weak, very weak, but very loving," p.63), while capitalizing on their sexual attractiveness. McClung considered these women parasites. Her 1925 novel, *Painted Fires*, gives a horrendous account of one of these, Eva St. John, a spoiled socialite who allows an innocent immigrant girl to be imprisoned for unwittingly obtaining the heroin St. John needed to feed her boredom-caused addiction.

The "indifference and slothfulness" of the gentle ladies was, for McClung, the very epitome of sin. She reminded her readers:

> *There is no resignation in Nature, no quiet folding of*
> *hands, no hypocritical saying, 'Thy will be done!'...*
> *Resignation is a cheap and indolent human virtue, which*
> *has served as an excuse for much spiritual slothfulness.*
> *(p. 9)*

For humanity as in Nature, struggle and growth are interlinked. To fight against injustice was the true meaning of "Thy will be done", for which we have as example not only Nature, but Christ himself.[30]

McClung and the Church

The 'divine' discontent[31] which characterized McClung's Christian feminism was not well-received by the church. Devoutly religious all her life, McClung was grieved by the opposition the call for women's rights received:

> When it is all over, the battle fought and won, and women are regarded everywhere as human beings and citizens, many women will remember with bitterness that in the day of our struggle, the church stood off, aloof and dignified, and let us fight alone. (p. 73)

Her vision of Canada required the church be at the forefront of social transformation, making Canada "the land of the fair deal." Yet despite its commitment to "building God's kingdom on earth" (as the Social Gospel urged), the church continually failed to extend the promise of equality to women.

McClung explores the problem in her essay "Women and the Church".[32] Written in 1915, it unfortunately reads as true today, an incisive account of the subordination of women within the Christian tradition. She begins her argument with the contention that God created man and woman in equality: "Whatever inequality has crept in since, has come without God's sanction (p. 68)." The source of inequality has been man's superior physical strength, which has increased as civilization advanced.[33] The biological difference is hardly a sign of male superiority in other respects, McClung reminds us:

> It is easy for bigger and stronger people to arrogate to themselves a general superiority. Christ came to rebuke the idea that brute strength is the dominant force in life. (p. 68)

Like other more recent feminist theologians, McClung finds the question of men's nature a problem. On the one hand, both sexes were created in the image of God. On the other, history has shown men to have an incredible inclination to aggression which seems to be absent from women. McClung did believe in a fundamental difference of perspective between the sexes, in part due to women's responsibilities as child-bearers, and describes the ancient division of labour rigidly enough to satisfy the most conventional anthropologist:

> Men fought and women worked. Men fought because they liked it; and women worked because it had to be done. (p. 14)

"But," she is quick to claim, "although men like to fight, war is not inevitable. War is not of God's making. War is a crime committed by men and therefore, when enough people say it shall not be, it cannot be." (p. 15)

This point, i.e., that war is not essential to God's creation, hence neither to men's nature, advances neither the patriarchal conservative or maternal feminist point of view. Rather, McClung argues a sophisticated radical feminist position. In McClung's view, men have been corrupted by the excess of power that physical strength and social dominance have given them.[34] They have named the world in their own terms, so that history, tradition, and even religion have been given a "masculine interpretation." (pp. 15, 70). Sheer survival, if not common humanity, demands that women's voice now be heard as well.[35]

As a male-dominated social institution, the church is understandably opposed to women's demands. By so acting, however, it is directly departing from Christ's teachings.[36] Even though scripture seems to confirm male domination, McClung dismisses that as inadmissible evidence:

> Christ's scribes were all men, and in writing down the sacred story they would naturally ignore the woman's part of it. (p. 69)

Secular works on women's nature are similarly suspect.[37] Indeed she speaks for every feminist when she sighs:

> What a glorious thing it will be when men cease to speak for us, and cease to tell us what we think, and let us speak for ourselves! (p. 85)

In perpetuating the inequality of women the church has unwittingly limited its own effectiveness by refusing to draw upon one-half of its resources. Worse still, it has done so for the most trivial of reasons. McClung dismisses the church's alleged reverence for women's delicate constitutions with the observation that men have never objected to female servants or factory workers. Rather, "it is the thought of women getting into comfortable and well-paid positions which wrings their manly hearts." (p. 52) In the end, opposition to feminism comes from a single source:

> The haunting fear of mankind—that the advancement of women will some time, some way, some place, interfere with some man's confort. (p. 32)

Then, as now, it is insufficient justification for inequality.

McClung offered many suggestions about how inequality between the sexes might be overcome. In addition to legal change, she supported women's access to all professions. Unlike liberal feminists, however, her view of emancipation did not require that women leave the home. She believed that "deeply rooted in almost every woman's heart is the love of home and children," adding, "but independence is sweet, and when marriage means the loss of independence, there are women brave enough and strong enough to turn away from it." (p. 86) Far from threatening marriage, feminism encouraged it, but marriage itself would have to change. Women's economic dependence had to end, whether by "wages for housework", cooperative housekeeping, or a total recasting of societal structures. She concludes:

> The time will come, we hope, when women will be economically free, and mentally and spiritually independent enough to refuse to have their food paid for by men; when women will receive equal pay for equal work, and have all avenues of activity open to them;...but free men and free women will marry for love, and together work for the sustenance of their families. It is not too ideal a thought. It is coming, and the new movement among women who are crying out for a larger humanity is going to bring it about. (p. 86)

Both supporters and detractors of Christian feminism must meet if the church is to flourish. While McClung assured her fellows that women would not desert the church, no matter how the church deserted women, many today would disagree. As the fight was still young, McClung could cheerfully remark that men were changing more every day, and those who did not change would eventually die. (p. 73) Prejudice, however, seems immortal. (p. 44) In the light of historical experience, the need for clarification of Christian feminist goals and strategies becomes even more apparent.

Feminism Within a Christian Context

It is clear that the patriarchal conservative stance of traditional Christianity is unacceptable from a feminist point of view. Separatism is likewise unacceptable from a Christian standpoint, although 'post-Christian' feminists such as Mary Daly develop a spirituality based upon that premise. Both perpetuate an antagonistic polarity of human experience, differing only in the sex to which they ascribe superiority.

Liberal feminism is congenial to Christian feminists who wish to expand women's responsibility in the church without tipping the boat they wish to gently rock (e.g., women ministers, but traditional liturgies). The liberal position is basically optimistic and women who find more aggressive demands for structural change unnecessarily antagonistic will find the liberal emphasis on education and gradual progress supportive to their view. Liberal feminism benefits from being sufficiently mainstream to participate within existing structures and, as such, has relative access to power. In practice, however, liberal feminists tend to use that power to increase women's access to the existing system rather than to change the system itself. Whether such structural transformation is needed, Christian feminists attracted to the liberal option must decide.

Despite its popularity in other theological arenas, Marxist analysis is less useful in service of the feminist cause. Marxist feminism recognizes that women's subordination is economically based and reinforced within that system. That in itself is invaluable, but its own subordination of women's struggle to a 'larger' Marxist program may seem to many a traditional patriarchal ploy.

Maternal feminism is gaining increased popularity, addressing precisely the questions Marxist feminism leaves unanswered. It affirms the worth of women's traditional activities, while giving them a significance and power the patriarchal world denies. Further, it assures women that they need not compete with men on men's terms. "Woman's world" is sufficient unto itself, although its range is greater than "man's world" admits. This scenario is both compelling and dangerous. The "special nature" view of women rightly celebrates women's unique perspective. It fails, however, to acknowledge the extent to which *all* experience has been informed by the dominant patriarchal culture. To say that singularly female activities such as motherhood are unconditioned by social reality flies in the face of the evidence; it also leaves the uncomfortable question of men's "special nature" unresolved.

While its appeal is understandable, special nature feminism fails to provide a basis for concrete action, short of the injunction to "be more womanly". Whatever its lure in theory, special nature feminism has proved in history to be singularly ineffective.

Perhaps the greatest resource for the development of a transforming and enduring Christian feminism lies in the radical feminist option. Despite its abrasive image, radical feminism is, at its heart, a call for a change in perception, a shift of focus somewhat like religious conversion. Far from requiring the abolition of home and family, it calls for a rehabilitation of relationship within them so that God's original intention of cooperative participation in equality is restored. The vision of radical feminism is not easily implemented, as we have learned from the example of Nellie McClung. The battles she fought fifty years ago are being fought today, and even the issues are little changed. Perhaps McClung spoke before her time; certainly neither the world nor the church heard all she had to say. In this she reflects one of radical feminism's weakest points: in calling for wholesale transformation it appears unreasonable, utopian, and uncompromising in its stand on immediate issues. While it is tempting to assume the prophetic role ("he who has ears, let him hear"), a more sober assessment must admit that the unpopularity of the radical feminist option is a problem. Those convinced of the revolution of thought required by radical feminism should be encouraged by the example of Nellie McClung, and draw strength from her memory. Both ridiculed and celebrated in life, and almost forgotten in death, she stands before us as a model of courage drawn from faith.

She reminds us too, that however the feminist call is formulated, however much we differ amongst ourselves and are opposed by others, the woman's movement is a spiritual movement, born of the hope for a better world. In engaging our present and retrieving our past we do God's work as well as our own. Let McClung's embodied conviction become our watchword:

> *The world needs the work and the help of the women, and the women must work, if the race will survive. (p. 66)*

R. R. Warne

Randi is a doctoral candidate in the Centre for Religious Studies, University of Toronto. The subject of her thesis is Nellie McClung, but she is interested in the whole range of early feminist literature and social activism.

Chapter 10 SIDE ROAD ON THE JOURNEY TO AUTONOMY: THE DIACONATE PRIOR TO CHURCH UNION

—Diane Haglund

SUMMARY

• The diaconate for women goes back to the early church. Deaconess had a limited liturgical role: they kept the doors and assisted at the baptisms for women. In Romans 16: 1, the King James Version of the Bible translates diakonos as servant.

The diaconate reappeared in the nineteenth century as a result of the urge to reform that grew out of the industrial revolution, and in women's search for fulfillment beyond the home. In 1836, Theodore Fleidner and his wife, Fredrika Munster, founded a deaconess training school in Kaiserwerth, Germany. Kaiserwerth supported a wide range of social services, including specialized hospitals and schools. The Centre quickly became well-known and prompted other churches to found orders. Efforts to establish the order in North America, however, met little interest when first proposed.

It is unlikely that a diaconate would have attracted many North American women at that time. By the mid-1860s, women found increasing opportunity in the mission field, education, or various reform societies. Then, too, the clergy attempted to put limitations on women. There were some radicals who challenged biblical translations and understandings, but for the most part women confined their activities to teaching Sunday school, organizing for prayer, organizing and working in the mission fields. The WMS has been described as the first great national organization to develop among women in Canada. The missionary societies gave women considerable power and an opportunity to serve denied them elsewhere.

The limits of women's participations in the courts of the church were clearly defined. In 1894, the Methodist General Conference refused to allow women to be members of church courts, a decision that held until 1922. Presbyterian women did not receive lay rights until after church union, and ordination for women in the United Church was denied until 1936. Interest in the office of deaconess began to emerge as it was felt that this office would grant women the chance to fulfill their ministry without usurping male power within the courts of the church. Canadians were aware of the work of Lucy Rider Meyer who founded the Chicago Training School and laid the foundations of the diaconate in North American Methodism. In 1893, after much effort, a Deaconess Aid Society was organized in Toronto Conference; the Canadian school was modelled on the Chicago one. In 1897, the Woman's Foreign Missionary Society of the Presbyterian Church established the Ewart Home as a training centre for women, both for foreign mission candidates and other Christian workers. The General Assembly of the Presbyterian Church endorsed the Deaconess Order in 1907. Both Presbyterians and Methodists looked to their new deaconesses as workers for the social gospel. Nursing and case-work were part of the duties of every deaconess in the first years of the movement, and self-sacrifice was the central code word.

From the beginning, churchmen expected the impossible from deaconesses. The ideal deaconess was to be a consecrated Christian and an excellent housekeeper with knowledge of music; she was to know the basics of nursing, be able to work as an exceptional teacher and take Sunday services when necessary. All this, showing the "bright side" of her personality!

The numbers of women expected to enter the deaconess order never materialized. The diaconate was in competition with teaching, nursing, and social work, as well as opportunities for mission service both at home and overseas.

Expectations surrounding the diaconate were unreasonably high. The deaconess was expected to retire after marriage, wear a uniform, and live in a supervised home. She was required to give all her time to her appointed duties as well as do part of the housework in her residence. The work was difficult and discouraging, and in the early days of the movement, training concentrated on biblical studies and did not help much with her social work. The low enrollment figures and high dropout rate reinforced the truth behind the image of "holy drudgery." By 1922, the orders were in crisis. General Conference was memorialized by deaconesses who said that the order did not occupy the place of importance in the church that it should; if the conference were not prepared to rectify the situation, the order should be disbanded.

The order was not disbanded, but even so, the early difficult days of the diaconate reinforced the limitations of the place of women. Indeed, in women's long journey to autonomy within the church, the diaconate represents a side road.

—editor

In 1894, the General Conference of the Methodist Church of Canada gave "hearty endorsement" to the establishment of an order of deaconesses which would give women a recognized place in church polity for the first time.[1] At the same conference, women were denied admission to the ordained ministry, and a decision was made to deny women's election to the church courts. The pattern was later repeated by the Presbyterian Church which endorsed an order of deaconesses in 1907. These decisions are only seemingly paradoxical. The diaconate, as it was introduced by these two churches, reveals much about women's place in mainline Protestantism in the nineteenth and early twentieth centuries.

The female diaconate had its roots in the early church. Although the office was suppressed in the Christian church, it was never abolished, and theologians who argued for the re-introduction of the office in the late nineteenth century believed that "a tolerably clear picture of the deaconess and her work" could be obtained from the *Apostolic Constitutions* of the fourth century.[2] These texts outline a limited liturgical role for women: the deaconess kept the doors and assisted at the baptism of women. Romans 16: 1 was cited as the scriptural authority for the office. Here Paul refers to "Phoebe our sister, which is a servant of the church which is at Cenchreae." Paul ascribes two titles to Phoebe: *diakonos,* translated as servant in the *King James Version,* and *prostatis,* usually translated as helper or patroness. Translators have generally chosen nouns which imply greater power when these same titles refer to male members of the church. This downplaying of the roles of early church women has long been questioned by feminist scholars: women in the early church probably were not limited from performing any missionary function because of their gender.[3]

Nineteenth-Century Revival

The diaconate reappeared in the complex social environment of the nineteenth century: an environment created by the periodic evangelical revivals common to North American society, Britain, and sections of Europe; the urge to reform that grew out of the industrial revolution; and in women's search for fulfillment beyond the home.

In 1836, Theodore Fleidner and his wife, Fredrika Munster, founded a deaconess training school at Kaiserwerth in Germany. Inspired by the work of deaconesses among the Mennonites of Holland, Fleidner's zeal for reform was an integral part of the Inner Mission Movement, an attempt by the Lutheran church to deal with a decline in church attendance and the social upheaval created by industrialization.

The Kaiserwerth order took the form of a sisterhood centred in a motherhouse and was designed to resemble family life. In continental Europe, deaconess orders provided the first acceptable alternative to the home, much as teaching and moral reform associations were doing for British and American women. At their peak, continental order numbered some 50,000 adherents.[4] Nursing, which developed as a separate profession in Britain and America, is generally associated with Protestant deaconess orders and Roman Catholic sisterhoods on the continent.

By the late nineteenth century, Kaiserwerth supported a wide range of social services including specialized hospitals and schools. The Centre quickly became well-known and prompted other churches to found orders. There was, however, considerable variation in form from one denomination to another. The Anglican diaconate was influenced by both the renewed interest in religious communities inspired by the Tractarian movement and by the considerable reform activities of women during this period, among them Florence Nightingale who received her formal nurse's training at Kaiserwerth. Other British denominations (Church of Scotland, English Baptists and Methodists), like their North American counterparts, did not establish orders until later in the century. Every denomination that established a diaconate for women would be influenced by the Kaiserwerth experiment. When the order was instituted in the Canadian Methodist Church, for example, the *Methodist Magazine and Review* carried several articles on the Centre. Offering a rationale for the introduction of the office into the Canadian Presbyterian Church, the convenor of the Committee on the Order of Deaconesses found reference to Fleidner's work "instructive and profitable."[5]

In 1849, Fleidner attempted to introduce the office into the United States when he accompanied four Kaiserwerth trained deaconesses to Pittsburgh at the invitation of German Lutherans there. It would be another four decades, however, before a diaconate would prosper in any denomination on this continent. Immediately following the Civil War, Annie Wittenmeyer and Susan M. D. Fry, two women renowned for their charitable enterprises, attempted to arouse interest in the office among Methodist churchwomen.[6] Their efforts seem to have met with little interest, and by 1874 the pair had turned their attention to the temperance cause.

It is unlikely that a diaconate would have attracted many supporters at this time. By the mid-1860s, those women who wanted a vocation in the church found increasing opportunity in the mission field. Teaching, of course, had become something of a standby for educated women who had to support themselves or for those who did not wish to marry. From early in the century the various reform societies had provided a rich sphere of activity for middle-class women. In fact reform was the only acceptable extra-familial activity for the married women.

It is also unlikely that Wittenmeyer and Fry would have found much support within the church. Although clerical views on their proposals are unknown, it is likely that they reflected those of a British bishop who in 1873 cautioned his American counterparts:

> *Sisterhoods should be under the direction of wise men. I have learned to fear female rule unless it be itself under authority, able to know all and capable of controlling or over-ruling.* [7]

This fear of female rule had been heightened by the early suffrage movement.

The Role of Women in North American Churches

In 1837, reformer Lydia Marie Child correctly assessed that "the sects called Evangelical were the first agitators of the women's question."[8] During the Second Great Awakening, American churchmen had sanctioned women's participation in reform as long as their activities could be accommodated to domesticity. Child, however, likened churchmen who had sought the help of women in the word of redemption to the sorcerer's apprentice:

> *Thus it is with you who urged women to become missionaries and to form tract societies. They have turned the household utensil to a living being and they have no spell to turn it into a broom again.* [9]

The conversion experience, as Nancy Cott points out, set up a direct relation to God's authority. Woman was "accountable only to her God" and so could defy the authority of men.[10] Early feminists "aspired to equal power in church and state" and both ordination and laity rights were contested issues in the period before the American Civil War.[11] The broom, to use Child's metaphor, was out of control. Religious reform became the arena in which many of the tensions surrounding women's role surfaced.

The clergy attempted to put limitations on the activities of those women who edged their activities beyond the accepted confines. Confronted with Pauline injunctions against their public activities, radicals like Sarah Grimke and Elizabeth Cady Stanton denied "that all pastors are better qualified to give instruction than women."[12] Grimke charged that men had purposefully translated the Bible to downgrade women. Stanton advocated that "all invidious distinctions based on sex" be struck from the Bible.[13] In 1895, she published *The Women's Bible,* a series of commentaries on those sections of the Bible that refer to women. The publication created an uproar and enraged the clergy. The Canadian religious press reprinted American articles which denied Stanton's arguments as "unworthy of confidence."[14]

211

Women like Grimke and Stanton were a minority. To win the confidence of ministers, the majority of women had hidden any individualistic motives and fallen back on the reasoning of domesticity or maternal feminism. By arguing that women had a right and a responsibility to extend their special nurturing qualities beyond the home, they expanded the boundaries set on their activities. Throughout the century, over clerical objections, they had sought and eventually won the right to organize for prayer, to teach Sunday School, and to enter and organize mission work. Ann Douglas suggests that this expansion of activity was tolerated because it did not confer "automatic entrée"[15] to the pulpit. Church government remained securely in male hands, even though by the late nineteenth century it was evident that North American Protestantism had become dependent on women's work.[16]

As early as 1836, a Canadian minister had the grace to admit that his work "would have been seriously handicapped but for the fact that the women organized and did most of the visiting."[17] In 1832, a Ladies Aid Society in Bathurst, N.B., recorded the purchase of "5 lbs. of candles" and "one bushel of oats" toward the maintenance of the minister and his horse. By 1848, their sisters in Bridgetown had taken over complete responsibility for furnishing and maintaining the manse in that community.[18] By late century, it was not unusual for women to raise the mortgage money for their congregations.

Many clergy deplored the "petty, worldly methods of raising money at church fairs, oyster suppers, pound sociables" which women had introduced to the church.[19] Dependence on women's support remained a thorn in clerical flesh until well into the next century. "Too much of the church is in the hands of the women," warned Dr. Hazelwood in *The Christian Guardian* of June 18, 1913; "the men need stirring-up and their interest in church work aroused." "If the men of the church were all and always as diligent," wrote a cleric in *The Presbyterian Record,* "what a work might be done".[20]

Lamentations about women's numerical superiority in the church had been heard for decades. Dougherty estimates that in 1888, women constituted five-eighths of American Methodism's membership.[21] Although figures are not available for the Canadian church, it is probably safe to assume a similar proportion. Douglas suggests, however, that the numbers themselves are not important:

> ...nineteenth century liberal ministers moaning over their largely feminine flocks as a signal of new disaster are telling as much about their own anxieties as about any statistical development. What is clear is that they felt increasingly dominated by their women members who had in the proliferating "societies" new arenas of activity.[22]

Particularly threatening were the woman's missionary societies. In the United States, women had agitated to serve as missionaries and to organize the missionary effort to women in India, China and Japan. Where the church had denied that right, women organized interdenominationally. The Women's Union Missionary Society, for example, was founded by various women's groups after a Baptist woman had been refused the right to organize by that church.[23] Incorporated in 1861, the Union Missionary Society became the model for the denominational boards set up between 1869 and 1888.

Throughout the history of the American missionary societies, and as late as 1923 in the American Presbyterian Church, one power play followed another as the male hierarchy tried to subordinate these groups and absorb them or bring them under the control of the general boards.[24] In Canada, the men asserted control from the beginning, apparently recognizing and benefitting from the mistakes of their American brethren. In both the Presbyterian and Methodist Churches, the women's societies were founded by men, and final authority for their activities rested with the male societies.[25] This authority undoubtedly chafed from time to time and tensions did exist.[26] Nonetheless, women quickly took advantage of the considerable autonomy granted to them.

Writing in 1916, Marjorie MacMurchy estimated that for the 250,000 women who belonged to an association in Canada, 200,000 belonged to a missionary society.[27] She described the WMS as "the first great national organization to develop among women in Canada."[28] In All Loves Excelling, Beaver comments on the keen insight for organization and publicity developed by WMS leadership. MacMurchy compared the societies to large business organizations and estimated that in the years before the first World War, the Canadian societies had raised, managed, and designated an income of between $400,000 and $500,000.[29] A historian of The Presbyterian Church in Canada estimates that these years up to one-third of the funds for the foreign mission effort by that church was raised by WMS members.[30]

The missionary societies gave women considerable power, and it was a power fully recognized by clergy. By the late nineteenth century, ministers, as Douglas suggests, "suspected—and rightly—that women had more chance of capturing the church than the senate."[31] The fact that the issue of ordination was being raised, and that district meetings in both the United States and Canada were attempting to elect women to Conference, confirmed their suspicions. Here, then, was a thorny dilemma for clergy. On the one hand they wished to preserve their own privileges; on the other, they realized that in time, simple justice would demand some reward.

Writers in the Canadian Methodist Magazine and Review recognized that women had long been the church's "most effective ministrants" since women "entered the lists." In 1894, the Rev. Dr. Thomas Webster, at 85 the oldest minister in the Canadian church, wrote:

213

> ...there has been scarcely a single great reform
> movement inaugurated...that has not borne the stamp of
> woman's mind...(there is) greater efficiency manifest in
> every department of Christian enterprise...[32]

Moreover, churchmen could scarcely ignore the gains being made by women in the larger society, particularly in the professions. Churchmen writing in the *Review* generally favoured women's larger involvement. "Happily, times have changed," declared Dr. Webster:

> ...the opportunity offered of acquiring knowledge has
> enabled them to demonstrate that they were and are the
> equals of their male competitors...[33]

While congratulating women on their success in other professions, Webster, like other writers, managed to avoid the issue of ordination. The subject, however, did occasionally raise its ugly head. In the "private opinion" of one writer, it was "not best" for women to preach, even though he conceded that:

> ...where in exceptional cases and with extraordinary
> gifts women go out of their way, and all by themselves,
> publicly...launch the lifeboat of the gospel, I say well done![34]

How women were to "launch" themselves in ordination was of course, a moot point.

The Formation of the Diaconate in North America

The bounds of women's sphere in mainline Protestantism were clearly defined. As noted in the Introduction, the Methodist General Conference of 1894 refused to allow women to be members of the church courts. These rights would be refused at each consecutive conference until 1922 when church leaders finally succumbed, influenced by the decision of the federal Government to grant the franchise to women in 1918. However, the right to ordination and the right to sit on the stationary committee were withheld. Presbyterian women did not receive lay rights until after Union. Ordination for women was denied by the United Church until 1936.

While not prepared to grant any office that would affirm women's autonomy, the male hierarchy in both churches would prove to be receptive to any office that could be accommodated to the separate spheres. The diaconate, as it was understood from the *Apostolic Constitutions*, filled the bill nicely.

Some two decades after Wittenmeyer and Fry had attempted to form "a devoted Christian Womanhood",[35] Methodist churchwomen again began to consider the possibilities of a diaconate. Interest in the office

214

developed as an outgrowth of their attempts to provide opportunities for theological education for themselves, and to deal with the appalling conditions created in North American cities by immigration and industrialization.

In 1885, Lucy Rider Meyer founded the Chicago Training School (CTS) and so laid the foundations of the diaconate in North American Methodism. A graduate of Upham Theological Seminary and Oberlin College, Rider Meyer had studied at the Women's Medical College, Philadelphia, and the Boston School of Technology, and completed her medical training at Northwestern University in 1887. While working as field secretary for the Illinois Sunday School Association in the early 1880s, Rider Meyer had been struck by the need for training for women in Bible study. Her idea for a school received ministerial support in principle, but she was left to raise the necessary funds herself.[36]

The idea of a school for women was not new. Indeed, the religious training school was a phenomenon of the late nineteenth century.[37] Initially established to provide training for woman missionary candidates, more than sixty of these institutions existed in North America prior to 1916. "Ministers receive years of training," wrote a Canadian churchwoman as the Presbyterian Woman's Foreign Missionary Society established the Ewart Training Home:

> What special training have we provided for our lady missionaries who in some measure, at least, are expected to do the same work as the pastor? We have been satisfied if they have evidenced their personal piety...by engaging in some quiet Christian work.[38]

Rider Meyer's school, however, was unique in that it was intended for women who would never see foreign service. As part of their training, her students carried the gospel to the Chicago slums. To help them relieve the distress they found there, Rider Meyer introduced basic nursing and "methods of work" (social work) to the CTS curriculum.[39]

The tradition of visiting is a long one in Protestantism and before the professionalization of social work was the principal means of social service. Rider Meyer was certainly not the first to attempt to formalize this activity. Numerous city missions organized by women were well established in both countries by this period; the Salvation Army's "Slum Sisters" were also beginning work in some American cities.[40]

Rider Meyer chose the diaconate as the appropriate model for the work of her students. It is also clear that she saw the office as an entry into church polity.[41] In May 1888, Bishop James Thoburn presented the case for the diaconate at the General Conference of the American Methodist Episcopal Church. A man of considerable ministerial influence, Thoburn was also a brother of one of Rider Meyer's colleagues in the CTS venture. The diaconate was endorsed (over the objections of some clergy), perhaps as a diplomatic concession, since this same conference denied laity rights to women. However, the decision by the Woman's Home Missionary Society to convert its home missions to deaconess institutions may well have provided the real impetus for the decision. Financially and administratively independent of the church, the WHMS had hired Jan Bancroft Robinson, author of *The Deaconesses of Europe and Their Lessons for America* and a scholar of some note, to oversee this project. By endorsing the CTS program, the male hierarchy may have been attempting to take the wind from the sails of what might prove to be another powerful female enclave. For many years the official diaconate existed side by side with the WHMS office while Rider Meyer and Bancroft Robinson debated the merits of a place in church polity as opposed to independence from male control.

The work of both orders soon became well-known to Canadian Methodists. By 1890, and undoubtedly with an eye to the upcoming Third General Conference, some clergy and a few women were mildly agitating in the pages of *The Methodist Magazine and Review* for establishment of the office.

Churchwomen writing in the *Review* demanded the simple justice of a reward for past services and if justice were to be done, that reward should be a place in church polity. "The time is fast approaching," wrote Mary Daniels "when the organized benevolent work of women must have a recognized place in the economy of the church."[42]

Miss Daniels sought to diminish the fears of those who thought that in instituting such an office, Methodism would be "aping the methods of the papal church."[43]

> ...the good features of the (Roman Catholic) sisterhoods are present...the evil has been eliminated. There is no vow, no renunciation of the dearest relations of life, nothing of the conventual systems.[44]

American Methodism's Bishop Ninde also reassured *Review* readers:

> Our order of deaconesses, without requiring any unscriptural views with its freedom from priests and Jesuitical arts and practices, is so radically different from Roman Catholic practices that we can hardly be charged with adopting the methods of the papal church.[45]

Miss Daniels asked those who objected on grounds that the diaconate was "abnormal and narrowing" to consider "if there are not many true and gifted women to whom the home and family life is not appointed."[46] Ninde reassured those who thought the office would remove women from their proper place and aid in the destruction of the home:

> I would ask God's blessing on that comparatively small

216

*class of women who are just as heartily content to forego
the blessing of a single home that they may mother
thousands of homeless ones.*[47]

The Methodist General Conference which convened in June was
memorialized by the Toronto and Montreal Conferences "to legislate for
the establishment of a Sisterhood." Conference, however, "feeling the
importance of a more definite recognition of women's work," recommended that each annual conference could "if deemed desirable" legislate for "a systematic organization of consecrated women."[48] The decision did not find favour with *Review* writers who apparently had expected
Conference itself to institute and oversee the office.

Miss Daniels began to play on Methodism's real fear that Roman
Catholicism and the Salvation Army were taking the lead in evangelizing
the slums.

> *We have our prisons, workhouses and hospitals calling
> for the loving ministries which only women can render. Yet
> to whom are these trusted?—in many places almost
> exclusively to the Roman Catholic Sisters of Charity. While
> the privilege of bearing the news to the poor and illiterate
> classes is given over chiefly to the Salvation Army.*[49]

The editor of the *Review* also expressed concern:

> *Are Protestant ladies less capable of devotion and
> humanity than Roman Catholic ladies? Roman Catholics of
> the highest, even of princely rank, enter the Sisterhoods of
> Rome. Are our children capable of emulating their zeal,
> while carefully avoiding what we regard as their errors?*[50]

In failing to implement the diaconate, was Methodism losing its women to
the Salvation Army? Miss Daniels wondered:

> *Perhaps if the churches opened their channel of
> usefulness there would be fewer eager, energetic women
> aglow with zeal to tell the tidings going out from us to the
> Army with its often objectionable features.*[51]

Finally, Miss Daniels brought forward churchwomen's ultimate threat.
Noting the spontaneous nature of some of the American work (presumably the WHMS), she challenged:

> *Perhaps the only answer…is the old one familiar to
> triteness, "the way to begin is to begin."*[52]

217

Sidonie Zilla, also writing in the *Review,* was more forthright. If the church would not begin the work then perhaps an appeal should be made "to some wealthy woman or women. It might be just as well for (an order) to be undenominational as the King's Daughters are."[53] There is no evidence, however, that Methodist women in this country attempted to organize a diaconate independently. That would be left to their Presbyterian sisters.

In 1893, on the initiative of a Methodist clergyman, a Deaconess Aid Society was organized in Toronto Conference. The Canadian school was modelled on CTS and its first three principals were graduates of the Chicago institution.

In 1897, the Woman's Foreign Missionary Society (WFMS) of the Presbyterian Church established the Ewart Home as a training centre for women. Established primarily for foreign mission candidates, "other Christian workers desiring to avail themselves of the training" were also accepted.[54] From the beginning, all students attended lectures at the Nursing At Home Mission, made rounds with Mission Nurses, "and shared with them in their ministrations to the suffering poor." Students also held services at the George Street Mission.

> This has opened the way for house-to-house visiting, and here has been found an open door and hearts waiting to receive the word....[55]

By 1900, students spent "most of the time not occupied in study in visiting the poor and sick."[56] While this may have been, as one Superintendent noted, "surely the very best training for foreign work,"[57] the WFMS executive had their sights on "a broader field" of activity. In the summer of 1901, three students were employed as "deaconesses" by congregations of the Presbytery of Toronto. WFMS leaders looked forward to "the time when the Ewart Home Deaconess (or Bible Women) will be in such request they will not be confined to (this) city."[58]

In 1904, the WFMS approached the executive of the Presbyterian General Assembly's Foreign Mission Committee (which held final authority for their activities) to request that the Ewart Home be made "a more recognized institution of the Church." Presumably they wanted a place in church policy for the deaconess. The WFMS also requested that the committee "*in conjunction with other committees of the Church* (author's italics) devise means to enlarge the scope of the Ewart Home".[59] Further study may well show that the WFMS leadership was asking the church to commit itself to the social gospel in advance of male leaders.

The General Assembly refused to change the WFMS Constitution, apparently fearful that division of effort would weaken the original purpose of the organization. *The Presbyterian* deplored the decision.

> *In view of the tidal wave of immigration which is flowing
> into our country and the grave individual and national
> dangers arising from religious neglect in the early days of
> settlement, it is felt that no available source of help must be
> overlooked.*[60]

Nothing daunted, the WFMS "pressed ahead" with the work. Ewart
Home students and graduates continued to serve as "deaconesses" until
the General Assembly finally endorsed the order in 1907.

The 1907 General Assembly also appointed Dr. J. G. Shearer as
Secretary of its Committee on Temperance, Social and Moral Reform. In
this action, the Assembly was following the example of the Methodist
General Conference of 1894 which, in addition to sanctioning the
Toronto Conference Deaconess Program, had received the first report
of its Committee on Sociological Questions. These, then, were the conferences at which the churches committed themselves to the social
gospel. The diaconate was just one of many new structures they would
adopt as they turned to reform.

"All resources must be brought into line," wrote the editor of *The
Presbyterian*, including "the banding together of our Christian women in
the work of holding Canada for Christ."[61] The *Review* editor hit upon the
reason which may, more than any other, have prompted his church to
take action.

> *We do not despair of having some days hundreds of
> sisters who, at their own cost, without receiving one penny
> from our churches, will do the kind of work we have
> indicated.* [62]

It was this need for "hundreds of sisters", for workers for the social
gospel, that finally gained women a foothold in church polity. In imple-
menting the office, male leaders would pay lip service to women's need
for a vocation and for increased status and dignity within the church.
This, however, was not the prime motive.

The diaconate was just one of the entirely new professions opening to
women at this time. The office shared much with the development of
nursing and social work; in fact nursing and "case work" were part of the
duties of every deaconess in the first years of the movement. Women's
professions reaffirmed their subordination. As Wayne Roberts suggests,
the term "helping profession" betrays the occupational limitations open
to women.

> *(Women) were not integrated into the professions as
> autonomous individuals...their professional existence was
> designed to extend the characteristics of familial
> subordination to the public arena, (to) reinforce the ideology
> of separate spheres....*[63]

219

Just as in nursing, the ideology developed for the diaconate was "long on responsibility and short on rights."[64] Self-sacrifice was the central code word in both professions. In the diaconate, however, it took on added meaning.

The doctrine of maternal feminism fitted in well with the social gospel theory. Isabelle Horton, an American Methodist deaconess, exploited both to develop a rationale for the diaconate. The Canadian orders produced no outstanding spokeswomen and, in the early years, Horton had considerable influence on the movement in this country.[65] Author of *The Burden of the City* and editor of *The Deaconess Advocate,* Horton spoke on several occasions in Canada including the commencement exercises of the Toronto Deaconess Training School in 1904. Dougherty uses Horton's work as an example of how male historians have ignored women's role in areas of study like the social gospel. Walter Rauschenbusch, generally credited as social gospel movement's theologian, published his *A Theology for the Social Gospel* in 1917. In 1904 Horton had espoused a similar "theology" in *The Burden of the City*. Like Rauschenbusch, she emphasized God as Love.

In an address printed in the *Methodist Magazine and Review* Horton argued that there "was a power above law, greater than law."

> *Human reason has figured it out that God is law; God is force. But inspiration says, God is love. The church has the secret of this power, if secret there be. To woman's hand especially has been committed the sceptre of its authority.*[66]

Not only did the church have the secret of that power, but in a deaconess order, properly directed and inspired, it could have an "arm of power" to reach the masses. Horton argued that the gospel of love, as preached by women, would reconcile capital and labour, bring the socialist back to the fold and Christianize the masses. Moreover, the masses were "more amenable" to the influence of women. "The great burden of the work...(could) only be done by the women folks."[67]

Miss Jean Scott, first principal of the Canadian Methodist Deaconess Home and Training School, agreed. The work the church "ought to do in the world" would only be half done, she argued, if men only were set apart to do it.

> *It is impossible for men to do all the work the church ought to do in the world. Whoever heard of a minister going round to nurse the sick? It is absurd on the face of it.*[68]

Miss Scott thought deaconesses stood "coordinate" with male officers of the church "and should be so recognized, while I do not believe their work is the same."[69] Horton seems to have been suspicious of the "different but equal" status granted the deaconess, but maternal feminism offered its reward:

> *What matter if we are not law-makers? We will conquer by the sign of the cross, the sign of utter sacrifice for love's sake.* [70]

Self-sacrifice through service was central to the ideology of the diaconate. At its most extreme, the language of the social gospel compared the deaconess to Christ. "The diaconate was bound to succeed," commented a clergyman in the *Review*, "because it opens up...in this age of emancipation an unbounded field of blessed Christ-like activity."

> *(The Deaconess) is not slow nor timid to sacrifice her all if called by God into the service of self-denying Christian charity...here is a communism of a kind the world wants but is not able to produce...a communism to love not to self....* [71]

"Like Christ," wrote Miss Scott, "the deaconess scours all Christendom...teaching, preaching, healing." [72] Bishop Ninde was not prepared to go that far, but he wrote:

> *When I see all about me these consecrated women...it seems to me...a ladder is lifted skyward with the angels of God ascending and descending thereon.* [73]

Maternal feminism asserted that woman's unique nurturing qualities gave her the right and responsibility to extend her activities beyond the home as a sort of social mother. In the church these qualities would form the basis of her ministry. "We ministers must not take on airs," wrote a Presbyterian cleric in 1905.

> *There is a ministry that is older and deeper and more patient than ours; it is the ministry that presides over the crib....* [74]

The affirmation of the diaconate, then, can be seen as an attempt by the church to "consecrate" the moral superiority that it had long attributed to women.

The Diaconate: The Image and The Reality

From the beginning, churchmen attempted the impossible; to infuse the actual with the ideal. According to *The Christian Guardian* of September 24, 1913, the ideal deaconess,

> *...will be a consecrated Christian, filled with the Holy Spirit, will have naturally, or will cultivate an unselfish, disposition, will be of a winsome, loving nature, filled with*

221

*the Christ love, going about doing good. She will have a
strong personality, firm, but kind, so that she may help
guide through various difficulties the lives of those with
whom she comes in contact.*

The ideal deaconess was also an excellent housekeeper and managed money "judiciously". She had a knowledge of music, was able to read aloud in an entertaining manner and was an accomplished platform speaker. She knew the basics of nursing. An exceptional teacher, she was able to assist with any activity or class in the church. When necessary she was able to take Sunday Service. Moreover, in performing any task she always showed "the bright side" of her personality.

*As superintendent of a home, she will feel the
responsibility of those with whom she is associated...as a
mother would...and will see that those in her care are not
overworked. She will look after her own health and
comfort, should provide herself with good, warm clothing in
winter, see that she has good shoes and rubbers...for the
task of an "ideal deaconess" is not an easy one, and she will
require a healthy body to do the work allotted her.*

That this paragon needed to be reminded about rubber boots (and deaconesses frequently were) is evidence that, from the beginning, the ideal and the actual clashed.

The "hundreds of sisters" whom the *Review* editor expected to flock into service never materialized. As early as 1899, an urgent call for candidates appeared in the magazine. The idealism associated with the orders was not as intense in the Presbyterian Church, but calls for candidates were heard frequently from both. "The labourers are few," lamented Superintendent Bishop in 1913:

*Is it the lure "of the life that now is" which overmasters
the love that constrains to self-sacrifice and which prevents
so many capable and cultured Christian women giving heed
to the call of the Master?*[75]

The diaconate was in competition with teaching, the emerging professions of nursing and social work, and the generally expanding employment opportunities in the secular society. Within the church, the orders were never able to compete with the opportunities for mission service offered by the Woman's Missionary societies. In 1913, enrolment figures for deaconess probationers remained the same as in the previous year, while the number of missionary candidates doubled. At Union, three times as many women were active in the foreign field as in deaconess work.[76]

Missionary service offered a romance that the diaconate could never possess. "Fiction appears weak and commonplace...beside...such a life," commented a writer in the *Review*. A typical article on the work in India, appearing in 1899, included engravings of camel carriages, temples and street scenes. Illustrations of beatific deaconesses surrounded by a clutch of kindergartners could not compete! The Methodist Church publicized the office extensively after 1900 but was never able to match the effective publicity machine of the WMS. The magazines produced by the various societies had a following and popularity that has perhaps only been matched by some television programs in our own day. Barbara Welther attributes the attraction of the mission field to "the rare combination of church and socially sanctioned activity and freedom" which women found there. The woman doctor, for example,

> ...found a far more interesting practice, an opportunity to perform operations, to study rare diseases, and to escape a professional life as poorly paid listener to female complaints, her probable lot had she remained at home.[77]

Opportunities in home mission work, which opened during the war, also provided competition for the orders. At Union, as many women had chosen that field of endeavour as the diaconate. An almost equal number had found employment with the Board of Evangelism and Social Service, self-supporting congregations, and in other areas of activity.[78] Since both churches had made provision to recognize suitably qualified applicants who had not graduated from church-sponsored programs, many women would have been eligible for membership in one or other of the orders. The fact that designation as a deaconess was obviously not sufficiently significant to a majority of women in the church says much about the status of the office.

Salary does not seem to have been an issue in discouraging potential recruits. Until 1917, when attempts were made to upgrade the order, Methodist deaconesses worked "for the love of Christ and in His Name." An allowance was paid—$10.00 per month in 1912—and provision was also made for a holiday allowance. On the other hand, Presbyterian deaconesses had always received a salary. The $30.00 per month they received in 1912 was the same salary paid to certified teachers and experienced settlement workers employed by the church. Even so, the Presbyterian order was only marginally more successful in attracting candidates. At Union in 1925, 61 Presbyterian deaconesses were engaged in some form of active service as compared to 47 of their Methodist sisters. The Methodist order had attracted 125 women to the order from its founding in 1894. The Presbyterian Church had designated 131 women, although in a shorter time period.

As in teaching and nursing, the deaconess was expected to retire after marriage. Like the nurse, she was required to wear a uniform and live in a home under the watchful eye of a superintendent. However, unlike the nurse, the deaconess had chosen a vocation and was required to "cheer-fully and willingly" give *all her time* to the duties appointed her.

The annual report of the Deaconess Society of the Methodist Church for 1912-1913 defined those duties as follows:

> *...to minister to the poor, visit the sick, pray for the dying, care for the orphan, seek the wandering, comfort the sorrowing, labour to save the sinning, and devote themselves to such forms of Christian work as may be suited to their abilities.*

Language in the Presbyterian order was never as full-blown, but the expectations surrounding the deaconess' role seem to have been as high. "In her desire to be 'all things'," wrote a number of that order, "the deaconess has reason to sigh for the wisdom of Solomon."[79] One deaconess described her daily routine in the *Christian Guardian* of March 18, 1903:

> *I made nine missionary calls, visited the hospital, gave away fifteen garments, supplied seven families with food and ended the day by leading a cottage meeting, speaking from the topic, "How Christ makes use of common lives."*

A Miss Lang spent 1500 hours on duty as a travellers' aide at Union Station in 1913. The following year her Presbyterian counterpart at the Vancouver docks wrote:

> *You forget the physical weariness which accompanies the strenuous effort of meeting so many strangers, and the necessity of giving so much practical help...when the port closes; listing, visiting and following all the Presbyterians occupy one, besides helping the distressed and relieving poverty.*[80]

Whatever their responsibilities, each deaconess performed part of the housework in the home in which she resided.

The deaconess seems to have been poorly equipped for the practical aspects of her work. Since "the supreme object of all deaconess work (was) to save the soul" a considerable part of the curriculum in both Presbyterian and Methodist orders was given over to Bible study and church history. Moreover, little direction, particularly in the early years, seems to have been given to them in their work. The deaconess was on her own, literally "climbing into attics, exploring dark cellars," seeking out misery in the urban slum and giving what aids she could. Often she did not have much aid to give.

In both orders, deaconesses were dependent on Aid Societies to raise funds, gather the clothing, and put up the preserves which she distributed.

Week after week, the deaconess column of the *Christian Guardian* carried appeals for assistance. However, the Aid Societies were never able to attract the level of support given to Women's Mission effort. "The whole work is much handicapped," wrote a Presbyterian deaconess involved in 'Ruthenian work',

> ...*an inadequate staff, lack of funds, supplies and equipment make connected effort difficult....*[81]

"We cannot measure results," wrote one of her sisters; "Faithfulness is what is required to Him."[82] Unfortunately, that faith could not always be mustered. Evidence appears even in the edited versions of the reports of individual deaconesses which appeared in the Church press or in Minutes of Conference or Assembly.

> *I found a sick mother and five little children, the eldest a newsboy, ten years of age, being the sole support of the family Oh, the dirt, the emptiness of that home!...A sense of helplessness swept over me....*[83]
>
> *One feels helpless in occasional visits to girls who are constantly surrounded by evil influence. They need...much closer touch than is possible from a deaconess whose time is fully occupied.*[84]

There is a poignancy about these young women carrying their "ministries of love and sympathy" alone into the slum. Isabelle Horton reminded *Review* readers that the deaconess "is simply a young women":

> *She has spent eight months, perhaps, in a training school. She has learned something of the Bible, something of history, something of many things that will be of use to her; but she has much to learn. She has barely skimmed the shores of the great ocean of misery and pain.*[85]

Horton and other commentators warned that the deaconess could not be "expected to bear the whole burden of the charitable work of the church ...on her inexperienced shoulders."[86] Addressing the Hamilton Deaconess Aid Society, Dr. Hazelwood chastised church members who were "taking advantage of these women."[87]

That the work was difficult and discouraging is attested to be the rest homes operated by most North American orders for their members, and by the liberal leaves of absence allowed. A letter in the Deaconess File of the Manitoba College papers indicates that at least one young woman withdrew from the work suffering from "nervous strain."[88] American Methodism's Bishop Thorburn, writing in the *Review*, lamented the popular image of the diaconate as a life of "holy drudgery". But the low enrolment figures and high dropout rate[89] indicate the substance behind the image.

During and immediately after World War One, new responsibilities were thrust upon the deaconess. A shortage of ministers meant that women in both Methodist and Presbyterian orders frequently conducted Sunday Service and carried out parish duties. Often they would serve a congregation for months at a time.

In the Presbyterian Church, several deaconesses found a welcome challenge as Home Missionaries. Initially hired as summer supplies on the same conditions and salary as male theology students, many women soon found permanent employment in the field. A similar opportunity later opened to Methodist women. "Without exception," wrote a church official in 1919, "these women have proven themselves to be faithful and successful preachers and pastors."[90] But no matter how successful they were, when a marriage had to be performed, or the sacraments administered, an ordained minister had to be called in.

"Our church can with profit continue their services" (as male replacements), wrote a Presbyterian cleric enthusiastically.[91] That women were no longer content "filling in the gaps" and serving as "efficient handmaidens" is evident in the declining membership of the orders. By 1922, only 43 deaconesses were engaged in active service in the Methodist Church compared to 71 in 1909. For a number of years the Deaconess Program, introduced to Manitoba College in 1922, provided a stopgap for the Presbyterian order. Of the twelve women designated to the order in 1924, for example, nine were Manitoba graduates.

By the twenties, deaconesses found their responsibilities shrinking as secular health and welfare agencies began to take over some aspects of their role. The deaconess program at Manitoba College included stenographic training on its curriculum, a sure death knell to the deaconess' unique ministry. The intense idealism associated with the diaconate as its founding would dissipate as enthusiasm for the Social Gospel waned. Increasingly, the modern Phoebe would find herself employed by a congregation, serving as secretary or organizing activities for girls and women. By 1922, the orders were in crisis.

That year, 26 of the 43 deaconesses in active service in the Methodist Church memorialized General Conference "calling attention to their opinion that deaconess work does not occupy the place of importance in the activities and religious life of the church that it ought to..." If Conference were not prepared to rectify the situation, the women suggested that the order should be disbanded.[92]

Here, then, was the dilemma of maternal feminism faced by women in both church and secular society. By suppressing autonomous motivations and relying on a rationale based on woman's unique nurturing qualities, the limitations of woman's sphere had been unwittingly reinforced.

226

In women's long journey toward autonomy in the church, the diaco-nate represents a side road. The office says much about women's relation-ship to mainline Protestantism, but ultimately, it represents a dead-end.

Diane Haglund

Diane is a student in the Joint Masters Program in History at the University of Winnipeg/University of Manitoba who was "struck by the extent to which secular historians writing on the early feminist movement have ignored the importance of the church in the lives of women." She hopes to use the research for this paper as the basis of her thesis.

Editor's note:

This paper represents one point of view of the diaconal ministry, and does not say anything about the diaconal ministry in The United Church of Canada after church union. See the Parsons' paper (chapter 8), for more infor-mation about the role of the diaconate today.

Chapter 11 LIBERATING CHRISTIANITY

—Margie Whynot

SUMMARY

Although women today make up fifty-five percent of the population of Canada, Christianity has been used both to elevate them and hold them down.

Throughout the centuries religion has been a system devised and defined by men. The stories of heroic women in the Bible and the early church have been suppressed; the liturgies of the Christian church have been male-centred and dominated by the male biblical characters. Even so, there have been dramatic changes in thinking in the past twenty years. With the advent of feminist theologians and an improving climate within society, women have been working toward change within the Christian church in general, and the United Church in particular.

One of the priorities for change must be the use of inclusive language, for as people become aware of the effects of words and phrases which leave out half the population, they will also gain an awareness of the broader issues of discrimination. There has been some work done on this issue by the United Church, and the Division of Mission in Canada has adopted guidelines to be used by their writers, editors, and artists, as well as their staff members.

As well as changing language, it is important that we challenge images which portray women as fragile, emotional, and incompetent to deal with the broader social issues. Each person needs to deal with issues of discrimination in her own way. Rather than accepting subordination to men as right and proper, women need to challenge the old symbols and traditions.

Freedom and equality of women will also have a positive effect on men, as both sexes will be freed of stereotypes. It is important for men and women to act together to reshape the imagery of the past and work for a future which is liberating for everyone.

—editor

Women make up fifty-five percent of the population of Canada. Christianity has been used both to enhance the status of this majority and to keep it in a subordinate position to men. The past twenty years, however, have seen dramatic changes in women's situation in The United Church of Canada and the beginning of a process which will liberate not only men and women but the church itself.

Throughout the centuries, people have "created" religions and shaped them, changing the shared meanings of language and symbols. In the first century of Christianity, Christians expected Christ to return almost immediately. As time passed, however, they changed their ideas and in effect, the "look" of that aspect of their religion. The Christian religion is not real in the sense that it is physical, like an object; Christianity is made up of the shared meanings of a group, "real" to the extent that there is some kind of group understanding about what it is. Unfortunately, what Christianity is has not been determined by the whole community, but by the part of the community which is male. As a result it has become a religion without female principles, a patriarchal system which serves man by taking away the power of woman.

One way to change the system is to redefine the religious language and symbols used to oppress. Language is extremely important in the development of a "self" and if we look at history, we can see why it has taken women so long to achieve enough self-esteem to work for change. From pre-Christianity to the present, they have been dominated by men in the structures of home, church and society. How many of us realize that Huldah (II Kings 22: 14ff) was an important prophetess in the Old Testament; that Deborah was a prophetess and judge (Judges 4: 4-5: 31); that Jesus and Paul knew and respected women who worked with them in their ministries (Romans 16: 1-16)? The loss of a heroic past has been one form of the oppression of women in the western, patriarchal culture.

Christianity, as it is commonly understood, has been oppressive in other ways as well. A young girl, taken to church, hears and observes people worshipping a Father God. She hears stories about male biblical characters, sings hymns full of male imagery, and takes part in a liturgy which ends with blessing in "the name of the Father, and the Son, and the Holy Spirit". We can understood how the girl internalizes the "maleness" of the Christian faith. The absence of "femaleness" in traditional Christianity affects her sense of her own worth as a human being as she grows into womanhood, and subtly reinforces the more open claims to male superiority.

To go against a tradition regarded sacred by others takes courage and vision; it is lonely and uncomfortable without support or a strong, positive reference group. All too often, women find they are like the Israelites in the wilderness: they cry out against their present hardship but elect the advantage of living in a state of oppression. The cost of liberation can be too great unless there are clearly defined, long-term goals.

With the advent of feminist theologians and an improving role in society generally, women have been working toward change within the United Church. For some, change has come through working within women's liberation movements; for others, it has meant a quieter transition from oppression to awareness, and then through the long, slow process of personal emancipation. For many women it has been a time of discomfort and even disbelief: to admit that oppression exists raises a problem that may require a costly solution.

The Importance of Language

Although many men and women oppose the changes that are slowly taking place, there is a growing, positive support for more equality even though it is not simple to change meanings and interpretations that have been accepted for centuries. One of the first priorities must be language that includes everyone, as it is almost impossible for women to develop a sense of themselves as complete persons when words and images shut them out. Inclusive language is important, for as people become aware of the effects of language that excludes half the population, they will also gain an awareness of the broader issues of discrimination. In addition, inclusive language used in this generation will be internalized by the next. The United Church has addressed the problems of language in a formal way:

> The Division (of Mission in Canada) has...recognized the need to deal with stereotyping and exclusiveness in (the) use of language and imagery. Since 1976 it has had guidelines on gender and God Language. In April 1982, the Division Executive adopted new guidelines which cover these areas: gender, religion, age, family structure, single people, people of exceptional need. The DMC Language and Image Guidelines are intended for use within the Division by writers, editors and artists, as well as program-planners and administrators, both staff and volunteer. In changing our use of language and imagery, the Division realizes that it also needs to work on the problems and issues that separate people. We are called to be an inclusive church and to do justly![1]

Those who think that the matter of language is trivial, or that the struggle to achieve a partnership of women and men in the church is unnecessary, often ground their arguments in scripture. In particular, fragments of Paul's letter are quoted, *even when they are at odds with the words and deeds of Jesus.* Letty Russell says:

> Over the years Christian tradition has been shaped around one-sided interpretations and isolated texts from the Bible in order to create an ideology of subjection for women. Sexism, like racism, communism, (and) capitalism is an ideology: a set of ideas created by men in order to shape reality in a certain way. This particular ideology was part of the Jewish-Hellenistic cultural context of Paul's writing and, over the centuries, the religious institutions of Western society have helped to make it "God's law" for many generations of women.[2]

The very way the Bible is written—by men for men—is a problem for many women. Others are willing to acknowledge its historical context and accept the fact that Jesus himself presents a different view of God and society. The four gospels indicate that Jesus did not spend all his time with the religious leaders of his day, or even with his own followers. He also spoke to and for the culturally disadvantaged. He talked to women about things that concern women, and there is no evidence that he considered them inferior to men, or unworthy of taking an active role in his service. In fact, his disciples included women, and the first resurrection appearance was to women. In spite of the record of Jesus' behaviour, however, there is still a segment of church society which ignores how Christ lived and invokes Paul's letters to prove the correctness of sexist attitudes.

Paul, writing out of the Jewish-Hellenistic culture in which he lived, did not intend to write scripture. He was simply writing letters to the Christian churches of his day, addressing the particular concerns of each. It could be that his admonition about women keeping silent was directed at the Montanist charismatic sect. Within that group, Priscilla and Maximilla, co-leaders with Montanus, were disturbing people by speaking in tongues. Since no one really *knows* why Paul wrote as he did, we can only look at other facts about his life. We do know that he worked with women as well as men.

> I commend to you our sister Phoebe, a deaconess of the church of Cenchreae, that you may receive her in the Lord as befits the saints, and help her in whatever she may require from you, for she has been a helper of many and of myself as well. (Romans 16: 1,2)

Rosemary Reuther, Mary Daly, and Dr. Phyllis Trible are prominent theologians who are helping Christians to discover their "female" biblical past. Trible's work, in particular, is extremely helpful in showing the Bible's potential for inclusiveness. By combining her method with the work of Mary Daly, it is possible to gain a new perspective on such stories

231

as the Creation and Fall, and on the importance of the use of language in that context. Daly, especially, wants to get "beyond God the Father" to a God that is also understood as Mother. It is through this new awareness of the feminine, and through a new sense of pride in a recovered past, that the relation between women and men can be healed. Freedom, in this sense, is a process of rebirth out of ignorance, apathy, and oppression into personhood. For women, this is not just a liberation from the home and domesticity, but from outdated ideas. The right to choose from the entire realm of human experience is essential to the development of each individual, whether male or female.

Challenging Past Images

To understand the importance of freeing the past by the use of inclusive language and feminist re-interpretation, it is helpful to understand why women act as they do. Women have been depicted as fragile, emotional, and incompetent to deal with the broader social issues. Since feminity is defined in terms of those qualities, many women behave accordingly, because to do otherwise would be "unfeminine". Others, perhaps with a stronger sense of self, construct alternate roles for themselves at the risk of being different or even labelled deviant.

In our present society, even a good education does not necessarily mean freedom if a woman lacks self-esteem and trust in her own experience. Brenda, a young university student studying for ordained ministry in the United Church, was just beginning to achieve some sense of herself when she was challenged by a fundamentalist leader opposed to the idea of women ministers. At a weekend retreat, using Paul's letters as his authority, he argued that women had no place in ministry. In spite of the fact that Brenda (not her real name) felt she had been called to a vocation within the church, she was shattered by his onslaught and considered a sex-change operation as an alternative to denying her call. She had attached so much value to his version of the "reality" of Christianity that she had permitted the man to oppress her. Her failure to respond out of her own "reality" only reinforced his claims as truth. Even Paul's "freedom" text did not ease Brenda's anxiety.

> For as many of you as were baptized into Christ have put on Christ. There is neither Jew nor Greek, there is neither slave nor free, there is neither male nor female; for you are all one in Christ Jesus. (Galatians 3: 27, 28)

Patriarchal powers appears to be "real", but it is only real as long as we accept patriarchal definitions of male and female roles. If, as a group, women were to act and work together on the basis of feminist meanings, social institutions (including the church) would change drastically. Many women have become aware of general oppression only after they have experienced some blatant form of discrimination in their own lives. As long as they are *comfortably* oppressed, they tend to slow down the process of redefinition by denying the problem. Unjust values, unconfronted, are taken to be legitimate values. By accepting a male view of Christianity, women justify male domination in the church and deny their own understanding of God and Godliness. Daphne Anderson, in *God's Hidden People*, quotes an "eminent United Churchman" speaking with the voice of authority in 1960:

> *The husband is the head of the family, according to the scriptures, and the wife is the heart. On all matters the wife ought to express her opinion and insist that it be considered. But when a decision has to be voiced in the outside world, the man is the spokesman.*[3]

Women in the United Church have come a long way since that statement was made. In fact, just twenty years later, Lois Wilson was elected Moderator. Throughout her two-year term she encouraged the use of inclusive language. Her commitment to male/female partnership was couched in a larger concern for all oppressed people. Sexism, for her, was a justice issue.

> *The challenge to the mainline churches today is to (act) out alternate models of authentic human community. It is to heal the yawning chasms between men and women, women and women, French and English, labourers and managers, native peoples and governments, etc. sic. And that is exactly what a growing number of Christian women are doing in Canada today. They are (wounded healers), standing with others in their pain and allowing the Holy Spirit to effect wholeness —or, conversely, allowing the Spirit to disturb, to make uncomfortable, and to pull them screaming and protesting, perhaps, into the world as it really is.*[4]

The pain, for women, of achieving full personhood in a culture which has systematically denied them such status, imparts a new, bittersweet meaning to the Hebrew prayer: "Blessed art Thou, O Lord our God, who hast not made me a woman."

Signs of Hope

Each person deals with the problem of discrimination in a different way and to a different degree. Janet, a social worker active in women's issues, provides an example of positive coping. She has reached the point in her "becoming" where she feels she is her own person. Although happily married, Janet (not her real name) maintains her individuality and uses her own name. She does not depend on her husband, a university professor and United Church clergy, to make her life complete. She has her own life and her own circle of friends, as does her husband. At every opportunity she speaks on behalf of women's rights—even from the pulpit of her husband's church.

Janet's story is typical of many others. She grew up working with her father, three sisters, and one brother on the family farm. During those formative years she first became aware of a double standard for girls and boys. Although she did her share on the outside—driving the tractor, forking hay, milking cows—equality stopped at the back door and there was no sharing of the household chores. Her fondest wish at that time was to see her father and brother do the dishes at least once! Housework, however, was left to her mother, sisters and herself.

Janet waited thirty-three years to speak out publicly against such social and psychological injustice. Her courage to do so resulted from her high self-esteem and the presence of a strong, positive support group which included her husband. Janet's sense of herself as a person had been strengthened by the growing body of women's writings and a community of women in her town, all struggling towards an understanding of freedom and equality. Only in such a nurturing context could she risk shaking the "comfortable pews". She is, in her corner of the world, helping to re-define what it is to be a woman and a Christian.

Because women, as well as men, have been brought up with patriarchal values, too many (like Brenda) see themselves as subordinate to men and accept this as right and proper. It is easier to stay the same than to change, and easier to follow than to choose, especially when the cost is so high. But Mary Daly sees the movement out of patriarchy as the only hope for *human* survival.

> *The freedom to fall out of Eden will cost a mirror-shattering experience. The freedom-becoming-survival of our species will require a continual, communal striving in be-ing in sisterhood that can surround non-being, forcing it to shrink back into itself...The power of sisterhood is not warfare. There have been and will be conflicts, but the Final Cause causes, not by conflict, but by attraction. Not by the attraction of a Magnet that is All There, but by the creative drawing power of the Good Who is self-communicating Be-ing, Who is the Verb from whom, in whom, and with whom all true movements move.*[5]

If women do not seek freedom, do not allow their creative individuality to "become", then the world is at risk. Women are presently challenging the old symbols and traditions of patriarchal Christianity which have resulted in oppression in God's name and the "God-on-our-side" warfare throughout the world.

Freedom and equality of women will also free men. As long as women are confined to stereotyped roles, men are also stereotyped. Betty Jane Wylie makes this point in *Beginnings: A Book for Widows*.

> *...It's a stereotype that says men have to be good at fixing toaster plugs and unstopping toilets while women sew on the buttons and make the porridge. If I lose a button I might as well throw the garment away. I'm three years behind in my mending.*[6]

The journey toward Be-ing is not a simple intellectual process. Each woman must come to understand that she is part of a sisterhood which shares the struggle toward wholeness. To be free is to be as God created her and, having achieved freedom, she will want others to be free as well. Only when all humans are liberated will each reflect the image of God.

> *When men discover their femininity and women their masculinity, then perhaps we can form a truly liberating and mutually enriching partnership.*[7]

The capacity to take the role of the others helps us to understand how and why people act and re-act as they do. Oppression will not disappear with the exchange of one oppressed group for another: the struggle for freedom within the church needs to be a corporate venture of men and women working together. If there is a central theme of Christianity, it is that the oppression of one is the oppression of all. If Christianity is to be understood as liberating, then it must be wrested from a past which has perverted its message in order to enhance the power of a particular group.

The symbolic imagery of our inherited faith is not absolute or fixed. Rather, we are permitted to interpret our symbols in a variety of ways. Women must assume their rightful place in church and society and, in partnership with men, set about the business of restoring God's kingdom on earth. The United Church, at its founding, was committed to the church that *could* be, not to the church that had been. As women rededicate themselves to a church which they are helping to shape, perhaps the God of Genesis will look upon creation again and find it not just "good", but "better".

Margie Whynot

> *Margie is a candidate for ordination in The United Church of Canada, who became interested in women's changing role in the church during the course of her studies at Mount Allison University.*

Chapter 12 POURING THE TEA AND
HIDING THE WINE BOTTLE:
REFLECTIONS ON THE ROLE
OF THE MINISTER'S MATE

—Andrea Shaver

SUMMARY

Traditionally, the role of the minister's spouse has been
carried by women, and her part has depended on the needs
of the minister as well as the expectations of each congregation. Her role has been in large part defined by tradition
and has basically been one of support: pouring tea, taking
leadership roles within the church, helping to visit the sick.
Marriage and parenthood have always been important
within the church, and the minister's wife has been
expected to provide a good example in this respect. In
many ways, she is a prototype for women's role within the
church itself: her duty is to serve, and recognition of her
work is minimal.

Ministers who pioneered in the opening-up of western
Canada were expected to be married and their wives often
combined their special ministry with the pioneering spirit.
One such woman was Emily Murphy, the first female police
magistrate in Canada and one of the key spokespersons in
the fight to have women declared persons under the law.
Attitudes about the role of minister's spouses reflected the
way women in general were regarded and treated. Education, moral reform, and moral leadership were in many
cases initiated and led by women. Influential leaders could
be found in people like Nellie McClung and Emily Murphy.
In spite of this, and in spite of the fact that the money raised
by women's groups went to a variety of reform causes,
women's entry into positions of power took years to
achieve. Even ordination of women into The United
Church of Canada did not take place until 1936, after years
of debate.

The expectations of the minister's spouse and women
in ministry have changed in recent years. The number of
women ministers has risen 150 percent since 1975; women's
enrolment at theological colleges is rising, and several United Church conferences have "networks" of women in
ministry. This change on the national and college level is not

always reflected on the local level. Some women ministers have found that ministers' wives have resented their ordination, while others being interviewed for ordination by conference boards have found that questions centred on their personal lives rather than on their theological understandings. In addition, when the minister's spouse is a man, difficulties may arise because the traditional expectations need to be revised. The minister's husband is not automatically expected to pour tea or attend UCW meetings!

The minister's spouse today needs to define his/her own role. A minister's marriage is much the same as any other, with some additional stress. Even so, the church would do well to consider the position of those who marry ministers: the different expectations attached to the role and work of the spouse can provide valuable insights into our attributes towards men and women.

—editor

*Q. I have been keeping company with a
theological student and we have fallen
deeply in love. I am a bit worried about
whether I could make it as a minister's
spouse. Are there not a great many extra
demands that will be made on me? What
do you think I should do?*

A. Go ahead and marry her.[1]

(The late Rev. Bud Morden in The
United Church Observer)

Asimple and benevolent answer, but is it a simple question? Would the answer have been different fifty, twenty, or even ten years ago? Would the question have come up? If the student were female would the answer be more complex? Although it has been said that ministers have a habit of marrying helpmates not lovers,[2] Mr. Morden seems to be denouncing such practice in his answer above. Conflicting views of this issue seem to be drawn largely along generational lines.

Because most ministers are men, most minister's spouses are women. Although the increasing number of men married to ministers will be considered, the focus in this article will be on the minister's wife. The role of minister's wife, unique and essentially undefined, has been tempered by manse living, the communal nature of the minister's work within the church, and the moral leadership the minister represents within the community. The part to be played by the wife depends to a great degree on the needs of the minister when he decides to marry, needs which change over the years. It is also affected by the expectations of each congregation the minister serves. Every member of a minister's family, even the youngest, realizes that she/he has a special place and certain obligations within the church community.

Church Union (in 1925) took place at a time of great upheaval for women. In the wake of the rejuvenated women's movement of the past two decades, it is interesting to see how the social climate has affected the lives of women so central to church life. The public nature of her role leads one to wonder what kind of woman accepts such a prominent scenario for her private life.

What's Expected

It is a common, if often unstated feeling among church members and clergy that a minister's spouse should feel a calling. This can be interpreted as an aptitude for church work with some sort of background in teaching, counselling or community work, plus a willingness to move far away from home for the sake of the minister's work. The adage that ministers tend to marry helpmates rather than lovers highlights this belief in working compatibility as an integral part of a minister's married life. There are many examples of well-trained women who were also ministers' wives. In 1868, Nathaniel Burwash married a former teacher at Wesleyan Female College in Hamilton, and Preceptress of the Ladies Academy in Sackville, New Brunswick. Many women met their husbands through church work in the first place. Even so, a background of church involvement does not automatically prepare one for life as a minister's wife.

Some women are married to men who decided to enter the ministry *after* marriage and after a certain way of life had already been established. Their reluctance to accept the special nature of clergy life could make the minister's job more difficult. One man, proceeding with his theological training despite such a situation, was questioned extensively by the Interview Board about his feelings toward women. He was encouraged to question whether the change in lifestyle he was willing to make was worth undermining his marriage. In an effort to explore his attitudes toward women the interviewers asked how he would feel about being an assistant to a woman minister. He admitted that the possibility had never entered his thinking![3]

The minister's position is not much different from that of a businessman who is asked to move around the country for the sake of his job. Indeed, ministers' choices are governed by the belief that a variety of pastorates is healthy for both clergy and parishes. This does not necessarily mean the minister's wife must become a docile follower: some men take into account the reluctance of their wives, and a compromise is reached. One woman said she tried to be as different as possible from what she considered a minister's wife should be. It was not until two years into ministry work that she underwent the kind of transformation that could be interpreted as a calling—a realization that she was doing what she was good at and what God wanted her to do.

Some women marry ministers with the subconscious need to realize a personal aspiration through their husbands.[4] Now, many are proceeding after marriage, to enter the ministry themselves. One woman admitted that she had started studying theology to understand and help her husband's career, and it was not until she was well into her studies that she realized that she herself would make a good minister. She had not recognized any sort of calling in becoming a minister's wife even though her family had been elated. Her subsequent decision to study theology and enter the ministry was accompanied by a "nagging sensation", her definition of a calling.

The role of a minister's wife is in large part defined by tradition: pouring tea, heading the UCW and other groups within the church, shaking hands with people at the door after services, helping her husband with his sermons and often typing them. It is basically a supporting role. Other duties are not always so straightforward. Ministers' wives take services when their husbands are away at meetings or ill; they visit the sick and counsel the distraught; they take on projects that need doing but lack leadership. How many congregational members are like the one who does not particularly appreciate the minister's work, but the splendid work of his wife with the youth groups balances that out? One female minister said that she encountered more hostility to her ordained role from ministers' wives than from other clergy precisely because so many of them have been doing ministerial duties without the ordination, the salary or the recognition—"unordained but usable".[5]

The wife is part of the special status of the minister and her time and energy are traditionally seen as available to the church when needed. In many ways she is a prototype for women's role within the church itself: her duty is to serve, and recognition of her work is minimal. Women are rarely policy-makers, and they usually have little recognized authority or power. A minister's wife is seldom seen on official boards of any kind: that would be seen as conflicting with her husband's work. Each is just another member of the congregation, and her duty is the duty of ministry given to every Christian. She is however, in a special class in that the dimensions of her ministry are larger than usual and her access to decision-making is smaller. Certainly, the church hierarchy recognizes the importance of the minister's wife's contribution. In the past, some couples seeking ordination have been advised that the wife should not seek ordination but go to her husband's charge and share ministry in that way. Does this mean they consider marriage to be as good as ordination?

Family has always been of central importance to the ministry of Christians, and one function of the clergy wife's role has been to provide an example of that centrality. That view formed the basis of the argument against female ministers as it was put forth in the 1920s and '30s:

> If women were to enter the ministry in great numbers, we should have a celibate clergy. For if a woman were to choose the ministry for her life's work she would have to renounce a family. History shows that the offspring of the manse are among the finest type of citizens, and countries that have a celibate clergy are of a lower moral tone than those where there are sons and daughters of the clergy to mingle with other people.
>
> Many young women who may have, in all sincerity, thought they could ignore that mating instinct, which is one of God's greatest gifts to his physical creatures, will find, after spending years of study and much money, that they must after all choose marriage and all its responsibilities. For of course no young woman who had heard the high calling of God in Christ Jesus would be presumptuous enough to say she could do more for the Lord as a minister than as a mother.[6]

At that time, the combination of marriage and motherhood was seen as the most appropriate career a woman could have. Indeed, the nature of the minister's work made his wife's involvement more of a career than was possible for many women.

Pioneering Roles

From an econimic standpoint, marriage was important to all professions in the opening-up of the Canadian West. That ministers be married was, by and large, a precondition of their pioneering placement. Working side by side in a difficult land gave pioneers a strong sense of partnership and a set of values based on principles of cooperation. The growth of social and political movements in the West at the turn of the century provides the background for the ecumenical movement that gave birth to the United Church.

The special ministry of the minister's wife combined with the pioneering spirit to produce women like Emily Murphy, the first female police magistrate in Canada and one of the key spokespersons in the fight to have women declared persons under the law. "For the first years of her marriage she channelled all her energies and interests into her life as the wife of a minister and the mother of three girls".[7] She used to copy inspirational quotes for her husband. She indexed his library and, in the lonely evenings when he was away on mission runs, she became a writer, known widely as Janey Canuck. Her writings were influential and through them, Emily Murphy became increasingly involved in social issues.

It is possible to draw a picture of the minister's wife by focussing on exceptional women like Mrs. Murphy, but it would not be an honest one. While such women found themselves in exceptional circumstances, many of their sisters led less noticeable lives. Certain aspects, however, were common. Ministers' wives were public figures, even in isolated charges. Marion Laing, a turn-of-the-century woman transplanted after marriage to Saskatchewan, wrote about the life of a pioneer minister whose days were taken up with calls to their scattered congregation. Mrs. Laing's personal sense of ministry led her to accompany her husband, something the parishioners had not experienced with their previous ministers in the East. "One woman told me she felt I was like one of themselves and they did not need to make strange with me, something to that effect. I felt quite flattered."[8] The pioneering of the West was part of the atmosphere wherein the United Church was born, and the work of women was an essential part of that climate.

At that time, women's place in society was in debate not only in the Supreme Court and the British Privy Council, but also in the committee on church union. The question of personhood was debated in all three bodies. The question of ordaining women, in a time of clergy shortage and national expansion following World War One, came up in 1923 and was dismissed every year until 1936 when the Rev. Lydia Gruchy was ordained. The issue was controversial and current. It could have irreparably damaged the cause of union but eventually served to move the United Church into the mainstream of the women's movement—if not by reasons of commitment, at least by practical and realistic considerations.

Women and the Church: Where Attitudes Begin

Women and the church accomplished much together. The Sunday School, often organized by ministers and run by women, was in many cases the foundation of the public educational system. Moral leadership in the uncivilized West was symbolized by the church and championed by women's organizations such as the Woman's Christian Temperance Union, the best organized women's group in the country. Influential leaders were Nellie McClung and Emily Murphy. McClung married a minister's son whose mother became an important role model for her work. The Social Gospel movement swept the West with a vigour that moved women into the forefront of social reform. Young, well-educated women travelled the country campaigning for social advancement:

> I was particularly excited to meet and have my work heartily endorsed by Nellie McClung and Judge Emily Murphy during a notable week in Edmonton. Always I was supported by women's groups and the editors of local papers. Unfortunately I met with no such unanimous responses from the clergy, even of my own church (Methodist). Many readily took up the challenge and you could always be sure of the support of those who had come under the influence of Salem Bland at Wesley College. Some were finicky about letting me speak from the pulpit and most were very curious about what I told their women and girls.[9]

Although the church did not always lead in matters of social reform, it provided an organization through which new ideas could reach the people and united women in awareness, if not in active concern. "People often set politics up in opposition to religion but that was hardly the case for me. Politics is working together to fulfil the needs of others as you would have them fulfil yours."[10] The coincidence of women obtaining the right to vote and the establishment of the United Church during the 1920s links the church to the concerns of women.

The work of women has always been vital to The United Church of Canada. As Canada was settled and cities established, women's leisure time was invested in social work through church organizations. Women proved to be excellent fund-raisers[11] and their money went to reform causes that were close to women's lives: temperance, half-way houses, education, and social welfare. They became political, moving from domestic life into social action. Ministers' wives, already public figures, provided role models for many. They led Sunday schools, CGIT, women's groups and mission societies, marshalling church women into action.

242

Women's entry into positions of power took much longer. Their work in the church went unrecognized for so long, largely as a consequence of the attitudes of women themselves. Born and bred to nurturing roles, their broadening perspective did not include concern about power. The message of feminism in turn-of-the-century social reform was dominated by views of maternalism. The writings of Nellie McClung describe maternal feminism as an extension of women's natural abilities as mothers into a more public forum. Admittedly idealized, this amplification was seen as the key to peace, social morality, and the preservation of the family. The radical element, apparent in the British feminist movement and introduced in Canada by the Pankhursts who lectured across the country, did not catch on. Women mainly responded to the arguments to which they could relate. Thus, when the social reform fervour and post-war prosperity ended, plunging Canada into the painful reality of the Depression, women's role and sphere of influence remained localized in the family and community and was directed toward the church, largely because of the understanding women had of the maternal nature of their role and influence.

The early arguments about the ordination of women illustrate the prevalent attitudes. Even today, some ordained women note that churchwomen are more often opposed to their ordination than men. Women have seen ministry and motherhood as an either/or proposition and their thoughts were, and still are, echoed by a large number of clergy. The reality of Lydia Gruchy's suitability for ordination could not be ignored. That she chose not to marry in her lifetime reflects not only her dedication to the work but also the social mores of her time.

The Rev. Mary Haggart, ordained in 1954, spoke to Grace Lane of the tension between marriage and ministry, as she has experienced it.

> *Her only complaint at present is with a problem she has faced before—loneliness. "I'm very busy and have many friends, but no one really close. You can't do the job properly," she feels. "Here's where the married man has an advantage—he can unwind to his wife, and hopefully she'll have a hot meal ready, at least now and then...Every vocation has its disadvantages and the advantages of mine far outweigh them. I wouldn't really want to be anything else."*[12]

The loneliness of a pioneer minister's job made marriage preferable, but a pioneer minister who was also a pioneer for *women* in the church was regarded differently. *Her* need for companionship was blurred by the image of wifely solicitude. She was thought of as the comfort, not the comforted. "Women may be equal in the eye of God but not always in the eyes of church and society."[13]

243

Changing Roles and Expectations

The advancement of the women's movement in recent years has focussed attention on the disparity in attitudes towards men and women. Women's growing awareness of broader fulfillment through employment, coupled with economic changes, dates back to the two World Wars when women worked outside the home out of necessity. For the first half of this century, ministers' wives generally fit into the role defined by Carolyn Blackwood in *The Pastor's Wife,* published in 1951. She characterized ministers' wives as helpmates: courteous, neat and cheerful, protective of the minister and his time, setting an example of gracious living on a modest income and being, essentially, a living example of a good Christian woman.[14] One might also add the quality of being taken for granted. The role Mrs. Blackwood describes is a static one which assumes stability as a basic value. This is the image younger ministers and their spouses have from childhood experience, and one which is supported in literary images:

> Still, Mrs. McKee doesn't bawl people out, nor look at their clothes. Mrs. McKee's clothes are none too hot, if it comes to that—old tweed skirts and kind of shrunken twin-sweater sets. Does Mrs. McKee like being the minister's wife? Morag would have it. Mrs. McKee, though tired-looking, doesn't seem to mind.[15]

The acceptance of a life of poverty is sometimes a difficult aspect of the role. The young Mrs. Chegwin, accustomed to every luxury in her eastern hometown, made her wedding trip to a tiny Saskatchewan parish at the turn of the century. Arriving at a deserted train station, she waited with her husband for five hours amidst her baggage until rescued at dusk by a chance passerby.[16] The stark reality of life as a minister's wife is brought home by stories of these pioneers. Mrs. Laing's habit of visiting parishioners in the early days of her husband's Saskatchewan parish left her with no time for housework. With the birth of her children, she found herself lonely and isolated while her husband travelled by himself.[17] It took courage for women like Mrs. Laing and Mrs. Chegwin to shape new lives in such alien settings.

It also took courage to set examples of Christian service far beyond the call of most church members. Mrs. Chegwin's family took in a young Chinese emigree who had arrived to marry a member of her church at a time when the Chinese were not highly thought of in the West. The immigration laws had only recently been eased and men were able to send for their fiancees and families to join them. Canadians were less than welcoming and any who were friendly, or tried to help, were frowned upon.[18] Christian values were often best exemplified by such people as the Chegwins who tread the middle ground between opposing ideas in their communities and within their own congregations.

244

Ministers' wives are well-acquainted with controversy. Coping with new frontiers, literally and figuratively, has resulted in a broadening of the role of minister's wife. Traditional expectations are gradually giving way. One minister makes it a point to remind the congregation of a new parish that they have not hired his wife and cannot, therefore, place obligations on her simply because she is his wife. Many congregations have expected new ministers' wives to inherit the UCW, Sunday School duties, the choir, and other involvements automatically. This attitude, according to a clergy wife, was more common in rural congregations and among women over fifty, especially since the minister's wife often was one of the few leaders with training and experience. Expectations today depend largely on the congregation's own experience. An increasing number of minsters' spouses have independent careers, are men, or are ministers themselves. How this affects the minister's work varies.

When the Minister is a Women

The number of women ministers has risen by 150 percent since 1975. In 1975 only ninety women had been ordained in the United Church.[19] Today, fifty percent of students studying theology are women; seventy-three percent have enrolled in Vancouver School of Theology.

The Division of Ministry Personnel and Education does not keep separate records for women ministers, ostensibly to minimize sexual differentiation, and focuses instead on the ministry as a whole. One woman felt this blurring of sexual lines helped to attract women with a vocation for ministry rather than those concerned with women's rights as a cause within the ministry. The church's stand on women's rights is negated in this way. In some areas there is no "networking" of female ministers, or attention given at the educational or adminstrative level to the unique problems of the woman minister. The situation, however, is improving. The Division of Ministry Personnel and Education has a committee on Women in Ministry. In addition, several conferences have "networks" of women in ministry and there is a special filmstrip available to encourage pastoral relations committees to consider women candidates for a vacancy. ("When Calling a Minister, Consider a Woman", is available from United Church Conference personnel officers.)

The national church's interest in equality tends to be general and abstract, seldom focussing on the reality of what's happening at the presbytery and congregational levels. The relevance of the church in the lives of its female members is questionable. One minister thought that clergy wives should shape their own lives because, in doing so, they help the cause of female ministers. This is not necessarily so. Women who have defined their lives in terms of their capacity to support a husband's work tend to resent the ordination of other women, especially if those ordained women are also married to ministers. There have been cases of United Church Interview Boards encouraging the female ordinand in a potential clergy couple to postpone ordination for awhile in the hope that she would find her role as a minister's wife at her husband's charge sufficiently fulfilling. Until recently, pregnant ministers were expected to take a leave of absence for the child's early years; in many circles this practice is still regarded as a wise move, since it fosters the stability of a family life. A minister who works in Toronto (her husband's church is in Hamilton) rejects this traditional view of family stability. She points out that one must decide whether it will be harder on the marriage *not* to accept a post, even if it means spending a good deal of time apart. She remembered that her discussions with the Interview Board prior to ordination had centred on her personal life and only marginally touched on theological questions. Other women had similar experiences. Two of them, serving on Interview Boards after their ordination, consciously focussed more on theological issues when interviewing ordinands.

Ironically, some ministers married to ministers did not feel that a shared theology was an important issue in their marriage. One woman, married to an Anglican minister, explained that she and her husband saw difficulties in both denominations and had chosen to remain in different churches because they were more comfortable in their own traditions. They have met with a great deal of disapproval over their decision. The husband's mother had converted from the United to the Anglican Church at marriage and expressed resentment that her daughter-in-law did not do likewise. The minister's wife in the United Church in which they were married opposed marrying them there, and United Church clergy in general have been less than understanding. An Anglican priest justified their decision in his own mind by regarding the Anglican Church as universal and the United Church as a provincial organization! Oddly enough, while several ministers and their wives do marriage counselling together, this particular couple does not feel suited to this kind of joint venture. Their styles of ministry are so different they would be incompatible in such work. Their involvement in each other's congregation is minimal, as it is for many married ministers with separate congregations. They seem to prefer it that way.

Separate careers in a marriage, more frequently a reality in current times, introduce many new elements into a minister's life. The option of owning a home rather than occupying a manse gives a new perspective to ministry in the eyes of both clergy and congregation. And the traditional role of minister's helpmate does not fit a spouse who happens to be male. Because many of the first women clergy did not marry, there are few precedents for the role of minister's husband. *He* is not automatically asked to chair the UCW and he is not asked to pour tea. It is essentially up to him to define the terms of his relationship with the congregation.

Whereas few minister's wives ever aspire to sit on the Official Board or the Board of Stewards, a man accustomed to such responsibilities prior to marriage would not think of avoiding such positions. Women find it difficult to differentiate the interests of minister and wife, but a husband, with separate career and valuable administrative experience in church work, presents quite different problems. One such husband accepted invitations to sit on boards by various congregations who recognized his expertise. Congregations saw him and his wife take opposing sides on administrative issues: he dealt with church work as any other parishioner. One congregation eventually requested his resignation from administrative duties, thinking he and his wife shared too much power. The situation reflected badly on his wife, and the controversy and bad feeling led to *her* resignation as well. This congregation could not accept a decidedly non-traditional relationship with their minister. Their minister did not live in a manse but in her own house, referred to by some of the congregation as the "mansion". Her husband's involvement in the church was welcomed and his administrative expertise brought excellent rewards. Unwilling to work with him, but seemingly unable to work without him, the congregation is struggling and may very well disintegrate over the divisions the situation has created.

The minister's husband was understandably confused and surprised by these developments. It had never occurred to him that his church work would in any way compromise his wife's position; there had never been any question of a power struggle between them. The realization of the uniqueness of the minister's husband's role has been brought painfully home through this tragic episode. He has decided that he may never again assume the administrative roles held in the past. At the same time, he will never experience the traditional expectations that confront ministers' wives. It is ironic that, as a minister's husband, he may never involve himself in some of the functions of church work in which he would like to participate, while many ministers' wives are forced into involvements they neither ask for nor want.

Defining a Personal Role Today

The struggle of ministers' wives to define their relationship with a congregation and the church in general has to be a personal one. Donna Sinclair outlines three distinct aspects to the life of a minster's wife: her relationship with her husband, her church, and herself. The clergy wife is her husband's helpmate and shares his responsibilities in her involvement in his work and work with the congregation. Many women find a great deal of fulfillment in assisting their husbands while maintaining a stable home life. They follow their husbands into their careers with enthusiasm and dedication, but there can be certain dangers in this role: "the major problem with this was an inevitable submergence of my identity into that of my husband...Breakfast sounded more like a meeting of the church staff than the sleepy conversation of newlyweds."[20] A problem also emerges when the minster's wife feels a responsibility to run her husband's life for him. It is more common, however, that she is a helpmate, living in her husband's shadow.

A transformation in self-identity often occurs when children are born. Ms. Sinclair saw herself as an enabler at one stage of her life. As her life became more private and homebound, the manse became her own

247

domain and she ran it smoothly to enable her husband to do the best job he could. In some ways her role affirmed the traditional role for women but, at the same time, she carried the responsibilities of the manse, maintaining its hospitality to parishioners and persons in need. This period allowed her to grow and learn, often painfully, the limits of her ability to care for her family, friends and parishioners, and still look after her own well-being.[21]

Another phase evolved as Ms. Sinclair grew older and her children became increasingly independent. She began to discover unrealized parts of herself and labelled this process "liberation". Many women at this stage of their lives return to a career suspended at marriage or mother-hood; some take up an academic program or become interested in sports. These developments often put clergy wives in conflict with the traditional role as they, their husbands, and congregations have come to define it. Ms. Sinclair notes: "I had rightly realized that if anyone expected me to be always gracious, or always thrifty, that was their problem (actually, fewer did than I thought)."[22] Because minister's wives are in the public eye they tend to be very sensitive to how others see them. One woman, whose experience of home ownership and employment has given her a liberated perspective, still admits that she wears a "Sunday face". Many women are aware that they are not really obliged to present an idealized view of marriage; one minister felt that people of *other* denominations expected their marriage to be exemplary. Still, a minis-ter's wife told about her habit of hiding the wine bottle when parishioners called, even though feeling she and her husband lived their beliefs and presented an honest example of a solid Christian marriage.

A minister's marriage is much the same as any other. Involvement in the church puts more stress on the importance of keeping it together, but church members are generally aware of the pressures a minister's lifes-tyle places on a marriage. One spouse complained of nuisance calls during dinner. Ministers try to keep regular mealtimes, too, he pointed out.

The United Church and its members would do well to consider the impact and position of those who marry ministers. The different expecta-tions attached to male and female clergy spouses can provide valuable insights into our attitudes as a church towards women and men. In the case of male ministers and clergy wives it seems we have been able, for years, to hire two people for the price of one. Any awareness of the special problems in being a minister's wife, and holding that unique position in the congregation, must also involve an awareness of her needs as a woman, as an individual in her own right, and of women's role in society generally.

Andrea Shaver

> *Andrea has been a student at the University of Toronto, pursuing her interests in women's studies and religion. Her fascination with the role of the minister's wife is not entirely academic, however; she was raised by one.*

Chapter 13 THE INFLUENCE OF RUTH TILLMAN ON WOMEN IN MINISTRY

—Marion Pardy

SUMMARY

- Ruth Tillman's life was both enriching and inspiring for the many men and women who came into contact with her over the years. Born in Hamilton, Ontario, Ruth entered full-time ministry in the United Church, first spending twelve years in Newfoundland ministering with and to children, youth, and adults in their homes, churches, and at camp. As well, she was national secretary for CGIT, and staff person for the Canadian Council of Churches.

    Marion Pardy chooses to concentrate on Ruth's influence on some of the women of Newfoundland with whom Ruth came in contact. Marion tells about Etta Snow, now ordained and serving in Ontario, who became a missionary in Angola; Helen James of Quebec City; Vera Moore, who became a deaconess at Metropolitan United Church in Toronto; Lorraine Mountford of Mississauga, Ontario; Myrtle Bickford of Cambridge, Ontario, a laywoman involved in a variety of church activities; Sandra Leja, who at the age of twelve travelled with Ruth to New York to present a UNICEF cheque on behalf of the children of Canada, now a nurse in St. John's Newfoundland; Betty McColgan, a colleague serving in Newfoundland when Ruth did; and of course, the author, Marion Pardy, now an ordained minister within The United Church of Canada with the position of children's ministry with the Division of Mission in Canada. No story about Ruth Tillman is complete without mentioning Nancy Edwards, her close and long-time friend, for many years well-known for her communications work with the United Church.

    Each of these women tells of how the warmth and humor, the leadership qualities, and the spiritual intensity of Ruth Tillman made a lasting impression on her life, and in many cases, influenced her decision for full-time ministry within The United Church of Canada.

—editor

When Ruth Tillman became National Secretary for CGIT in 1962, she wrote her first National Secretary's letter for *The Torch* from Loon Bay Camp, Newfoundland. She begins:

> *This letter is being written during the middle of a CGIT Camp at Loon Bay, Newfoundland. As I think of the intermediate girls in this camp, I try to visualize teenaged girls across Canada who will have had similar experiences this summer. The other morning at our outdoor chapel, my mind wandered to the many young people who have made important decisions in this place set aside for worship. Then I thought of two of the members of the staff who, not too many years ago, were campers themselves.*
> *(The Torch, Oct./Nov., 1962)*

Ruth modestly neglected to say that one of those staff members had made a decision to enter professional ministry, and that Ruth herself significantly influenced that decision. I know: I was that staff person!

When Ruth died on November 23, 1978, I became aware that there were many women who could witness to Ruth's influence in their lives. Neither space nor time permits an exhaustive commentary on these persons. Rather, I propose to focus on Ruth Tillman's contribution to the church through the lives of women primarily from Newfoundland Conference, where she served for twelve years (1949-61) ministering with and to children, youth, and adults in their homes, their churches, and at camp. By sharing the Good News with them through word, music, and exemplary living, she encouraged each to become the person God would have her be.

Etta Snow

Etta Snow, presently a minister in the Guthrie/Hawkstone Pastoral Charge, Ontario, comes from Bay Roberts, Newfoundland. Etta recalls meeting Ruth while teaching at Shoal Harbour between the years 1948 and 1950. In those days, school teachers in Newfoundland were expected to be involved in the church; Etta was no exception. In addition to teaching school during the week, Etta was a leader in Mission Band, Explorers, and NGIT (Newfoundland Girls In Training prior to Confederation in 1949), a Sunday School teacher, and a member of the Women's Auxilliary. When Ruth Tillman, as Bonavista Presbytery WMS Christian Education worker, came to visit, Etta had many questions, and Ruth had many ideas. Etta found herself as a summer camp leader and cook's helper (Ruth was the cook) at Thwart Island Camp, begun by Ruth and Nancy Edwards, Ruth's close friend and colleague serving, at that time, as Twillingate Presbytery WMS Christian Education worker and living in Gander.

Etta was initially impressed by Ruth's vibrant personality, her encouragement, her wealth of ideas, and her voice. As their relationship developed, Etta also became aware of her depth, her insights into scripture, the world church, and her ability to tell Bible stories, especially those from the Old Testament. "We sat with our mouths opened," Etta recalls. For Ruth, faith was alive, vibrant and meant to be lived.

Ruth's gift to Etta was vision, enabling her to see the "more" in life. Ruth herself raised the question: "Have you ever considered 'full-time' church work?" At that time Etta's academic credentials consisted of a Newfoundland teaching certificate granted after one year of study at Memorial University, St. John's. When Etta indicated interest, Ruth continued to provide support, encouraging her to apply to the United Church Training School as a full-time student. While Etta attended from 1950-52, Ruth continued to keep in touch through letters and personal visits.

Like most other women interviewed, Etta found it difficult to talk about Ruth without mentioning Nancy Edwards. In Newfoundland they complemented one another well; Nancy as director of camp and Ruth as business manager. They worked well together; they argued; they were friends.

It is no coincidence that upon graduation from the United Church Training School, Etta Snow went to Angola as a missionary. She had been exposed to Ruth's global concern, and when she entered the Training School she was influenced by Dean Harriet Christie, another global person. Harriet often invited missionaries as guests to the school, and during Etta's graduation year in 1952, the Rev. Tommy Tucker and Pastor Fredico Mussill from Angola spoke of the great need for missionaries there. From 1952 to their evacuation in 1975, Etta served as a missionary in Angola. Her work towards ordination upon her return to Canada was motivated by a desire to return to Angola as an ordained minister. That was not possible and she accepted a call to Guthrie/Hawkstone.

It was indeed fitting that Etta Snow was the person to pay tribute at Ruth's funeral on November 26, 1978. In that message she articulated the thoughts of many:

> *I speak for a number of people in Newfoundland today who can give witness to the fact that their lives have been richly blessed and enriched because of their contacts with Ruth...Some of these persons were inspired and challenged to continue that ministry and to give themselves to full-time service in the church. This afternoon I am particularly*

251

*honoured and proud to be one of a number from
Newfoundland who can say that it was Ruth Tillman's
influence, support and encouragement that led me into the
church's ministry.*

Helen James (Smith)

Helen James is now living in Quebec City, married to the Anglican
Dean of Quebec; they have two teenaged daughters. Her home was
Grand Bank, Newfoundland, and it was at camp near Grand Bank, when
she was about sixteen years old, that she first met Ruth. This initial
contact developed through Vacation Bible School and leadership training
courses. Helen indentifies Ruth as a powerful, continuing influence in her
life, enabling her to believe in herself as a child of God with potential. The
quality that most movitated Helen was Ruth's sincerity and her gift of
enabling others to value their own lives and appreciate their own worth.
Helen writes:

> *It's difficult to write of Ruth's influence on my life without
> mentioning Nancy—together they worked as a team—
> supportive of one another. Through their influence I moved
> to Ontario and lived for one year at Five Oaks under the
> directorship of Bev Oaten. Great things have happened in
> my life through the dedication of these three people...When
> Ruth died, I was so thankful that I had known her.*

Vera Horaki (Moore)

Vera Moore was away to the "Mainland"—a social worker in
Montreal—when Ruth and Nancy first met Vera's family in Grand Falls,
Newfoundland. A few years later Vera returned to Newfoundland and
continued her career there. Shortly after meeting Ruth and Nancy, Vera
found herself at camp: leading Bible study, crafts, recreation, and assuming the numerous other responsibilities undertaken by camp leaders in
Newfoundland at that time. "I had never been to camp before," Vera
recalled. That experience was the beginning of a long-lasting friendship,
which resulted in Vera's move to Toronto in 1962, where she worked at
Metropolitan United Church, and lived with Nancy and Ruth until her
marriage. When speaking of Ruth, Vera smiles: "I can vividly picture
her—her warmth and humour—how she could laugh!"

Lorraine Mountford (Roberts)

Lorraine Mountford comes from St. John's, Newfoundland, and
attended the United Church Training School from 1957-59. During the
summers of 1958 and 1959, she was employed by the Woman's Missionary Society to do caravanning and camp leadership and worked at Loon
Bay Camp with Ruth Tillman as her supervisor. Lorraine found Ruth to
be an inspiring and caring person—"I learned a lot from her." She also
recalled Ruth as very helpful, approachable, outgoing, knowledgeable,
and interested in many things. There were some difficulties: Ruth was an

energetic person with a forceful personality and a temper that erupted easily in certain situations. Working with Ruth meant devoting excessive time and energy to the job! On the other hand, Ruth called forth the best anyone could offer, and people found themselves capable of leadership they had previously though impossible.

Lorraine now lives in Mississauga and is an active member of her church there.

Marion Pardy

Ruth reprimanded me for sneaking from my cabin after lights out. She chided me to "cherish health": "Your smile would be so bright with your front teeth filled" (dentists were sparse in Newfoundland in those days). I experienced the impact of her temper when I had to be called constantly, or was caught in some mischievous misdemeanor. "Tilly" (as Ruth was known at Loon Bay Camp) was an assertive, robust woman who did not hesitate to praise or criticize. I was a fun-loving child and teenager, and it was much more adventuresome to walk the dark path late at night to the "john" furthest from the cabin than go to the one nearby! The adventure, of course, was in smothering giggles and not "getting caught", for that usually resulted in strong reprimands from Ruth. During my first experience of Loon Bay Camp, I recall approaching her in fear and trembling the morning after such an escapade. I quickly learned, however, that Tilly carried few grudges. She seemed able to respond to each situation as it occurred, and the scolding lasted for that situation only.

Anger and laughter, joy and sadness were natural responses for Ruth Tillman—she was an integrated, complete person. As a teenager at camp I stood in awe of her, valuing all she said and did. Ruth touched my own sense of fun with her songs, her stories, her games, her contagious laughter, and she touched my serious nature with her depth and intensity, her integration of faith and life. In conversation I was embraced by her intensity of concern—no question seemed irrelevant. I recall her at vespers around campfire at night, the glow of the fire enhancing the depth that shone in her face and eyes as she led us in "Jesus Walked This Lonesome Valley", "Lord, I Want to be a Christian", "We are Climbing Jacob's ladder" (before the days of "dancing Sarah's circle"), "Kum Ba Yah", and numerous other spirituals and songs. When she spoke her words flowed from a faith in a global and personal God who called us to respond to life. Through Ruth I experienced the Christian faith as vibrant and through her, I envisaged ministry within the church as life abundant. The fun of camp, the serious group gatherings, the quiet moments of "morning watch" all personified in Ruth Tillman—made me want to pass on all that I had received through professional church ministry.

I was fortunate to be a leader at camp when Ruth was business manager and leader, and it was a privilege to continue that peer relationship with her when I moved to Ontario. Ruth's and Nancy Edwards' support continued through my years in Belleville as I completed academic admission requirements to Covenant College, through my students days at Covenant College, and throughout my career. Ruth Tillman was a woman who touched people's lives. She touched my life and its direction was significantly changed. I mourned her death, experiencing a personal sense of loss. Her legacy is present in my life and in the lives of countless women and men throughout the church.

Myrtle Bickford

Myrtle Bickford now lives in Cambridge, Ontario. Her church activities are numerous: Sunday School Superintendent; UCW programming: member of Christian Development Committee; Cradle Roll; Summer Vacation School. I met her at Five Oaks during a South Pacific Event (November 1982), and the name of Ruth Tillman arose in conversation.

Myrtle first met Ruth at Maritime CGIT Camp Council in 1965. Ruth attended in her capacity as National Secretary of CGIT while Myrtle was camp leader. She vividly remembers Ruth, identifying her as a powerful, continuing influence. Ruth's gifts to Myrtle were a vision of the church as a world-wide community, the ability to face and tackle difficult issues such as suicide and abortion, and to accept people as they are. She saw Ruth as an unpretentious person of utter honesty whose love of young people shone through. Myrtle captures the spirit of Ruth in these words:

> I really loved and admired her and though she was the busiest of people, she amazed me with her always finding time for friends—either writing or visiting...At camp the girls admired her so much. Her group was always popular— either when teaching new songs, games and dances from around the world, or on life situations. She always gave herself fully to her work and nothing or no one seemed unimportant to her. I felt it was a real privilege to know her.

Sandra Leja (Taylor)

In *The Torch*, October 1960, an article appeared entitled "Sandra Goes to New York". The occasion was the presentation of a cheque of $200,000 from the Canadian UNICEF Association to Maurice Pate, UNICEF's Executive Director in the United Nations building. "Sandra" was a 12-year-old member of CGIT: Sandra Taylor from Fraser Road United Church, Gander, Newfoundland. Accompanying Sandra on this very exciting, scary trip was Ruth Tillman, Newfoundland Conference Christian Education Secretary. A trip to New York City for a twelve-year-old Newfoundlander was no ordinary experience. It was a "once-in-a-lifetime" event. A proud and excited Sandra made this speech:

> On behalf of the thousands of children across Canada who shared their treats with children all over the world on Hallowe'en, I would like to present this cheque for $200,000 to UNICEF. This gift comes to you with our love and we sincerely hope that our pennies will help UNICEF to cure more and more children of sickness and hunger.

254

The *Torch* article stated that Ruth "helped spark the project", an action typical of Ruth's ministry of global concern. Ruth not only broadened people's horizons through her own personal gifts, but sought opportunities to expose Canadians to people from other countries.

What Sandra remembers about Ruth on that trip was her friendliness and how she helped her to relax, feel at ease, and enjoy herself. When she later became Provincial President of CGIT, her job included executive meetings with Ruth in St. John's to plan the next CGIT Camp Council at Loon Bay. Sandra recalls Ruth's sense of humour and how easy it was to communicate with her.

Sandra is now a registered nurse at the Grace Hospital, St. John's, Newfoundland, and the mother of two children.

Betty McColgan

Betty was the WMS Christian Education worker for Twillingate Presbytery from 1957-61, and then Newfoundland Conference Staff in Christian Education (1951-63) after the integration of WMS and WA. Her first place of residence in Newfoundland was Lewisporte where she boarded with Minnie and Fred Small, and worked from an office that was a former barber shop. Betty recalls the exclamation of small children as they peered through her office window: "I tought 'dis is were they cuts 'air."

Known at the United Church Training School as Betty "camping in the Maritimes" McColgan, Betty was initially attracted to Newfoundland by Loon Bay Camp which offered promise and invited challenge. (Betty's home was Saint John, New Brunswick.) At Loon Bay, Betty worked closely with Ruth Tillman, getting to know her as they waited for trains delivering campers at Notre Dame Junction during the early hours of the morning, shopped for groceries, or did the banking at Lewisporte. Betty spoke knowingly of Ruth as an in-depth conversationalist, a person who loved to sing, a hard worker with a great concern for people, for justice, for the environment, and for ecumenicity. Even though she had an explosive temper, Ruth never held a grudge. In all, she was a person with boundless energy who called forth excellence in herself and others.

Some people did not respond positively to Ruth's outspokenness. At one time church polity decreed that a deaconess could only speak at Presbytery and Conference by a motion from the floor. Sometimes Ruth would not be granted that privilege. But Ruth carried on making her concerns heard where she could, especially at camp. There she lived her beliefs and that modelling of faith was contagious.

In response to the question, "What was she like to work with?" Betty provided some illustrations of Ruth's high standards, full-time commitment to ministry, humour, concern, and flexibility. One night Betty left the campsite to pick up a new car in Gander. She decided to stay there overnight (probably the only night away from camp during the summer) and upon her return, Ruth "blew her stack", partially from concern that an accident had occurred, but also feeling that Betty was shirking her duties. Ruth fought with the camp committee, usually over camp standards (e.g. the need to have water tested) and development funds. Although she expected much, she didn't expect anything she wasn't prepared to give herself.

Ruth's humour was brought out by the Lieutenant Governor's visit to Loon Bay Camp. There was only time (or money) to paint one side of the main camp house prior to his arrival, and someone was delegated to prevent these distinguished guests from walking around the house!

During her ministry in Newfoundland, Betty moved to St. John's and lived with Ruth. There the two exchanged roles, with Betty in the Conference Office responsible for Ruth's administrative work, and Ruth in Twillingate Presbytery doing Betty's field trips. Betty affirms: "Ruth aimed for the highest common denominator for the good of others."

Betty is presently minister at Birch Cliff United Church, Scarborough—a long way in time and environment from Newfoundland. But Newfoundland remains a memorable experience, easy to recall. Betty also contributed greatly to the church there, leaving her mark on many people

Nancy Edwards

When Nancy Edwards from Vancouver, British Columbia, first met Ruth Tillman from Hamilton, Ontario, at the United Church Training School in 1945, she didn't think she was going to like this woman "from the East" who wore bright lipstick and nail polish! Little did she realize, at the time, that this woman would become a life-long friend. Ruth was the one who invited Nancy to room with her at the Training School when because of late registration, Nancy had to find her own accommodation.

Upon graduation both Nancy and Ruth were appointed by the Woman's Missionary Society to Winnipeg—Nancy to MacLean United and Ruth to Stella Mission. One year later, Nancy and Ruth journeyed together to their next posting with the WMS in Newfoundland Conference—Nancy to Twillingate Presbytery and Ruth to Bonavista Presbytery. In those days in Newfoundland lack of transportation made visiting difficult, and Ruth and Nancy were together only for the major holidays. During the summer, however, they coordinated their efforts in Vacation Church School and camping. In this context, others experienced Ruth and Nancy as a collegial team, using their unique gifts in the Christian education and leadership development of children, youth, and adults.

Nancy has vivid memories of those days: sharing a berth on that first train journey from Port Aux Basques to Gander (because they didn't have sufficient funds) and counting their money and halving it (less than $5.00); Nancy disembarking at Gander, leaving Ruth to continue the trip to Clarenville; their first summer camp in a school in Clarenville; camping at Thwart Island; negotiating, planning, and developing the campsite at Loon Bay. They co-led numerous camps with Nancy ("Neds") as director and Ruth ("Tilly") as business manager, and enjoyed a tenting trip to Newfoundland during the summer of 1978, just prior to Ruth's death. They shared a beautiful, close friendship and, in her Christmas letter of 1978, Nancy wrote:

> Ruth and I have tented in every province of Canada and nothing "pleased" Ruth more than getting that little blue and yellow tent up—complete with safari cots—and eating and picnicking outdoors...My own memories are of Ruth's beautiful contralto singing voice; her easy swing from fun to discussing the depth of any subject; watching children or young people—as she preached, taught or sang. They knew she was sharing her "real" self and vision of the "whole" Body of Christ. She never talked down to them. From the time we were put together as roommates (United Church Training School) and discovered we had mutual friends in the Canadian Japanese evacuees, until now—I have great reason to thank God for Ruth's warm, stimulating, demanding, giving, caring friendship, and I'm sure you share my feelings. You could disagree with her—but never question her motives, her dedication and her love.

The memories are still fresh for Nancy in her Christmas letter of 1981: "...I remember thankfully, Ruth at many campfires singing with her warm, deep voice, "He's Got the Whole World in His Hand", and the fire bright on the upturned faces."

Brigalia Bam from the World Council of Churches' Education and Renewal Unit vacationed with Nancy and Ruth in Halifax on their return from Newfoundland during the summer of 1978. When she heard of Ruth's death, Brigalia wrote a warm, caring letter of sympathy to Nancy. An excerpt of that letter contains these words:

> I join those many people who give thanks to God for Ruth's life. You were so close to her, I know your life can never be the same again. I will remember you in my prayers.

Nancy maintains direction and purpose while living in official retirement. She talks willingly, easily, and longingly about Ruth, and with sadness for the loss of a special friend. Although life is drastically different for her, Nancy speaks with thanksgiving for the friendship they shared and for Ruth's great gift to the church.

Conclusion

Not one phrase but many summarize Ruth Tillman's influence on others: depth; humour; intensity; acceptance; calling forth of excellence; demanding; biblical passion and insight; gift of music; global consciousness; camp enthusiast. Although none explicity attributed women's consciousness-raising to Ruth, it was an activity that loomed large in her ministry. The struggle for women's rights was not a politicized activity for her in Newfoundland, but she embodied the values of the movement as she encouraged and enabled women to develop their God-given potential to the fullest.

What prepared Ruth for such depth, intensity, and calibre of ministry? How did her passion for Bible studies and global consciousness arise? These questions are raised in an attempt to identify some of the environmental influences in her life.

An intriguing fact is the lack of parental and personal church involvement until her later teen years. For example, Ruth did not attend CGIT as a teenager. Her mother, although not active in the church, attended fairly regularly and is described by Helen Currie, Ruth's high school friend, as a woman of German background with a deep religious faith. Except on special occasions, Ruth's father, also of Roman Catholic background, did not attend. He, however, was very interested in music and both Ruth and her brother, Ted, seemed to have inherited their gift of music from him. Even though her parents were not active church people, Ruth's home life was a considerable influence in terms of personality and faith. Ruth Kipling, another high school friend, describes the Tillman house as her "second home". Another person, George Affleck, describes Ruth's home in a similar way. George, now a retired minister living in Parksville, British Columbia, was director of the Forward Movement. In a letter to Nancy Edwards shortly after Ruth's death, he states, "She and her Mother and Dad made their home my home in those years when we were travelling by faith rather than by any organized support, and I have never forgotten it." In a recent telephone conversation with George, he described Ruth's mother as "warmhearted", and their home as his "headquarters". He and Ruth were close friends.

During Ruth's teens, her sister committed suicide. This tragic experience, says Ruth Kipling, deepened her faith. George Affleck, a source of strength during this time, maintains that Ruth's zest for faith and the church was a result of personal discovery and for that reason, both held a deep significance for her. Mrs. Perrin (now Mrs. Outerbridge), a Sunday School teacher, was a quiet woman who often invited her class to her home and took a genuine interest in them. It was through this experience that Ruth became interested in the church and joined the Young People's Union. And it was through YPU that the Forward Movement, camping, Bible Study, and world-awareness entered Ruth's life to shape its direction.

The Forward Movement was an organization begun in 1939 by five students from Emmanuel College: George Affleck, Harold Bailey, Bert Scott, Jack Thompson, and George Petrie. They travelled around the country to Young People's groups and Sunday worship services to recruit for overseas missions. As the Movement developed, the purpose became more evangelical, bearing witness to the faith and encouraging

258

young people to establish ongoing Bible Study groups in their own setting. The purpose became threefold: prayer, study, action. As a result of this understanding of integrated faith and action, many young people decided to enter professional ministry. All were challenged to demonstrate their faith through financial giving and through active contact with places of need. Work camps were a primary expression of this faith in action, and many participants in the Movement found themselves with shovels, hammers, and saws.

The church, approving the Movement, deferred George Affleck's placement so that he could act as director. He was financially dependent on the hospitality of individuals and the generosity of the groups to which he spoke, and it was in this context that Ruth first encountered him and the Forward Movement, at Ryerson Camp. The organization, described as a "Movement of the Spirit", significantly influenced Ruth's life, through camping, work camps, Bible study, and YPU. After one experience at work camp she commented to Helen Currie that she now knew why men lean on their shovels! Work camps demanded arduous labour, and Ruth's commitment to any task was total. She became very active in YPU and, for a time, was YPU President from Hamilton Conference. George Affleck recalls:

> When anyone asked her to do anything, she never counted the cost if she felt that was what God was calling her to do; she loved fun, was a song leader, and her leadership emerged wherever she went.

Eventually Ruth decided that full-time professional ministry was her calling.

According to her friend, Ruth Kipling, Ruth left school with two completed subjects in her "middle school" (Grade XI) to enter the world of office work and banking. She returned to night school and, within three years, while continuing to work full-time, completed her Senior Matriculation. Having accomplished the academic requirements for entrance to the United Church Training School, she was admitted as a student—a gift to the church.

Ruth's background sheds some light on her Newfoundland ministry: her camping enthusiasm, her biblical and global awareness, her genuine encouragement of others, her acceptance of us as we were, and her challenge to us to "become". Lack of education was in Ruth's view no barrier. Having made a decision, we were supported and encouraged to obtain the necessary education to implement that decision. Words from scripture capture the spirit of her ministry:

> "I came that they may have life, and have it abundantly." (John 10: 10b)
> "For I received from the Lord what I also delivered to you...." (I Corinthians 11: 23A)

259

George Affleck's summation of Ruth, amply illustrated in this paper, is shared by the writer:

"She embodied the Spirit of Christ." And we were richly blessed!

Marion Pardy

Marion is an ordained minister in The United Church of Canada. She has recently taken on a challenging role as Special Assistant, Ministry with Children, in the Division of Mission in Canada. Like Ruth Tillman's, I'm sure Marion's ministry will influence both the institution and the people of our church.

Photos

2. The Rev. Lydia
Gruchy preaching

1. The Rev. Lydia Gruchy, first
woman to be ordained in The
United Church of Canada: St.
Andrew's United Church,
Moose Jaw, Saskatchewan,
1936

3. The Very Rev. Lois
Wilson

4. The Very Rev. Lois Wilson,
first moderator of The United
Church of Canada; elected in
Halifax, Nova Scotia, 1980

FIRSTS AMONG WOMEN

5. Viola Halpenny, first non-staff woman appointed to the Executive and Sub-Executive of General Council

6. Olive Ziegler, one of the founders of the CGIT movement

7. A former United Church women's group

8. Working at a clothing depot

9. The care and nurture of children and youth

10. Worshipping at a Truro Presbyterial meeting held in Wentworth, Nova Scotia

WOMEN AT WORK AND WORSHIP

11. Banner-making for a local congregation

12. Aiko Carter of Japan, Lina Voklus of Papua New Guinea, and Lois Boice of Vancouver express their concerns about the nuclear issue to UCW groups from the western provinces

13. The class of '54 at the United Church Training School

14. Nellie McClung

WOMEN WHO TAUGHT US

PHOTO: WOLF KUTNAHORSKY, BERKELEY STUDIO

15. Ruth Tillman

PHOTO: WOLF KUTNAHORSKY, BERKELEY STUDIO

16. The Rev. Karen Mitchell at a table group at the 1980 General Council

PHOTO: WOLF KUTNAHORSKY, BERKELEY STUDIO

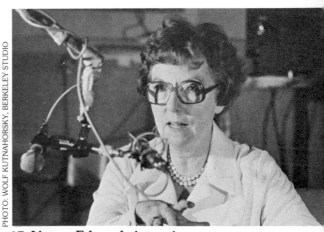

17. Nancy Edwards interviews

8. Stella Burry, Newfoundland
Deaconess

19. Mabel Louise Dubbin

20. Gwenyth Hubble

21. Nell Langford Rowell, graduate
of Victoria University in 1895,
teacher at Alma College, spouse
and supporter of lawyer Newton
Rowell who sucessfully fought
the Persons case of 1928, which
in 1929 won women the right to
be appointed to the Senate.

267

22. The early days of overseas missionary work: Dr. Choni Oliver

AT WORK OVERSEAS

23. Dr. Ruth Taylor, overseas missions secretary for WMS

24. Dr. Florence Murray and Ada Sandell (r.) in Korea

25. The Rev. Elda Struthers with students in Korea

Notes and Acknowledgements

NOTES AND ACKNOWLEDGEMENTS

NOTES ON SECTION 1   OUR STORY: CHRISTIAN LIBERATION

Chapter 1: Women Together: The Call to Collective Action
Chapter 2: Faith and Finances
Chapter 3: Social Change Reflected in Women's Work and Worship
Chapter 4: The Past as a Guide to the Future

NOTES ON SECTION 4   INVESTIGATING WOMEN, WORK AND WORSHIP

Chapter 8: Women and Power in The United Church of Canada
Chapter 9: Christian Feminism in the United Church: Resources in Culture and Tradition
Chapter 10: Side Road on the Journey to Autonomy: The Diaconate Prior to Church Union
Chapter 11: Liberating Christianity
Chapter 12: Pouring the Tea and Hiding the Wine Bottle: Reflections on the Role of the Minister's Mate

ACKNOWLEDGEMENTS

Contributors to the Women, Work and Worship Project
Nancy Rowell Jackman
Shirley Davy

NOTES AND ACKNOWLEDGEMENTS

SECTION 1

Chapter 1: Women Together: The Call to Collective Action.

All materials, including letters, that were submitted to the Woman, Work and Worship project, have been deposited in the United Church Archives at Victoria College in Toronto. They have been catalogued by Conference, and numbered. For example, a submission from Saskatchewan may include several items. Its catalogue reference would be WWW (denoting that it was part of the project research material); Saskatchewan (denoting that it was from Saskatchewan Conference); #3 (denoting that it was the third listing for Saskatchewan); Item 2 (denoting that it was the second of several items included in the submission). There is a file card index accompanying the Women, Work and Worship material, and readers are welcome to make use of the submissions for future research projects. Maritime Conference has been subdivided into Maritime—N.B. and Qué., Maritime—N.S., and Maritime—P.E.I. Québec has been included with the Maritimes because items were received from that area of Québec which is in the Maritime Conference.

FOOTNOTES

1. WWW, London, #1, Item 29, submitted by Kay Brodie on behalf of the Algoma Women, Work and Worship Committee.

2. Dr. Christine MacInnes, *Window on the Past: The Story of the Halifax Wesleyan Female Benevolent Society* (Maritime Conference, The United Church of Canada, 1966), p. 3, included in WWW, Maritime—N.S., #3, submitted by Marilyn Livingston.

3. WWW, Saskatchewan, #26, submitted by Vera Miller.

4. WWW, Toronto, #17, submitted by Mary Rowell Jackman.

5. *First-St. Andrews: 150th Anniversary Special* (London, 1982), p. 8, included in WWW, London, #11, submitted by Jean MacMillan.

6. *The Golden Years: Mount Paul United Church 1928-1978* (Kamloops, 1978), p. 11, included in WWW, British Columbia, #8, submitted by Mabel Burnett.

7. WWW, Manitoba, #6, submitted by Sylvia Doran.

8. J. R. Spencer, *Our Corner of the Vineyard* (Souris, P.E.I., 1978), p. 45, included in WWW, Maritime—P.E.I., #1, submitted by Olga J. Leard.

9. WWW, Alberta, #7, submitted by Donna Minor.

10. See the chapters written by Warne, Haglund and Parsons for more information about women's involvement in the Social Gospel Movement.

11. WWW, Maritime—P.E.I., #2, submitted by Winnie MacMillan.

12. See chapter 9 written by R. Warne for a fuller explanation of "maternal feminism".

13. John Webster Grant, *The Church in the Canadian Era: The First Century of Confederation* (Toronto: McGraw-Hill Ryerson, 1972), pp. 81-82.

14. WWW, Saskatchewan, #29, submitted by the Watrous UCW History Committee.

15. "A Brief History of the World Day of Prayer", Women's Inter-Church Council of Canada, Toronto. (This pamphlet is available free from WICC, 77 Charles Street West, Toronto M4S 1K5.)

16. WWW, Manitoba, #6, submitted by Sylvia Doran.

17. WWW, Saskatchewan, #29, submitted by the Watrous UCW History Committee.

18. WWW, Saskatchewan, #28, submitted by Frances McDougall.

19. J. R. Spencer, *Our Corner of the Vineyard*, included in WWW, Maritime—P.E.I., #1, submitted by Olga J. Leard.

20. *The Story of Blackstock United Church* (1975), p. 11, included in WWW, Bay of Quinte, #9, submitted by Thelma Wright.

21. Dr. Ruth Taylor, quoted from a taped interview with Heather Dau, at Berkeley Studio, March 11, 1975.

22. Charles Frederick Allison, quoted by Prof. John C. Reid in "The Education of Women at Mount Allison, 1854-1914: The Clash of Academic and 'Ornamental' Traditions", 1982 (unpublished), p. 14. This paper has now been published in *Acadiensis: Journal of the History of the Atlantic Region*, Vol. XII, No. 2, Spring 1983.

23. *Ibid.*, p. 14

24. "Profiles of Women in Pictou Presbyterial at Work and Worship" (New Glasgow, 1982), p. 1, included in WWW, Maritime—N.S., #6, submitted by Phyllis Gunn.

25. Grace Johnston, *History of South Gloucester United Church at Johnston's Corners: 1834-1980* (Gloucester, 1980), p. 19, included in WWW, Montreal and Ottawa, #2, submitted by Grace Johnston.

26. Quoted from a talk given by Vida Wellwood, "History of Early Church Women", Comox, B.C., September 1982, included in WWW, British Columbia, #4, submitted by Comox UCW.

27. W. Morrison Kelly, *The History of the Congregations Forming St. Andrew's United Church* (Toronto, 1969), pp. 49-50, included in WWW, Toronto, #20, submitted by the women of St. Andrew's United Church.

28. Grace Lane, *Saskatchewan's Sturdy Strands of Faith* (Saskatchewan, 1980), p. 15, included in WWW, Saskatchewan, #3, submitted by Grace Lane.

29. WWW, Alberta, #5, submitted by Beth Tachit.

30. WWW, Alberta, #9, submitted by Marion Cabelka.

31. WWW, London, #1, Item 29, submitted by Kay Brodie on behalf of the Algoma Women, Work and Worship Committee.

32. WWW, Saskatchewan, #16, submitted by Janet Loveridge.

33. WWW, Maritime—N.B., #9, submitted by Clotilda Ellis.

34. WWW, Toronto, #5, submitted by Gladys Coxon.

35. WWW, London, #1, Item 29, submitted by Kay Brodie on behalf of the Algoma Women, Work and Worship Committee.

36. WWW, Manitoba, #3, submitted by Edith Shiells.

37. WWW, London, #1, Item 38, submitted by Kay Brodie on behalf of the Algoma Women, Work and Worship Committee.

38. Mrs. G. C. Ashton, *The Story of Women's Groups in Brooklyn Sunday School—Harcourt Memorial United Church: 1887-1982* (Guelph, 1982), p. 32, included in WWW, Hamilton, #7, submitted by Ruth G. Kaufman.

39. WWW, Maritime—N.B., #10, Item 2, submitted by Gwen MacRae.

40. WWW, Manitou, #1, submitted by Bernice Bowmans.

41. Elva Richards McGaughey, *A Firm Foundation: A History of St. Paul's United Church* (Prescott, Ontario, 1980), p. 56, included in WWW, Montreal and Ottawa, #3, submitted by Enid Arscott.

42. Elizabeth Howell Verdesi, *In But Still Out: Women in the Church* (Philadelphia: Westminster Press, 1976), p. 38.

43. Dr. Christine MacInnes, *Window on the Past*, p. 6. (See note #2.)

44. *Victoria Square United Church: 1880-1980* (1980), p. 29, included in WWW, Toronto, #2, submitted anonymously.

45. Bert Platt, *Trinity United Church, Beeton: 1878-1978* (1978), pp. 56-57, included in WWW, Toronto, #7, submitted by Muriel Reynolds.

46. WWW, Montreal and Ottawa, #2, submitted by Grace Johnston.

47. Bert Platt, *Trinity United Church, Beeton: 1878-1978*, p. 60, included in WWW, Toronto, #7, submitted by Muriel Reynolds.

48. *Victoria Square United Church: 1880-1980*, p. 30, included in WWW, Toronto, #2, submitted anonymously.

49. Elizabeth Howell Verdesi, *In But Still Out: Women in the Church*, p. 43.

50. See Parsons' Discussion about General Council Responses to the WA and WMS.

51. Grace Lane, *Saskatchewan's Sturdy Strands of Faith*, p. 26, included in WWW, Saskatchewan, #3, submitted by Grace Lane.

52. WWW, British Columbia, #8, submitted by Mabel Burnett.

53. M. Joyce Dicken, "Ministry", *Exchange*, Spring-Summer, Vol. 1, No. 3, 1977, pp. 13-14, included in WWW, Saskatchewan, #4.

54. Orrin E. Klapp, *Collective Search for Identity* (New York: Holt, Rinehart and Winston, 1969).

55. "God-wardness" is a term used by M. Joyce Dicken in "Ministry". (See note #53.)

56. Mrs. G. C. Ashton, *The Story of Women's Groups in Brooklyn Sunday School—Harcourt Memorial United Church: 1887-1982*, pp. 28-29, included in WWW, Hamilton, #7, submitted by Ruth G. Kaufman.)

Chapter 2: Faith and Finances

FOOTNOTES

1. WWW, Saskatchewan, #13, Item 1, submitted by Gwendolyn Mills.

2. WWW, British Columbia, #3, submitted by Audrey Sawchuck and Violet E. Stewart.

3. WWW, British Columbia, #19, submitted by Trudi Mathias.

4. WWW, Manitoba, #15, Item 3, submitted by Laura Warsaba.

5. WWW, Manitoba, #15, Item 3, submitted by Laura Warsaba.

6. WWW, Saskatchewan, #15, submitted by Shellbrook UCW.

7. WWW, Saskatchewan, #28, submitted by Frances McDougall.

8. WWW, British Columbia, #8, submitted by Mabel Burnett.

9. WWW, Alberta, #7, submitted by Donna Minor.

10. WWW, British Columbia, #3, submitted by Audrey Sawchuck and Violet E. Stewart.

11. WWW, Alberta, #2, submitted by Violet Hackett.

12. Bert Platt, *Trinity United Church, Beeton: 1878-1978* (1978), p. 39, included in WWW, Toronto, #7, submitted by Muriel Reynolds.

13. Jean Gordon Forbes, *Wide Windows: The Story of the Woman's Missionary Society of The United Church of Canada* (Toronto: Literature Dept., WMS, UC., 1951), p. 3.

14. WWW, British Columbia, #3, submitted by Audrey Sawchuck and Violet E. Stewart.

15. WWW, Manitoba #15, Item 14, submitted by Laura Warsaba.

16. WWW, Hamilton, #4, submitted by D. Aileen Farrell and Margaret E. Hicks.

17. WWW, British Columbia, #1, submitted by Ena Archer, Mary Douglas, Evelyn Torrance.

18. Minnie M. Haight, *An Historical Sketch of the Women's Auxiliary to Emmanuel Evangelical United Brethren Church in Waterloo, Ontario 1903-1963*, p. 4, included in WWW, Hamilton, #10, Item 1, submitted by Helen Hall.

19. WWW, Alberta, #5, submitted by Beth Tachit.

20. WWW, Maritime—New Brunswick and Québec, #13, submitted by Winnifred Gray.

21. WWW, Manitoba, #9, Item 1, submitted by Maud Lelond.

22. WWW, Manitoba, #9, Item 6, submitted by Maud Lelond.

23. WWW, Manitoba, #10, Item 1, submitted by Margaret De La Mare.

24. WWW, Saskatchewan, #24, Item 3, submitted by Joyce M. McManus.

25. Mary F. Bailey, *A History of Mansonville United Church, 1873-1973*, p. 35, included in WWW, Montreal and Ottawa, #5, Item 3, submitted by Jean McNeil.

26. WWW, British Columbia, #17, submitted by Trudi Mathias.

27. WWW, Saskatchewan, #15, submitted by Shellbrook UCW.

28. WWW, British Columbia, #10, submitted by Nora McEwen.

29. WWW, Maritime—Nova Scotia, #2, Item 10, submitted by Jean M. Curtis and Grace Kilcup.

30. WWW, Maritime—P.E.I., #5, Item 6, submitted by Mrs. Henry Moyse.

31. WWW, Manitoba, #5, submitted by Marjorie Sissons.

32. WWW, Saskatchewan, #12, p. 6, submitted by Eileen McLeod.

33. "The Fellowship of the Least Coin", pamphlet. Available free from Women's Inter-Church Council of Canada, 77 Charles Street West, Toronto M5S 1K5.

34. WWW, Toronto, #5, submitted by Gladys Coxon.

35. *Victoria Square United Church: 1880-1980* (1980), p. 16, included in WWW, Toronto, #2, submitted anonymously.

36. WWW, Maritime—Nova Scotia, #2, Item 3, submitted by Gladys Fraser.

37. WWW, Manitoba, #6, Item 1, pp. 3-4, submitted by Birtle UCW.

38. WWW, Manitoba, #15, Item 21, p. 2 and 4, submitted by Laura Warsaba.

39. WWW, British Columbia, #2, p. 4, submitted by Margaret Huntington.

40. WWW, Manitoba, #6, Item 1, p. 7, submitted by Birtle UCW.

41. WWW, Saskatchewan, #16, submitted by Janet Loveridge.

42. WWW, Hamilton, #10, Item 4, p. 2, submitted by Helen Hall.

43. WWW, Manitoba, #13, Item 3, pp. 3-4, submitted by Ida Berglund.

44. WWW, Maritime—P.E.I., #3, p. 4, submitted by Ruby Matheson.

45. Steven Chambers, compiler, *This Is Your Church: A Guide to the Beliefs, Policies and Positions of The United Church of Canada* (Toronto: *The United Church Observer*, 1982), p. 114.

46. "Statement of the Secretary of the Division of Mission in Canada regarding Staff Support for the UCW and Men's Networks", issued by Howard Brox, Secretary, DMC, April 14, 1983.

47. Steven Chambers, compiler, *This Is Your Church: A Guide to the Beliefs, Policies and Positions of The United Church of Canada*, p. 28.

48. Elizabeth Howell Verdesi, *In But Still Out: Women in the Church* (Philadelphia: Westminster Press, 1976), p. 24.

49. Reba Patterson, President of the Continuing Board of the Women's Missionary Society of The United Church of Canada, in a letter to Lynda Newmarch, Editor, *Exchange*, The United Church of Canada.

Chapter 3: Social Change Reflected in Women's Work and Worship

FOOTNOTES

1. David Lochhead with Betty-Jean Klassen, *Living Between Memory and Hope* (Toronto: The United Church of Canada, 1981), p. 27)

2. Daphne Anderson: "A Working Paper on Women in the Church", Division of Congregational Life, British Columbia Conference, The United Church of Canada, 1976, p. 27. (Subsequently published by Division of Mission in Canada as *God's Hidden People.)*

3. John Webster Grant, *The Church in the Canadian Era* (Toronto: McGraw-Hill Ryerson, 1972), pp. 106-107.

4. This was the case of Dr. Chone Oliver, medical missionary to India. Included in WWW, British Columbia, #20, p. 1, submitted by Glenna Jamieson.

5. WWW, Maritimes—P.E.I., #5, Item 8, p. 1, submitted by Mrs. Henry Moyse.

6. Dr. Beatrice Wilson, interviewed on tape by Heather Dau, Berkeley Studio, Toronto, January-February 1980, side A.

7. WWW, Bay of Quinte, #8, p. 20, submitted by Betty Thompson.

8. "The Woman's Christian Temperance Union and the Building of Willard Hall, Toronto", *National Reference Book on Canadian Men and Women* with other General Information for Library, Newspaper, Educational and Individual Use", Sixth Edition, Canadian Newspaper Service Registered, 1940, pp. 931-944.

9. Elizabeth Ross, cited by Jean Gordon Forbes in *Wide Windows: the Story of the Woman's Missionary Society of The United Church of Canada* (Toronto: Literature Dept., WMS, U.C., 1951), p. 28.

10. Jean Gordon Forbes, *Wide Windows*, p. 31.

11. John Webster Grant, *The Church in the Canadian Era*, p. 92.

12. Genevieve Leslie, "Domestic Service in Canada, 1880-1920", *Women at Work Ontario, 1850-1930*, J. Acton, P. Goldsmith and B. Sheppard, eds. (Toronto: Women's Press, 1974) p. 95.

13. The Duchess of Sutherland, speaking to the Staffordshire branch of the UBWEA in 1894. Cited "Domestic Service in Canada, 1880-1920", *Women at Work Ontario, 1850-1930*, p. 102.

14. John Webster Grant, *The Church in the Canadian Era*, p. 103.

15. Cited in John Webster Grant, *The Church in the Canadian Era*, p. 114.

16. Ceta Ramkhalawansingh, "Women During the Great War", *Women at Work Ontario, 1850-1930*, p. 262.

17. John Webster Grant, *The Church in the Canadian Era*, p. 116.

18. Grace Johnston, *History of South Gloucester United Church,* included in WWW, Montreal and Ottawa, #2, p. 23, submitted by Grace Johnston.

19. *Historical Sketch of Algoma Presbytery,* London Conference, 1979, p. 23, included in WWW, London, #4, submitted anonymously.

20. WWW, Alberta, #5, submitted by Beth Tachit.

21. John Webster Grant, *The Church in the Canadian Era,* p. 137.

22. *Ibid.,* p. 138.

23. WWW, Manitoba, #4, submitted by Audrey Tohue.

24. WWW, British Columbia, #20, p. 2, submitted by Glenna Jamieson.

25. Daphne Anderson, "A Working Paper on Women in the Church", p. 28.

26. WWW, Maritime—Nova Scotia, #2, Item 2, submitted by Rev. Frances MacLellan.

27. Cited in John Webster Grant, *The Church in the Canadian Era,* p. 150.

28. *Mount Paul United Church: the Golden Years, 1928-1978,* p. 11, included in WWW, British Columbia, #8, submitted by Mabel Burnett.

29. WWW, Maritime—Nova Scotia, #2, Item 2, submitted by Rev. Frances MacLellan.

30. WWW, Saskatchewan, #29, p. 2, submitted by History Committee, Watrous United Church.

31. WWW, London, #1, Item 46, submitted by Kay Brodie.

32. John Webster Grant, *The Church in the Canadian Era,* p. 161.

33. *Ibid.,* p. 162.

34. Margaret Louise Shortiss, interviewed on tape by Heather Dau, Berkeley Studio, January 1978.

35. WWW, London, #1, Item 3, p. 3, submitted by Kay Brodie.

36. WWW, Bay of Quinte, #11, p. 3, submitted by Ruby Imeson.

37. WWW, Maritime—Nova Scotia, #2, Item 12b, p. 2, submitted by Lillian (MacKinnon) Piercey.

38. WWW, Manitoba, #15, Item 21, submitted by Laura Warsaba.

39. WWW, Saskatchewan, #20, p. 2, submitted by Clair Scott.

40. Roy Webster, interviewed on tape by Heather Dau, Berkeley Studio, December 1979.

41. *Recalling Our Heritage: 1962-1982,* pp. 3-4, included in WWW, British Columbia, #15, submitted by Lillian Soya.

42. WWW, Bay of Quinte, #11, submitted by Ruby Imeson.

43. WWW, British Columbia, #11, submitted by Nell Hanna.

44. WWW, Manitoba, #7, p. 5, submitted by Georgia Hyndman.

45. WWW, Manitoba, #15 Item 12, submitted by Laura Warsaba.

46. WWW, Saskatchewan, #12, p. 2, submitted by Eileen McLeod.

47. *The United Church Observer,* 50th Anniversary Issue, January 1975, p. 34.

48. *The United Church Observer,* Reference Edition, 1963, p. 33.

49. *Proceedings of General Council,* Edmonton, Alberta, September 1960, p. 227.

50. *Ibid.,* p. 228.

51. *Ibid.,* p. 236.

52. WWW, London, #1, Item 3, p. 5, submitted by Kay Brodie.

53. WWW, Toronto, #10, p. 1, submitted by Hopeville UCW, Dundalk.

54. WWW, London, #13, Item 3, p. 6, submitted by Marion E. Marshall.

55. WWW, London, #10, submitted by Dorothy R. Joslin.

56. WWW, London, #13, Item 3, p. 3, submitted by Marion E. Marshall.

57. WWW, Toronto, #17, p. 3, submitted by Mary Rowell Jackman.

58. Anne M. Squire, *Women in the Church* (Toronto: Division of Mission in Canada, The United Church of Canada, 1978), p. 1.

59. *Ibid.*, pp. 2-3

60. See Rosemary Agonito, ed. *History of Ideas on Woman: A Source Book.* New York: G. P. Putnam's Sons, 1977).

61. Graeme S. Mount and Michael J. Mulloy, *A History of St. Andrew's United Church, Sudbury,* p. 93, included in WWW, Manitou, #2, Item 3, submitted by Tina Hansen.

62. Pat Clarke, "Christian Feminism", *The United Church Observer,* March 1981, p. 30

63. Statement taken from "Questionnaire Regarding Inclusive Language Guidelines", circulated within Muskoka Presbytery, November 1982.

64. Pat Clarke, "Christian Feminism", p. 30.

Chapter 4: The Past as a Guide to the Future

FOOTNOTES

1. WWW, Saskatchewan, #32, Item 7, submitted by Eleanor Haw.

2. WWW, British Columbia, #7, p. 11, submitted by Lillian Soga.

3. *Ibid.*, p. 12.

4. *Ibid.*, p. 12.

5. WWW, Montreal and Ottawa, #3, letter, submitted by Enid Arscott.

6. For further reading on this subject, see Rosemary Agonito, ed. *History of Ideas on Woman: A Source Book* (New York: G. P. Putnam's Sons, 1977). Also, Mary F. Lefkowitz and Maureen Fant, eds. *Women in Greece and Rome* (Toronto: Samuel-Stevens, 1977).

7. The Cornwall Collective. *Your Daughters Shall Prophesy: Feminist Alternatives in Theological Education.* (New York: The Pilgrim Press, 1980), p. 7.

8. WWW, British Columbia, #2, p. 3, submitted by Margaret Huntington.

9. *Recalling Our Heritage: 1962-1982* (Vancouver South Presbyterial United Church Women) p. 20, included in WWW, British Columbia, #15, submitted by Lillian Soga.

10. WWW, Montreal and Ottawa, #6, submitted by Katherine M. Crawford.

11. Grace Johnston, *History of South Gloucester United Church at Johnston's Corners: 1834-1980* (Gloucester, 1980), p. 35. Included in WWW, Montreal and Ottawa, #2, submitted by Grace Johnston.

12. WWW, Manitoba, #15, Item 16, p. 1, submitted by Laura Warsaba.

13. *Recalling Our Heritage: 1962-1982*, p. 19. (See note #9.)

14. WWW, Maritime—Nova Scotia, #2, Item 3, p. 4, submitted by Gladys Fraser.

15. Elva Richards McGaughey, *A Firm Foundation: A History of St. Paul's United Church: 1830-1980* (Prescott, Ontario), p. 74, submitted by Enid Arscott.

16. Gert Beadle, Thunder Bay poet who proudly describes herself as a hag and a crone, in a letter to Shirley Davy, dated June 28, 1982.

17. Nancy J. Van Scoyoc, *Women, Change and the Church*, Ezra Earl Jones, ed. (Nashville: Abingdon, 1980), pp. 95-96.

18. WWW, Maritime—New Brunswick, #9, submitted by Clotilda Ellis.

19 WWW, Montreal and Ottawa, #4, submitted by Christine Judge.

20. Christine Frye, "This song of praise and thanks", *Through the Darkness: psalms of a survivor*. (Winfield, B.C.: Wood Lake Books, 1983), p. 66.

SECTION 4

Chapter 8: Women and Power in The United Church of Canada

FOOTNOTES

1. Elizabeth Clark and Herbert Richardson. *Women and Religion, A Feminist Sourcebook of Christian Thought* (New York: Harper and Row, 1977), p. 12.

2. Rosemary Reuther and Eleanor E. McLaughlin. *Women of Spirit: Female Leadership in the Jewish and Christian Traditions.* (New York: Simon and Schuster, 1979), p. 105.

3. *Ibid.*, p. 116.

4. J. Plaskow and Carol Christ, ed. E.S. Fiorenza, "Women in the Early Christian Movement", in *Womanspirit Rising: A Feminist Reader in Religion* (New York: Harper and Row, 1979), p. 87.

5. Rosemary Reuther, "Virginal Feminism in the Fathers of the Church" in *Religion and Sexism* (New York: Simon and Shuster, 1972), p. 163.

6. *Ibid.*, p. 169.

7. *Ibid.*, p. 217.

8. Interview with Genevieve Carder.

9. *General Council Proceedings, 1926,* Woman's Missionary Society Report, p. 349.

10. Jean Forbes, *Open Windows* (Toronto: Woman's Missionary Society, 1952), p. 14.

11. *The New Outlook,* 1925, June Issue, p. 28.

12. *General Council Proceedings, 1926,* Woman's Missionary Society Report, p. 349.

13. Forbes, *op. cit.,* Introduction, p. vii.

14. Forbes, *op. cit.,* p. 15.

15. Hazel Hefren, *thesis,* p. 34.

16. *General Council Proceedings,* 1940, p. 380.

17. *General Council Proceedings, 1954,* Woman's Missionary Society Report, p. 520.

18. *General Council Proceedings,* 1954, pp. 516, 517.

19. *General Council Proceedings, 1930,* p. 34.

20. *General Council Proceedings, 1954,* p. 505.

21. Interview with Dr. Beatrice Wilson.

22. *The New Outlook,* November 18, 1936.

23. *Ibid.,* June 23, 1935, p. 76.

24. *General Council Proceedings, 1928,* p. 25.

25. *General Council Proceedings, 1962,* p. 76.

26. *The New Outlook,* 1925, June, "Women's Page", p. 28.

27. *General Council Proceedings, 1932,* p. 277; *1946,* p. 109.

28. Board of Women, Division of Mission in Canada, Research Report, *Church Women—Figures and Facts,* p. 34.

29. *General Council Proceedings, 1960,* p. 696.

BIBLIOGRAPHY

Clark, Elizabeth and Richardson, Herbert. *Women and Religion, A Feminist Sourcebook of Christian Thought.* New York: Harper and Row, 1977.

Forbes, Jean. *Open Windows.* Toronto: The United Church of Canada, 1952.

Hefren, Hazel. "The Ministries of Women in the United Church as Seen Against Their Historical Background", thesis, Vancouver School of Theology, 1965.

Plaskow, J. and Christ, Carol, ed. *Womanspirit Rising: A Feminist Reader in Religion.* New York: Harper and Row, 1979.

Reuther, Rosemary Radford, ed. *Religion and Sexism.* New York: Simon and Schuster, 1972.

Reuther, Rosemary and McLaughlin, Eleanor, ed. *Women of Spirit.* New York: Simon and Shuster, 1979.

Wollstonecraft, M. *Vindication of the Rights of Women.* 2nd ed. Pelican Books, 1975.

Board of Women Research Report, *Church Women—Figures and Facts,* Toronto: Division of Mission in Canada, 1972.

General Council Proceedings of The United Church of Canada, Toronto: The United Church of Canada, 1925-1980.

Chapter 9: Christian Feminism in The United Church: Resources in Culture and Tradition

FOOTNOTES

1. Patricia Clarke, "Christian Feminism", *The United Church Observer*, March 1981, pp. 29-38.

2. This section draws upon Alison Jaggar's valuable article, "Political Philosophies of Women's Liberation" in *Feminism and Philosophy*, Ed. Mary Vetterling-Braggin et al. (Totowa: Littlefield and Co., 1977), pp. 5-21. See also Carol S. Robb, "A Framework for Feminist Ethics", *Journal of Religious Ethics*, Vol. 9/1, Spring 1981, pp. 48-67.

3. While we tend to think of this polarization in terms of Victorian "separate spheres", historically there has been considerable variation and overlap. For example, women were economically dominant in the cottage industries of pre-industrial England, and in the Jewish shtetls of eastern Europe. The only consistency is that men's work is given greater status.

4. For example, Luther argued, "Men have broad shoulders and narrow hips, and accordingly they possess intelligence. Woman (sic) have narrow shoulders and broad hips. Women ought to stay at home; the way they are created indicates this, for they have broad hips and a wide fundament to sit upon, keep house and bear and raise children", cited in *Not In God's Image*, Ed. J. O'Faolain and I. Martines (Toronto: Fitzhenry and Whiteside Ltd., 1973), p. 197.

5. Mary Daly is the foremost theological proponent of this position, which is given its fullest treatment in her latest work, *Gyn/Ecology* (Boston: Beacon Press, 1978).

6. Laurel Galana, "Radical Reproduction: X Without Y", *The Lesbian Reader* (Oakland: Amazon Press, 1975), pp. 122-137. A fascinating early treatment of the possibility of an all-female society can be found in Charlotte Perkins Gilman's utopian novel, *Herland* (New York: Pantheon Books, 1979), originally published in 1915.

7. The suggestion that motherhood be considered a service to the state was first made by Mary Wollstonecraft, in 1972 in *A Vindication of the Rights of Women*. Wollstonecraft herself died of childbed fever.

8. It would seem that liberal feminists should therefore support the right of individual women to choose motherhood as a career. However, as the liberal view tends to see biology as something to be overcome, and the work in the home as private and therefore of secondary value, the overwhelming emphasis of liberal feminism is upon bringing women into a male-dominated work force in the public sphere.

9. "The first condition for the liberation of the wife is to bring the whole female sex back into public industry." Friedrich Engels, *The Origin of Family, Private Property and the State*, quoted by Jaggar, p. 10.

10. Ephesians 5: 22 ff., *Holy Bible, Revised Standard Version* (Cleveland: The World Publishing Company, 1962).

11. For a full discussion of this question, see Rosemary Ruether, *New*

Woman/New Earth: Sexist Ideologies and Human Liberation (New York: The Seabury Press, 1975).

12. Persons interested in the story of McClung's life should read her two-volume autobiography, *Clearing in the West* and *The Stream Runs Fast*. Candace Savage's *Our Nell: A Scrapbook Biography of Nellie McClung* (Saskatoon: Western Producer Prairie Books, 1979) provides valuable background material on McClung, and gives a vivid picture of the Canadian society of McClung's day.

13. Rather than consider the feminist position seriously, the anti-feminist will: 1) *trivialize*—claim that the issue is not important, that things are "being taken out of proportion" (What woman has not been told she is getting worked up over nothing?); 2) *sexualize*—disparage the position by maligning the physical attraction of its author. (In the NFB film, "Not a Love Story", women demonstrating against pornography are told they are doing so out of jealousy, being "too ugly" for porn films themselves); 3) *emotionalize*—assume feminist conviction is a result of emotional imbalance, belligerence, or sheer bad temper.

14. Stephen Leacock, "The Woman Question", *The Social Criticism of Stephen Leacock,* Ed. and Introduction by Alan Bowker (Toronto: University of Toronto Press, 1973), pp. 53ff. It is instructive to compare Leacock's essay with McClung's *In Times Like These,* published in the same year (1915).

15. *Ibid.,* p. 55

16. This differentiation and specialization of function was considered a sign of evolutionary advance. The more a woman concentrated on a single activity (motherhood), the more refined and pure a specimen of womanhood she was taken to be. That most women did not have this dubious luxury and instead found themselves working in sweatshops or as servants in the "true woman's" home was taken as scientific proof of their evolutionary inferiority.

17. Nellie McClung, *In Times Like These* (Toronto: University of Toronto Press, 1972), p. 70. This 1915 volume of McClung's essays remains her most concise and thorough treatment of the social issues of her day. All further quotes will be from this volume, indicated in the body of the text by page number.

18. Which meant in practice, "The hand that rocks the cradle should never rock the boat". McClung called such platitudes "dope", *In Times Like These,* p. 38.

19. Being "guardian of the race" invested women with a certain positive status, provided they accepted their role and the world was functioning relatively smoothly. Any disruption, however, could be logically construed as women's failure to do their job properly. The intensity with which many Victorian women pursued the ideal of moral purity is understandable in the context of this impossibly great responsibility, a fact which the stereotype of Victorian "prudishness" completely overlooks.

20. The WCTU deserves a far fuller treatment than can be given here. What material does exist tends to reflect the stereotypical assumption of Victorian prudery and repression characteristics of dominant scholarship's treatment of women's issues.

21. Frances Willard, *Women and Temperance* (New York: Arno Press, 1972), p. 43.

22. *Ibid.,* p. 238.

23. *Ibid.,* p. 26.

24. McClung, *In Times Like These,* p. 87. Famed Social Gospel leader, J .S. Woodsworth was another. His *Strangers Within Our Gates* ranks the desirability of immigrant groups on the basis of "national character".

25. Terry L. Chapman, "Early Eugenics Movement in Western Canada", in *Alberta History,* Autumn 1977, 25(4).

26. "It does not seem to the thoughtful observer that we need more children nearly so much as we need better children, and a higher value set upon all human life." *In Times Like These,* p. 88.

27. Richard Allen, *The Social Passion. Religion and Social Reform in Canada 1914-1928* (Toronto: University of Toronto Press, 1973). "I have purposely not suggested that the women's movement was a subsidiary, auxiliary part of a 'larger' movement for social reform. The historical record is characteristically skewed to reflect men's activities, despite women's overwhelming creation of and participation in organizations for social reform." Even Allen concentrates exclusively upon male church and labour leaders; McClung is mentioned twice, by name only. The place of women in conventional history is a subject worthy of fuller exploration, particularly for those engaged in feminist analysis. A good beginning is Gerda Lerner, *The Majority Finds Its Past* (New York: Oxford University Press, 1979).

28. On ordination, see Mary Hallett, "Nellie McClung and the Fight for the Ordination of Women in The United Church of Canada", *Atlantis,* Spring 1979, 4(2), pp. 2-16. Catherine Cleverdon's *The Woman Suffrage Movement in Canada* (Toronto: University of Toronto Press, 1974), originally published in 1950, remains the most thorough treatment of the suffrage question to date.

29. "...the new movement among women is a spiritual movement...women, whose work has been taken away from them, are now beating at new doors, crying to be let in that they may take part in new labours, and thus save womanhood from the enervation which is threatening it. Women were intended to guide and sustain life, to care for the race; not feed on it", *In Times Like These,* p 64.

30. "It was the people who did not like to be disturbed who crucified Christ—the worst fault they had to find with him was that he annoyed them...", *In Times Like These,* p. 10.

31. "Discontent may mean the stirring of ambition, the desire to spread out, to improve and grow. Discontent is a sign of life, corresponding to growing pains in a healthy child", *In Times Like These,* p. 44.

32. *In Times Like These,* pp. 68-79.

33. This precisely the contention made by Rosemary Ruether in *New Woman /New Earth,* written fifty years after McClung's essay. Ellipses such as this are far too common in women's history, and stand as a sober reminder to optimists who feel progress to be inevitable and irreversible.

34. "Superior physical force is an insidious thing, and has biased the judgement of even good men", *In Times Like These*, p. 69.

35. "The world needs the work and help of the women, and the women must work, if the race will survive", *In Times Like These*, p. 66.

36. "The Christian Church has departed in some places from Christ's teaching—noticeably in its treatment of women. Christ taught the nobility of loving service freely given; but such a tame uninteresting belief as that did not appeal to the military masculine mind. It declared Christianity was fit only for women and slaves", *In Times Like These*, p. 69.

37. *In Times Like These*, p. 70. The psychoanalytic theory of Carl Jüng is often taken by feminists to be a positive resource. To the contrary, Jüng's archetypes are drawn from a German Romantic tradition wherein woman's place was symbolically rich, but socially and politically poor. As representatives of the "Unconscious", women are denying their true nature by speaking for themselves.

BIBLIOGRAPHY

Allen, Richard. *The Social Passion: Religion and Social Reform in Canada 1914-1928.* Toronto: University of Toronto Press, 1973.

Bacchi, Carol. *Liberation Deferred? The Ideas of the English Canadian Suffragists 1877-1918.* Toronto: University of Toronto Press, 1983.

Chapman, Terry L. "Early Eugenics Movement in Western Canada." *Alberta History.* Vol. 25 No. 4, Autumn, 1977.

Clarke, Patricia. "Christian Feminism", *The United Church Observer.* March 1981.

Cleverdon, Catherine. *The Woman Suffrage Movement in Canada.* Toronto, University of Toronto Press, 1974.

Daly, Mary. *Gyn/Ecology: The Metaethics of Radical Feminism.* Boston: Beacon Press, 1978.

Gilman, Charlotte Perkins. *Herland.* New York: Pantheon Books, 1979.

Galana, Laurel. "Radical Reproduction: X Without Y". *The Lesbian Reader.* Oakland: Amazon Press, 1975.

Hallett, Mary. "Nellie McClung and the Fight for the Ordination of Women in The United Church of Canada". *Atlantis.* Spring, 1979.

Holy Bible, Revised Standard Version. Cleveland: The World Publishing Company, 1962.

Jaggar, Alison. "Political Philosophies of Women's Liberation" in *Feminism and Philosophy*, ed. Mary Vetterling-Braggin *et al.* Totowa: Littlefield and Co., 1977.

Kraditor, Aileen. *Ideas of the Woman Suffrage Movement 1890-1920.* New York: Columbia University Press, 1965.

Leacock, Stephen. "The Woman Question" in *The Social Criticism of Stephen Leacock*, ed. and Introduction by Alan Bowker. Toronto: University of Toronto Press, 1973.

Lerner, Gerda. *The Majority Finds Its Past*. New York: Oxford University Press, 1979.

McClung, Nellie L. *In Times Like These*. Toronto: University of Toronto Press, 1975.

————————. *Painted Fires*. Toronto: Thomas Allen, 1925.

————————. *Purple Springs*. Toronto: Thomas Allen, 1921.

O'Faolain, J. Ed. and L. Martines. *Not In God's Image*. Toronto: Fitzhenry and Whiteside Ltd., 1973.

Robb, Carol S. "A Framework for Feminist Ethics", *Journal of Religious Ethics*. Vol. 9. No. 1. Spring, 1981.

Ruether, Rosemary R. *New Woman/New Earth: Sexist Ideologies and Human Liberation*. New York: The Seabury Press, 1975.

Willard, Frances. *Woman and Temperance*. New York: Arno Press, 1972.

Chapter 10   Side Road on the Journey to Autonomy

FOOTNOTES

1. John Henry Riddell, *Methodism in the Middle West* (Toronto, 1946), p. 239.

2. W. A. J. Martin, "Report of Committee on an Order of Deaconesses," in *Acts and Proceedings of the Thirty-Fourth General Assembly of The Presbyterian Church in Canada*. (Toronto, 1908), p. 312.

3. Elizabeth Schüssler Fiorenza, "Word, Spirit and Power: Women in Early Christian Communities," in *Women of Spirit: Female Leadership in the Jewish and Christian Traditions,* ed. Rosemary Ruether and Eleanor McLaughlin. (New York: Simon and Schuster, 1979) p. 36.

4. Frederick S. Weiser, "The Origin of the Modern Diaconate for Women" in *Servants of Christ: Deaconesses in Renewal,* ed. Donald G. Bloesch (Minneapolis, 1971) p. 19. I am indebted to Weiser for this account of Fleidner's work.

5. Martin, *op. cit.,* p. 312.

6. Mary A. T. Dougherty, *The Methodist Deaconess 1885-1918: A Study in Religious Feminism,* unpublished Doctoral Dissertation (University of California/Davis, 1979), p. viii.

7. Barbara Welther, "She Hath Done What She Could: Protestant Women's Missionary Careers in Nineteenth-Century America", *American Quarterly,* Vol. 30, No. 5 (Winter: 1978), p. 635.

8. Dorothy C. Bass, "Their Prodigious Influence: Women, Religion and Reform in Antebellum America, *Women of Spirit: Female Leadership in the Jewish and Christian Traditions,* ed. Rosemary Ruether and Eleanor McLaughlin (New York: Simon and Schuster, 1979), p. 280.

9. *Ibid.* (page number not available)

10. Nancy Cott, *The Bonds of Womanhood* (New York, 1977), p. 154.

11. Ann Douglas, *The Feminization of American Culture* (New York, 1977), p. 68. Quoting early reformer Grace Greenwood, ©1853.

12. Bass, *op. cit.,* p. 295, quoting Sarah Grimke.

13. *Christian Guardian,* June 3, 1885.

14. *Ibid.* (page number not available).

15. Douglas, *op. cit.,* p. 134.

16. Page Smith, *Daughters of the Promised Land: Women in American History* (Boston and Toronto: Little, Brown & Co., 1970), p. 178.

17. Grace Lane, "The Women Who Made History" in *The United Church Observer,* (Dec. 1, 1961), p. 8.

18. *Ibid.,* p. 9.

19. J. Balcom Shan, "Women and the Church" in *The Presbyterian Record* (XXXIV, No. 9), Sept. 1909.

20. *The Prebyterian Record* (XXXIV, No. 10), October 1909, p. 433.

21. Dougherty, *op. cit.,* p. v.

22. Douglas, *op. cit.,* p. 117.

23. R. Pierce Beaver, *All Loves Excelling: American Protestant Women in World Mission,* revised edition (Grand Rapids, 1980), p. 91.

24. *Ibid.,* p. 80.

25. Harriet Louise Platt, *The Story of the Years: A History of the Woman's Missionary Society of the Methodist Church of Canada 1881-1906* (Toronto, 1908). This official history credits a Dr. Sutherland as the "source" of inspiration.

26. George N. Emery, *Methodism on the Canadian Prairies 1896-1914: The Dynamics of an Institution in a New Environment* (Ottawa, 1970), p. 195. Emery, for example, describes tensions between the WMS and male church officers re funds for home mission work.

27. Marjory (Lady Willison) MacMurchy, *The Woman—Bless Her: Not as Amiable a Book as it Sounds* (Toronto, 1916), p. 3.

28. *Ibid.,* (page number not available).

29. *Ibid.,* (page number not available).

30. John S. Moir, *Enduring Witness: A History of The Presbyterian Church in Canada* (Hamilton, 1924), p. 180.

31. Douglas, *op. cit.,* p. 131.

32. *Methodist Magazine and Review,* Vol. XXXIX, January-June 1894, p. 157.

33. *Ibid.,* p. 156.

34. *Ibid.,* Vol. XXXIV, July-December 1891, p. 449.

35. Dougherty, *op. cit.,* p. ix.

36. *Ibid.,* p. 30ff.

37. Y. L. Brereton and C. R. Klein, "American Women in Ministry: A History of Protestant Beginning Points", in *Women of Spirit: Female Leadership in the Jewish and Christian Traditions,* ed. Rosemary Ruether and Eleanor

McLaughlin (New York: Simon and Schuster, 1979), p. 309.

38. *The Presbyterian Church in Canada,* Sixteenth Annual Report—Of the Woman's Foreign Missionary Society—Western Division (Toronto, 1892).

39. Dougherty, *op. cit.,* p. 46ff.

40. Norris Magnuson, *Salvation in the Slums: Evangelical Social Work, 1865-1920.* (Metuchen, N.J. 1977), p. 34.

41. Dougherty, *op. cit.,* p. 52ff.

42. *Methodist Magazine and Review,* Vol. XXI, January-June, 1890, p. 44.

43. *Ibid.,* Vol. XXXV, January-June, 1892, p. 594.

44. *Ibid.,* Vol. XXXI, January June, 1890, p. 53.

45. *Ibid.,* Vol. XXXV, January-June, 1892, p. 595.

46. *Ibid.,* Vol. XXXI, January-June, 1890, p. 53.

47. *Ibid.,* Vol. XXXV, January-June, 1892, p. 595.

48. *Journal—Third General Conference of the Methodist Church* (Toronto, 1890), p. 321.

49. *Methodist Magazine and Review,* Vol. XXXI, January-June, 1890, p. 52.

50. *Ibid.,* Vol. XXXII, January-June, 1890, p. 139.

51. *Ibid.,* Vol. XXXI, January-June, 1890, p. 53.

52. *Ibid.,* Vol. XXXIV, July-December, 1891, p. 257.

53. *Ibid.,* Vol. XXXIV, July-December, 1891, p. 372.

54. *The Presbyterian Record* (XXII, No. 10), October 1897, p. 261.

55. *Twenty-Third Annual Report of the Woman's Foreign Missionary Society of The Presbyterian Church in Canada (Western Division),* (Toronto, 1901), p. 61.

56. *Twenty-Fifth Annual Report of the Woman's Foreign Missionary Society of The Presbyterian Church in Canada (Western Division)* (Toronto, 1908), p. 62.

57. *Thirty-Second Annual Report of the Woman's Foreign Missionary Society of The Presbyterian Church in Canada (Western Division)*(Toronto, 1908), p. 61.

58. *Twenty-Sixth Annual Report of the Woman's Foreign Missionary Society of The Presbyterian Church in Canada (Western Division)* (Toronto, 1902), p. 66.

59. *Twenty-Ninth Annual Report of the Woman's Foreign Missionary Society of The Presbyterian Church in Canada (Western Division)* (Toronto, 1905), p. 22.

60. *The Presbyterian,* May 19, 1903, p. 586.

61. *Ibid.,* (page number not available).

62. *Methodist Magazine and Review,* Vol. XXXII, January-June, 1890, p. 139.

63. Wayne Roberts, "Rocking the Cradle for the World: The New Woman and Maternal Feminism 1877-1914", in *A Not Unreasonable Claim: Women and Reform in Canada 1880-1920,* ed. Linda Kealy (Toronto, 1979), p. 39.

64. *Ibid.,* p. 37.

65. The Editor of the *Methodist Magazine and Review* describes Horton as influential in the establishment of the Canadian Methodist Order (Vol. LIV, July-December, 1901), p. 84.

66. *Methodist Magazine and Review,* Vol. LXII, July-December, 1904, p. 503.

67. *Ibid.,* (page number not available).

68. *Ibid.,* Vol. LXV, January-June, 1897, p. 520.

69. *Ibid.,* (page number not available).

70. *Ibid.,* Vol. LXII, July-December, 1905, p. 503.

71. *Ibid.,* Vol. XL, July-December, 1894, p. 408.

72. *Ibid.,* Vol. LXV, January-June, 1897, p. 520.

73. *Ibid.,* Vol. XXXV, January-June, 1892, p. 596.

74. *The Presbyterian Record,* February, 1905, p. 80.

75. *The Christian Guardian,* September 3, 1913 (The Deaconess Work Column).

76. The United Church of Canada, "Report on Employed Women Workers", *The Record of Proceedings of General Council* (Toronto, 1928), p. 254.

77. Welther, *op. cit.,* p. 634.

78. The United Church of Canada, *op. cit.,* p. 254.

79. The Presbyterian Church in Canada, *Acts and Proceedings of the Fortieth General Assembly* (Toronto, 1914), p. 205.

80. *Ibid.,* (page number not available).

81. The Presbyterian Church in Canada, *Acts and Proceedings of the Forty-Third General Assembly* (Toronto, 1917), p. 180.

82. The Presbyterian Church in Canada, *Acts and Proceedings of the Thirty-Ninth General Assembly* (Toronto, 1913), p. 269.

83. *The Christian Guardian,* April 29, 1903, p. 114.

84. The Presbyterian Church in Canada, *Acts and Proceedings of the Forty-Second General Assembly* (Toronto, 1916), p. 209.

85. *Methodist Magazine and Review* Vol. XIVIII, July-December, 1898, p. 212.

86. *Ibid.,* (page number not available).

87. *The Christian Guardian,* June 25, 1913.

88. Manitoba College Papers, Deaconess File. Letter from Principal J. M. McKay to Barbara Henderson, November 20, 1920.

89. Doughtery estimates that American Methodist deaconesses served an average of 4.6 years.

90. The Presbyterian Church in Canada, *Acts and Proceedings of the Forty-Fifth General Assembly* (Toronto, 1919), p. 37.

91. *Ibid.,* p. 29.

92. Methodist Church—"The Order Was Not Disbanded" in *Journal of the Eleventh General Conference* (Toronto, 1922), p. 331.

BIBLIOGRAPHY

Books

Allen, Richard. *The Social Passion.* Toronto: University of Toronto Press, 1973.

Beaver, R. Pierce. *All Loves Excelling: American Protestant Women in World Mission,* revised edition. Grand Rapids, 1980.

Bloesch, Donald G. ed. *Servants of Christ: Deaconesses in Renewal.* Minneapolis, 1971.

Cott, Nancy. *The Bonds of Womanhood.* New York, 1977.

Douglas, Ann. *The Feminization of American Culture.* New York, 1977.

Kealy, Linda ed. *A Not Unreasonable Claim: Women and Reform in Canada 1880-1920.* Toronto , 1979.

MacMurchy, Marjory (Lady Willison). *The Woman—Bless Her: Not as Amiable a Book as it Sounds.* Toronto, 1916.

Magnuson, Norris. *Salvation In The Slums:* Evangelical Social Work, 1865-1920. Metuchen, N.J. 1977.

Moir, John S. *Enduring Witness: A History of The Presbyterian Church in Canada.* Hamilton, 1924.

Platt, Harriet Louise. *The Story of the Years: A History of The Woman's Missionary Society of The Methodist Church of Canada 1881-1906.* Toronto, 1908.

Riddell, John Henry. *Methodism in The Middle West.* Toronto, 1946.

Ruether, Rosemary and McLaughlin, Eleanor eds. *Women of Spirit: Female Leadership in the Jewish and Christian Traditions.* New York: Simon and Schuster, 1978.

Smith, Page. *Daughters of The Promised Land: Women in American History.* Little, Brown and Co., Boston and Toronto, 1945.

The United Church of Canada. *The First Fifty Years, 1895-1945: The Training and Work of Women Employed in the Service of The United Church of Canada.* Toronto, 1945.

Articles

Bass, Dorothy C., "Their Prodigious Influence: Women, Religion and Reform in Antebellum America", in *Women of Spirit: Female Leadership in the Jewish and Christian Traditions,* ed. Rosemary Ruether and Eleanor McLaughlin (New York: Simon and Schuster, 1979).

Brereton, Y. L. and Klein, C. R. "American Women in Ministry: A History of Protestant Beginning Points", in *Women of Spirit: Female Leadership in the Jewish and Christian Traditions,* ed. Rosemary Ruether and Eleanor McLaughlin (New York: Simon and Schuster, 1979).

Fiorenza, Elizabeth Schussler, "Word, Spirit and Power: Women in Early Christian Communities", in *Women of Spirit: Female Leadership in the Jewish and Christian Traditions.* Ed. Rosemary Ruether and Eleanor McLaughlin (New York: Simon and Shuster, 1979).

Lane, Grace, "The Women Who Made History", *The United Church Observer* (December 1, 1961).

Magney, William, "The Methodist Church and The National Gospel 1884-1914" in *The Bulletin of The Archives of The United Church of Canada* (No. 20, 1968).

Roberts, Wayne, "Rocking the Cradle for the World. The New Woman and Maternal Feminism 1877-1914", in *A Not Unreasonable Claim: Women and Reform in Canada 1880-1920*, ed Linda Kealy (Toronto, 1979).

Weiser, Frederick S. "The Origin of the Modern Diaconate for Women", in *Servants of Christ: Deaconesses in Renewal* ed. Donald G. Bloesch (Minneapolis, 1971).

Welther, Barbara, "She Hath Done What She Could: Protestant Women's Missionary Careers in Nineteenth-Century America", in *American Quarterly*, Vol. 30, No. 5 (Winter, 1978).

Theses

Dougherty, Mary A. T., *The Methodist Deaconess 1885-1918: A Study in Religious Feminism*, unpublished Doctoral Dissertation (University of California/Davis, 1979).

Emery, George N., *Methodism on the Canadian Prairies 1896-1914: The Dynamics of an Institution in a New Environment* (Ottawa: National Library of Canada—Canadian Thesis on Microfilm, 1970).

Periodicals

The Christian Guardian, January-December 1885: January-December 1903; January-December 1913; January-December 1914.

The Methodist Magazine and Review, Vol. XXI, 1890-Vol. XXXIX, 1894; Vol. XLV, 1897-Vol. XLVII, 1898; Vol. LIV 1901-Vol. LXII, 1905.

The Presbyerian, Vol. 1, July, 1902-Vol. 13, December 1914.

The Presbyterian Record, Vol. XV, 1890-Vol. XXII, 1897; Vol. XXX, 1905-Vol. XXXIV, 1909.

Documents and Records

Methodist Church, *Journal of The Third General Conference* (Toronto, 1890).
_____, *Journal of The Fourth General Conference* (Toronto, 1894).
_____, *Journal of The Fifth General Conference* (Toronto, 1898).
_____, *Journal of The Sixth General Conference* (Toronto, 1902).
_____, *Journal of The Seventh General Conference* (Toronto, 1906).
_____, *Journal of The Eighth General Conference* (Toronto, 1910).
_____, *Journal of The Ninth General Conference* (Toronto, 1914).

——————————, *Journal of The Tenth General Conference* (Toronto, 1918).

——————————, *Journal of The Eleventh General Conference* (Toronto, 1922).

Presbyterian Church in Canada, *Acts And Proceedings of The Twenty-third General Assembly* (Toronto, 1897).

——————————, *Acts And Proceedings of The Twenty-fourth General Assembly* (Toronto, 1898).

——————————, *Acts And Proceedings of The Twenty-fifth General Assembly* (Toronto, 1899).

——————————, *Acts And Proceedings of The Twenty-sixth General Assembly* (Toronto, 1900).

——————————, *Acts And Proceedings of The Twenty-seventh General Assembly* (Toronto, 1901).

——————————, *Acts And Proceedings of The Twenty-eighth General Assembly* (Toronto, 1902).

——————————, *Acts And Proceedings of The Twenty-ninth General Assembly* (Toronto, 1903).

——————————, *Acts And Proceedings of The Thirtieth General Assembly* (Toronto, 1904).

——————————, *Acts And Proceedings of The Thirty-first General Assembly* (Toronto, 1905).

——————————, *Acts And Proceedings of The Thirty-second General Assembly* (Toronto, 1906).

——————————, *Acts And Proceedings of The Thirty-third General Assembly* (Toronto, 1907).

——————————, *Acts And Proceedings of The Thirty-fourth General Assembly* (Toronto, 1908).

——————————, *Acts And Proceedings of The Thirty-fifth General Assembly* (Toronto, 1909).

——————————, *Acts And Proceedings of The Thirty-sixth General Assembly* (Toronto, 1910).

——————————, *Acts And Proceedings of The Thirty-seventh General Assembly* (Toronto, 1911).

——————————, *Acts And Proceedings of The Thirty-eighth General Assembly* (Toronto, 1912).

Presbyterian Church in Canada, *Acts And Proceedings of The Thirty-ninth General Assembly,* (Toronto, 1913).

——————————, *Acts And Proceedings of The Fortieth General Assembly* (Toronto, 1914).

——————————, *Acts And Proceedings of The Forty-first General Assembly* (Toronto, 1915).

——————————, *Acts And Proceedings of The Forty-second General Assembly* (Toronto, 1916).

——————————, *Acts And Proceedings of The Forty-third*

General Assembly (Toronto, 1917).

————————————————————, Acts And Proceedings of The Forty-fourth General Assembly (Toronto, 1918).

————————————————————, Acts And Proceedings of The Forty-fifth General Assembly (Toronto, 1919).

————————————————————, Acts And Proceedings of The Forty-sixth General Assembly (Toronto, 1920).

————————————————————, Acts And Proceedings of The Forty-seventh General Assembly (Toronto, 1921).

————————————————————, Acts And Proceedings of The Forty-eighth General Assembly (Toronto, 1922).

————————————————————, Acts And Proceedings of The Forty-ninth General Assembly (Toronto, 1923).

————————————————————, Acts And Proceedings of The Fiftieth General Assembly (Toronto, 1924).

————————————————————, Acts And Proceedings of The Fifty-first General Assembly (Toronto, 1925).

————————————————————, Sixteenth Annual Report of The Woman's Foreign Missionary Society—Western Division (Toronto, 1892).

————————————————————, Seventeenth Annual Report of The Woman's Foreign Missionary Society—Western Division (Toronto, 1893).

————————————————————, Eighteenth Annual Report of The Woman's Foreign Missionary Society—Western Division (Toronto, 1894).

————————————————————, Nineteenth Annual Report of The Woman's Foreign Missionary Society—Western Division (Toronto, 1895).

————————————————————, Twentieth Annual Report of The Woman's Foreign Missionary Society—Western Division (Toronto, 1896).

————————————————————, Twenty-first Annual Report of The Woman's Foreign Missionary Society—Western Division (Toronto, 1897).

————————————————————, Twenty-second Annual Report of The Woman's Foreign Missionary Society—Western Division (Toronto, 1898).

————————————————————, Twenty-third Annual Report of The Woman's Foreign Missionary Society—Western Division (Toronto, 1899).

————————————————————, Twenty-fourth Annual Report of The Woman's Foreign Missionary Society—Western Division (Toronto, 1900).

————————————————————, Twenty-fifth Annual Report of The Woman's Foreign Missionary Society—Western Division (Toronto, 1901).

————————————————————, Twenty-sixth Annual Report of The Woman's Foreign Missionary Society—Western Division (Toronto, 1902).

——————————————————, *Twenty-seventh Annual Report of The Woman's Foreign Missionary Society—Western Division* (Toronto, 1903).

——————————————————, *Twenty-eighth Annual Report of The Woman's Foreign Missionary Society—Western Division* (Toronto, 1904).

——————————————————, *Twenty-ninth Annual Report of The Woman's Foreign Missionary Society—Western Division* (Toronto, 1905).

——————————————————, *Thirtieth Annual Report of The Woman's Foreign Missionary Society—Western Division* (Toronto, 1906).

——————————————————, *Thirty-first Annual Report of The Woman's Foreign Missionary Society—Western Division* (Toronto, 1907).

——————————————————, *Thirty-second Annual Report of The Woman's Foreign Missionary Society—Western Division* (Toronto, 1908).

The United Church Of Canada, *The Record Of Proceedings of General Council* (Toronto, 1926).

——————————————————, *United Church of Canada Yearbook* (Toronto, 1928).

Papers

University of Winnipeg Archives, *Manitoba College Papers* (Deaconess File).

——————————————————, *Paper Of Principal J. M. McKay.*

Chapter 11: Liberating Christianity

FOOTNOTES

1. The United Church of Canada, *Year Book*. (Toronto: 1982), p. 105.

2. Letty M. Russell. "Women's Liberation in a Biblical Perspective" in *Concern*, Vol. 13, No. 5 (New York: The National Board, YMCA, May-June, 1971) p. 19.

3. *The United Church Observer* as quoted by Daphne Anderson in *God's Hidden People*. (Toronto: Division of Mission in Canada, The United Church of Canada, January, 1980), p. 17.

4. The Very Rev. Dr. Lois M. Wilson, "Rockers of the Cradle/Rockers of the Boat", in *Women in the Church*, Vol. 8, No. 2 (Montreal: Religious Studies Dept., McGill University, Spring, 1981), p. 8

5. Mary Daly, *Beyond God the Father*. (Boston: Beacon Press, 1973), p. 198.

6. Betty Jane Wylie, *Beginnings: A Book for Widows*. (Toronto: McClelland and Stewart, 1982, revised ed.), p. 63.

7. Sheila D. Collins, "Toward a Feminist Theology", in *Christian Century*. (New York: Christian Century Foundation, August 2, 1972), p. 4.

BIBLIOGRAPHY

Anderson, Daphne. *God's Hidden People*. Toronto: Division of Mission in Canada, The United Church of Canada, 1980.

Chambers, Steven, compiler. *This is Your Church*. Toronto: *The United Church Observer*, Publisher, 1982.

Christ, Carol P. and Judith Plaskow, ed. *Womanspirit Rising*. San Francisco: Harper and Row, 1979.

Clark, Elizabeth and Richardson, Herbert, ed. *Women And Religion*. New York: Harper and Row, 1977.

Collins, Sheila D. "Toward a Feminist Theology" in *The Christian Century*. August 2, 1972. New York: The Christian Century Foundation.

Daly, Mary. *Beyond God the Father*. Boston: Beacon Press, 1973.

Golfman, Rosalyn. "The Changing Roles of the Jewish Woman" Unpublished essay—on loan from Dr. Eldon Hay, Mount Allison University, Sackville, N.B.

Hewitt, John P. *Self and Society: A Symbolic Interactionist Social Psychology,* second edition. Boston: Allyn and Bacon, 1979.

Hunt, Gladys. *Ms Means Myself*. Grand Rapids, Michigan: Zondervan Publishing House, 1972.

Mollenkott, Virginia Ramey. *Women, Men and the Bible*. Nashville: Abingdon Press, 1978.

Palmer, Rev. Carolyn. "Women and the Ministry". Unpublished essay—from her personal file. Sackville, N.B.

Price, Eugenia. *God Speaks to Women Today*. Grand Rapids, Michigan: Zondervan Publishing House, 1964.

Reuther, Rosemary. *New Woman: New Earth*. New York: Seabury Press, 1975.

Reuther, Rosemary, ed. *Religion and Sexism*. New York: Simon and Shuster, 1974.

Riedel, Eunice, Thomas Tracey and Barbara Moskowitz. *The Book of the Bible*. Toronto: Bantam Books, 1979.

Robertson, Roland, ed. *Sociology of Religion,* Baltimore: Penguin Books, 1969.

Russell, Letty M. "Women's Liberation in a Biblical Perspective", *Concern,* Vol. 13, No. 5. New York: The National Board, YMCA, May-June, 1971.

Sayers, Dorothy L. *Are Women Human?* Grand Rapids, Michigan: William B. Eerdmans, 1971.

Schaller, Lyle E., ed. *Women as Pastors*. Nashville: Abingdon Press, 1982.

Shteir, Ann B., ed. *Women on Women*. Toronto: York University Press, 1978.

Swidler, Leonard. *Biblical Affirmations of Women*. Philadelphia: The Westminster Press, 1979.

Trible, Dr. Phyllis. *God and the Rhetoric of Sexuality*. Philadelphia: Fortress Press, 1978.

The United Church of Canada. *Year Book*. Toronto: General Council of The United Church of Canada, 1960, 1970, 1982.

Van Scoyoc, Nancy J. *Women, Change and the Church*. Nashville: Abingdon Press, 1980.

Wallace, Ruth A. and Wolf, Alison. *Contemporary Sociological Theory*. Englewood Cliffs, N.J.: Prentice-Hall, Inc., 1980.

Washbourn, Penelope. *Becoming Woman*. New York: Harper and Row, 1977.

Weidman, Judith L., ed. *Women Ministers*. San Francisco: Harper and Row, 1981.

Wilson, Very Rev. Dr. Lois M. "Rockers of the Cradle/Rockers of the Boat", *Women in the Church*, Vol. 8, No. 2. Montreal: Religious Studies Dept., McGill University, Spring, 1981

Wylie, Betty Jane. *Beginnings: A Book for Widows*, revised ed. Toronto: McClelland and Stewart, 1982.

Chapter 12: Pouring the Tea and Hiding the Wine Bottle

FOOTNOTES

1. From "Question Box" column by the late Bud Morden, in *The United Church Observer* (Toronto: The United Church of Canada, August 1982).

2. Barbara Bagnell, "Why Ministers' Marriages Break Up", in *The United Church Observer*, June 1972, p. 15.

3. Much of the research for this essay was compiled through interviews and correspondence with ministers, spouses and parishioners. They will remain anonymous for the most part because they have requested that of me.

4. Donna Sinclair, *The Pastor's Wife Today* (Burlington, Ontario: G. R. Welch Co. Ltd., 1981), p. 62.

5. Quoted from a letter sent to me by a minister's wife.

6. From a letter to the editor written June 6, 1928 by Anne Cottingham of Sioux Lookout and reprinted by *The United Church Observer*, January 1975.

7. Byrne Hope Sanders, *Canadian Portraits* (Toronto: Clarke, Irwin and Co. Ltd., 1958) p. 116.

8. From a letter by Marion Noble Laing to her mother, November 17, 1905, excerpts of which were published in the historical booklet produced to commemorate the Centennial of St. Andrew's Church, Fort Qu'Appelle, Saskatchewan, 1981.

9. R. Allen, Editor, *The Social Gospel in Canada.* Papers of the Interdisciplinary Conference on the Social Gospel in Canada, March 1973, University of Regina. (Ottawa: National Museums of Canada, 1975), pp. 51-52.

10. *Ibid.,* p. 52.

11. *Ibid.,* p. 56.

12. Grace Lane, "Mary Haggart—at home on the range," in *The United Church Observer,* February 1975.

13. Muriel Duncan, "You haven't made it until we've all made it" in *The United Church Observer,* March 1975, p. 12.

14. *Ibid.,* see Foreword by Lyle E. Schaller.

15. Margaret Laurence, *The Diviners* (New York: Alfred A. Knopf, Inc., 1974), Seal Edition, 1978, p. 78.

16. From a letter written to me by Mrs. Ethel Johnson, November 3, 1982.

17. *Op. cit.,* Letters of Marion Noble Laing.

18. *Op. cit.,* Letter from Mrs. E. Johnson.

19. *Op. cit.,* Duncan article, p. 12.

20. *Op. cit.,* Sinclair, p. 29.

21. *Ibid.,* See Chapter 2, "The Enabler", pp. 42-59.

22. *Ibid.,* p. 67.

BIBLIOGRAPHY

Allen, R. Ed. *The Social Gospel in Canada.* Papers of the Interdisciplinary Conference on the Social Gospel in Canada. Held March 1973, University of Regina. Ottawa: The National Museums of Canada, 1975.

Couch, Tim. "How to Keep Your Pastor", Parts V and VI of VIII, in the *Presbyterian Communique,* Pottstown, Pa: Presbyterians United for Biblical Concerns, Spring 1982.

Gibson, E. *When the Minister is a Woman.* New York: Holt, Rinehart and Winston, 1970.

Laurence, Margaret. *The Diviners.* New York: Alfred A. Knopf Inc., 1974. Seal Edition, 1978.

St. Andrew's United Church Centennial Booklet. Fort Qu'Appelle, Saskatchewan, 1981.

Sanders, Byrne Hope. *Canadian Portraits.* Toronto: Clarke, Irwin and Co. Ltd., 1958.

Sinclair, Donna. *The Pastor's Wife Today.* Burlington, Ontario: G. R. Welch Co. Ltd., 1981.

Studies of the Royal Commission for the Status of Women in Canada. #8—*Cultural Tradition and Political History of Women in Canada.* Ottawa: Information Canada, 1971.

The United Church Observer. Toronto: The United Church of Canada.
    —Bagnell, Barbara. "Why Ministers' Marriages Break Up", June 1972.

—Duncan, Muriel. "You haven't made it until we've all made it", March 1975.
—Krotz, Larry. "Mr. and Mrs. Minister", September 1975.
—Lane, Grace. "Mary Haggart—at home on the range", February 1975.
—Milton, R. and Manly E. "Liberation: His and Hers", August 1975.
—Morden, Bud. "Question Box" Column, August 1982.
—"A Women's Place—over 50 years it changed", January 1975.

I gratefully acknowledge the candour and eloquence with which ministers, ministers' spouses and parishioners spoke to me. The insights they provided gave inspiration and colour for this essay.

I would also like to thank Prof. Jane McAuliffe, Marion Laing, and the people at the United Church Archives at Victoria Univesity for their invaluable assistance.

ACKNOWLEDGEMENTS

We would like to thank all of those listed below who submitted materials to the Women, Work and Worship project. We also thank those of you who wrote anonymously and had your work submitted by others. You are the true authors of this book.

WWW, Alberta

#1	Ruth Gray
#2	Violet Hackett
#3	Coaldale UCW
#4	Elvira Jackson
#5	Beth Tachit
#6	Brenda Skeith
#7	Donna Minor
#8	Elaine Brown
#9	Marion Cabelka
#10-#20	Mary Thomas (Includes materials written by Shirley Sunby, Helen L. Pierce, Verda M. Ullman, Edna Williams, Irene Hinman)
#21	Olive Fissell (25 items)
#22	Olive Fissell (16 items)
#23	Rev. Mary Thomas (Includes material by Helen Leprus)
#24	Helen Mack

WWW, Bay of Quinte	#1	Mrs. Howard Jackson, Mrs. David Magahay, Jeannette McKague
	#2	Jeannette McKague (Includes materials written by Joan Gladwin, Frances Cooper, Eunice Nicholls, Carol Clark)
	#3	Mrs. Ivan Dorman
	#4	Jean Sheridan
	#5	Marguerite Cluff
	#6	Mrs. Ross Ketcheson
	#7	Peggy Heard (Includes materials by Rev. J. N. Clarry, Jean Wagar)
	#8	Betty Thompson
	#9	Thelma Wright
	#10	Joan Chalovich
	#11	Ruby Imeson, Ruth Turner
WWW, British Columbia	#1	Ena Archer, Mary Douglas, Evelyn Torrance, Marie Fogg
	#2	Margaret Huntington
	#3	Audrey Sawchuk, Violet E. Stewart
	#4	Comox UCW
	#5	Mildren Fahrni
	#6	Armstrong UCW
	#7	Lillian Soga
	#8	Mabel Burnett
	#9	Celina A. Piercy
	#10	Nora McEwen
	#11	Nell Hanna
	#12	Mrs. Jack Andrews
	#13	Mrs. H. R. Koops
	#14	Esther Faubert
	#15	Lillian Soga
	#16	Muriel Kilgour
	#17	Trudi Mathias
	#18	Vera Young
	#19	Trudi Mathias, Florence Burroughs
	#20	Glenna Jamieson
WWW, Hamilton	#1	Freda Moulton
	#2	Katherine Best
	#3	Barb Van de Komer

	#4	Margaret E. Hicks, D. Aileen Farrell
	#5	Marion Martin
	#6	Centenary UCW
	#7	Ruth Kaufman
	#8	Mary Potter
	#9	Doreen Wilhelm (Returned)
	#10	Helen Hall (Returned)
WWW, London	#1	Kay Brodie (50 items)
	#2	Kay Brodie
	#3	Tarentorous UCW
	#4	Kay Brodie
	#5	Lynn Hudson
	#6	M. Jean Kelly, Marguerite E. Murray
	#7	Betty (Gibson) McConnell
	#8	Wilma Forrest
	#9	Marion Anderson
	#10	Dorothy E. Joslin
	#11	Jean MacMillan
	#12	Warsville UCW
	#13	Mrs. Peter Vanrooyen (7 Items) (Includes materials by Marion Marshall, Margaret Ford)
WWW, Manitoba	#1	Ellen Rowatt
	#2	Jean Hutchings
	#3	Edith Shiells
	#4	Audrey Tohue
	#5	Marjorie Sissons
	#6	Birtle UCW (4 items) (Includes materials by Eleanor Woods, S. A. Doran)
	#7	Georgia Hyndman
	#8	Alice Green
	#9	Maud Lelond (8 items) (Includes materials by Liela E. Brown, Merle Argue, Jean McCallum, Evelyn MacLeod)
	#10	Margaret De La Mare
	#11	Adelene E. Leonard
	#12	Mrs. J. V. Horsman
	#13	Ida Berglund
	#14	Marjorie E. Brooks

	#15	Laura Warsaba (23 items)
		(Includes materials by Eileen Jackson,
		Emma Thornborough, Lena Steel,
		Doris Magarrell)
WWW,	#1	Bernice Bowman
Manitou	#2	Tina Hansen (6 items)
WWW, Maritime—	#1	Maritime Conference UCW
New Brunswick	#2	Jean Cormack
and Québec	#3	Christine Oliver
	#4	Sackville UCW
	#5	Elaine Hannan
	#6	Lorena Green
	#7	Wanda Harding
	#8	Queen N. Linton
	#9	Clotilda Ellis
	#10	Gwen MacRae (7 items)
		(Includes materials by Inez Colpetts)
	#11	Ruth Boothroyd
	#12	Phyllis Gard
	#13	Winnifred Gray
	#14	Marion Court
	#15	Susan M. Short
	#16	Olive C. Firlotte
WWW, Maritime—	#1	Rev. Frances MacLellan
Nova Scotia	#2	Rev. Frances MacLellan (12 items)
		(Includes materials by Gladys Fraser,
		Mildren Pirie, Mrs. E. .S. Arnold, Kathleen
		Conrad, Doris M. C. Lisling, Audrey Hill,
		Jean Curtis, Grace Kilcup, Mrs. A. D.
		MacKinnon, Lilian Piercey)
	#3	Marilyn I. Livingston
	#4	Alice W. Harrison
	#5	Evelyn Price
	#6	Phyllis Gunn
	#7	Ann McKee
	#8	Marion MacLean
	#9	Jessie MacLeod
		(Includes materials by Elsie Percy)
	#10	Connie Crossley

WWW, Maritime—	#1	Olga J. Leard
Prince	#2	Winnie MacMillian
Edward Island	#3	Ruby Matheson
	#4	Florence T. Roper
	#5	Mrs. Henry Moyse (18 items)
		(Includes materials by Blanche M. Warren, Grace Jay, Myrtle Wood, Pauline Townshend, Stanhope UCW, Margaret MacDonald, Mrs. George MacMillian, Annie Simmons)

WWW, Montreal	#1	Galdys Major
and Ottawa	#2	Grace Johnston
	#3	Enid Arscott
	#4	Christine M. Judge
	#5	Jean McNeil
	#6	Katherine H. Crawford
	#7	Lois Martineau
	#8	Christine M. Judge (4 items)

WWW,	#1	Mrs. W. G. Manning
Newfoundland	#2	Gertrude Locke
WWW,	#1	Land UCW
Saskatchewan	#2	Cyprus Hills UCW
	#3	Grace Lane
	#4	M. Joyce Dickin
	#5	Hazel Lyall
	#6	Anne Hokanson
	#7	Anne Kokanson
	#8	Vera Laing
	#9	Thelma Baldock
	#10	Rosemary Bren
	#11	Kathy Anderson
	#12	Eileen McLeod
	#13	Gwendolyn Mills
	#14	Marjorie Eldred
	#15	Shellbrook UCW
	#16	Janet Loveridge
	#17	Kathleen Ellison
	#18	Mrs. M. McQuoid
	#19	Blanche Dennis
	#20	Jean Sandness
	#21	Marion Serviss

	#22	Ida P. Hingten
	#23	Rita M. Klassen
	#24	Joyce M. McManus
	#25	Margaret Groat
	#26	Vera Miller
	#27	Millie Boucher
	#28	Frances McDougall
	#29	Watrous UCW
	#30	Irene Baumgartner
	#31	Alice Pitt
	#32	Florence Fowke (13 items) (Includes materials by Sonja Herter, Joy Frain, Eleanor Haw, Herma Bailey, Bernice Chalmers, Olive Whitby, Lillian McBean, Sheila McLeod, Lucille Sorensen)
	#33	Thelma McConnell
	#34	Submitted anonymously (re Sylvia [Johnson] Humphreys)
WWW, Toronto	#1	Sandhill UCW
	#2	Victoria Square UCW
	#3	Muskoka Presbyterial UCW
	#4	Leonora Wilson
	#5	Gladys Coxon
	#6	Florence J. Morson
	#7	Muriel Reynolds, Laurene Ellison
	#8	Miriam Little
	#9	Mrs. L. E. Marrs
	#10	Hopeville UCW
	#11	Ruth Torrance
	#12	Shirley Endicott Small
	#13	Hilda Rowan
	#14	Helen Whitney
	#15	Mrs. A. Coatsworth
	#16	Mrs. H. V. Vick
	#17	Mary Rowell Jackman
	#18	Isabel Uren, Fumiko Ioi, Molly Bryce
	#19	Mrs. V. Bassingthwaite, Mrs. K. Spence
	#20	Evelyn Shaw

Materials have also been received from the following contributors:
Frances Dunham, Mary Green
Eileen Isaac

Jean Newans
Ruby Alexander
Pat Stuart
Martha Walker
Catherine Barrick
John G. Reid
Mary Landry
Margaret Torrance
Marion Logan
Rev. Glenn Lucas
Hide Shimizu

PHOTO: THE GLOBE AND MAIL

Nancy Rowell Jackman

Nancy Jackman believes that money has no politics. Even so, this United Church woman uses her wealth to pursue social justice for women. Through the family foundation, she has funded many women's issues and interests which include an annual scholarship to the University of Toronto for studies in feminist theology; responsibility for the two-year project and publication of *Women, Work and Worship;* support of the National Action Committee for the Status of Women; grants for the Cruise Missile Conversion Project, the Diaconal Association, immigrant women's placement centre, Womynly Ways musical productions, etc.

Nancy inherits her feminism from her maternal grandmother whose husband, Newton Rowell, a Methodist lawyer and Liberal politician, fought one of the most celebrated Canadian legal battles. It was known as the Persons case of 1928, and in 1929 it won women the right to be appointed to the Senate.

"I've always had a passion for social justice. I have kept bumping into it all my life." Her father was MP for Rosedale, and his riding was one which includes families of wealth and poverty. In the 1930s, her mother started the Bond Street nursery, probably one of the first daycare centres in Toronto. Both parents gave Nancy a global perspective and a sense of social responsibility.

Her allegiance is to The United Church of Canada with which she has had a stormy professional relationship. The church was a strong tradition in her family, but she never considered making it her life until "I had a conversion experience" in Bali, working in a refugee project sponsored by the World Council of Churches. While Nancy was in Indonesia, she had a letter from Ruth Tillman, then national secretary for CGIT, asking her to write an article for *The Torch*.

When Nancy returned to Toronto, she wanted to work for the church. She called Ruth Tillman who advised her to see Jean Parker, who at that time had the care and education of deaconesses as part of her portfolio at United Church House. Jean sent her to Covenant College. Nancy graduated with a theology diploma in 1967, went on to receive her B. A. in political science at York University, studied Bible at the Hebrew University in Jerusalem, and worked in Amsterdam as a goldsmith before joining the staff at Naramata Centre in British Columbia. While at Naramata, she studied on weekends at Wentworth College in Spokane, Washington, and received her M.A. in the applied behavioural sciences, specializing in Organizational Development.

In 1975, she was commissioned a deaconess by British Columbia Conference—but not before her first application was turned down. A few years later, she was dropped from the ministerial rolls when Toronto Area Presbytery recommended her removal. She chose to defend herself before the judicial committee of the 1980 General Council, even though she knew that she could have sued the church in the civil courts. She won her case on a point of justice and was reinstated, along with the other ten who had also been dropped from the Toronto Conference rolls. A year later, after painful reflection, tired of fighting with an organization that didn't seem to have room for her, she resigned.

Scarred by her experiences, she resolved that "if the church wanted me, it would have to come and get me." Recently she was asked to speak to Toronto Conference on the Charter of Rights and its implications for women. She is now a member of the Women's Concerns Committee of Toronto Conference and represents them on conference executive.

Nancy continues to work for what she believes is appropriate to her faith as a Christian and a feminist. Indeed, if the church is to receive her support, it will have to change from what she feels is lackluster commitment to such women's issues as "better pension packages for women, freedom from clergy harassment, non-sexist architecture, hymns and prayers, more and better staff appointments for women." She looks forward to the day when "women are treated as humans, not just sources of sin, sex, and money."

Shirley Davy

Shirley Davy, project coordinator for Women, Work and Worship, brings a diverse background in the social sciences and religious studies to her consideration of women in The United Church of Canada. Her academics, however, are well grounded in the practical world of work, marriage and motherhood. For the past several years "work" has consisted of writing, teaching and developing affirmative action programs for business, government and educational institutions.

As a "committed but often frustrated" member of the United Church herself, Ms Davy also brings her many years of congregational work (volunteer) to Women, Work and Worship. She has recently relocated from Toronto to Parry Sound, Ontario, and is looking forward to becoming part of another church family tree.

In addition to Women, Work and Worship, Shirley has written a women's studies textbook, suitable for use by women's groups, which will be published in the spring of 1984. That, she says, is just another aspect of the same ministry that brought her to the Women, Work and Worship project.

311